The New York Times

GUIDE TO

PERSONAL FINANCE

The New York Times GUIDE TO PERSONAL FINANCE

SAL NUCCIO

Harper & Row, Publishers
New York, Evanston, and London

LIBRARY OF CONGRESS CATALOG CARD NUMBER: 65-21019

ACKNOWLEDGMENTS

Top billing here should go to my wife, Edwina, and our children. "Togetherness" was all too rare for our family during the months it took me to prepare this book.

Next are my colleagues on the *New York Times.* The Personal Finance column made its first appearance in the *Times* less than four weeks after Thomas E. Mullaney took over as business-financial editor. He gave the feature prominence and allowed the necessary latitude to mold it to readers' needs by providing me with a generous share of a newspaper's most precious commodity—space. Robert E. Bedingfield, assistant to the business-financial editor and a most prodigious and enthusiastic reporter, sustained me through the feature's embryonic development, and thereafter served as advocate, adviser, and constructive needler.

Much assistance also came from other department colleagues, particularly my pinchhitters, among them John Hibbs Allan, Elizabeth M. Fowler, Robert Metz, and Leonard Sloane. Help came from persons in other sections of the paper too, most notably Glenn Fowler, real estate editor.

Other expert individuals and organizations were extremely cooperative in my research efforts for the columns and the book. While it would be impossible to mention them all, I would like to single out a few.

Thus, specific thanks to David Gotterer and Eli Mason of the New York accounting firm of Mason & Company; to Oscar Lasdon, financial consultant and associate editor of the *Banker's Magazine;* to Robert Waldron and Fred DeLuca of the Health Insurance Institute; Charles C. Clarke at the Insurance Information Institute; Milton Amsel and Joseph McCarthy of the Institute of Life Insurance; Harvey Greenfield, Paul Hundt, Ernest Meyers, and Joseph Shapiro, all lawyers; to Charles Ferber, manager of the Social Security Administration's midtown Manhattan office; and to Richard Stephens, who provided a quiet refuge in which I could work.

Other helpful organizations were the Better Business Bureau of Metropolitan New York, the National Better Business Bureau, the New York Stock Exchange, the National Association of Securities Dealers, the Investment Company Institute and various federal agencies, including the Securities and Exchange Commission, the Internal Revenue Service and the Departments of Labor; Commerce; and Health, Education and Welfare.

I am especially obliged to Jeannette Hopkins, my editor at Harper & Row, and to her assistant, Barbara Kaplan.

In the final analysis, of course, any errors this book may contain are on my head.

SAL NUCCIO

CONTENTS

INTRODUCTION

As life becomes more and more complicated, the family without financial guidance finds it increasingly difficult to manage its money wisely. As personal income has risen and all of us engage in the pursuit of happiness, we are surrounded by a great array of sellers of goods and services, by companies eager to extend "easy credit," by institutions advertising loans, by organizations offering the "best" savings plan and the "best" investment plan. Making the right decisions requires knowledge and keen analysis. The average family is constantly concerned with matters of personal finance and constantly weighing its various aspects, for it knows that its decisions will determine whether it is getting the most value for every dollar—in effect, utilizing its income to best advantage.

In response to the public's desire for regular information on money management, *The New York Times* introduced on August 26, 1963, a Personal Finance column by Sal Nuccio. Originally a Monday feature, it now appears twice a week. In the first column Mr. Nuccio discussed the amount of life insurance a man needs and since then he has covered many aspects of insurance, investment, taxation, estate planning, consumer economics and other subjects that affect every person's pocketbook.

Successive columns generated an increasing volume of letters and telephone calls from readers seeking more guidance or suggesting new topics. In addition, a record number of requests were made by business concerns, trade associations, Government agencies and other organizations for permission to reprint many of the articles. In view of this response, The *Times* decided to expand the Personal Finance column and since May, 1965, it has run on Thursdays as well as Mondays.

The decision to produce *The New York Times Guide to Personal Finance* was in a sense made by the readers of the column.

They kept requesting a compilation of Mr. Nuccio's articles or a book by him to which they could turn for guidance.

During the planning stages we agreed with Mr. Nuccio that a volume containing reprints of his columns under subject headings might be too unwieldy. So the book that Mr. Nuccio has written, while drawn primarily from his columns, is essentially a brand-new work, as cohesive as it is comprehensive.

The author has the kind of diversified background that is vital to expertise in the personal finance field. In a duplex and sometimes triplex career since he graduated from college 20 years ago, Mr. Nuccio has, among other things, conducted an insurance business, worked in Wall Street, in advertising and in the automobile and other sales fields. Most important, however, he has also been a newspaperman during the major part of that time and has the ability to convey to his readers in clear and simple language all that he has learned through experience, reporting and research.

THOMAS E. MULLANEY
Business-Financial News Editor
The New York Times

October, 1966

The New York Times

GUIDE TO

PERSONAL FINANCE

1

MAPPING A FAMILY FINANCIAL PROGRAM

"It used to kill me to have to go to my mother-in-law every Tuesday night for the 50 cents my wife and I needed to go to the movies. I always repaid her the next day, when I got paid, but I could never have the money ready for the next Tuesday movie. That was 30 years ago, but the memory still bothers me."

The memory may linger to disturb this now successful executive, but it has taught him little. He has continued on a much larger scale the often depressing practice of dipping into tomorrow's income to finance today's pleasures—and needs, for that matter. Though earning $25,000 a year, and having earned more than $10,000 a year for the last 20 years, he has found it necessary to refinance his home mortgage to put his son through college, to utilize the fly-now-pay-later plan for several vacations, and to use his credit as currency when buying a car, a boat, major appliances or other big-ticket items. When prudently used, credit can be a blessing—few homes could be bought without it, for example—but there are obvious pitfalls in overuse.

Just as this man and his wife could have forgone one Tuesday-night movie and disciplined themselves to save the 50 cents for pay-as-you-go entertainment the following Tuesday, so could they have been provident later in preparing for bigger expenditures. It would have saved them money for other pleasures and needs; credit buying is expensive. Perhaps they would have recognized this if the mother-in-law had been conscientious-parent enough to ask 60 cents in repayment for each 50 cents borrowed. The executive, and through his example his entire family, had not yet learned to achieve what some psychologists consider to be the highest degree of maturity: the ability to postpone pleasure when necessary. He had failed to carry into his personal life the management abilities for which he was so well paid by his employer. In this respect he is on a par with most Americans in this affluent society.

That personal financial problems are widespread is apparent in many statistical studies and surveys. For example, in a recent American Bar Association survey* of "judges, friends of the court and commissioners of domestic relations" in the 50 states and Puerto Rico, 89 per cent of the respondents cited financial difficulty as one of the two prime causes of divorce. The other was drinking, to which economically distressed people sometimes turn.

That the economic problems generally can be solved is equally apparent. Much can be done by most families to get more out of their dollars—so much more that dreams could become concrete plans. It takes realistic long-term financial planning within the limits of present and potential income, budgeting that helps to maintain discipline without being stifling, sensible buying (good shoppers are made, not born) and some degree of optimistic determination, which generally grows stronger with each economic "success." Most important, the emotional pressures of financial distress tend to ease with sound money management, and life becomes more enjoyable.

While there is need for personal financial guidance, if not rehabilitation, at all levels of our society, surveys indicate that the proportionately greatest need is among persons in the middle and upper-middle income brackets, and they usually are not getting it. These individuals and families may have difficulty with management of so-called discretionary income, that is, money above the amount required for basic living needs. A few unwise decisions of magnitude, or just plain overspending, can shove a family into a whirlpool of "indiscretionary" credit living, destroying its ability to meet even basic expenses.

This was the observation, too, of Sidney Margolius, a writer and

* The survey was conducted by the Support Committee of the association's Family Law Section, under the guidance of Mrs. Una Rita Quenstedt, Assistant Corporation Counsel for the District of Columbia, and Col. Carl E. Winkler, chief of the Legal Assistance Division of the Army's Office of the Judge Advocate General.

lecturer on consumer affairs, who said: "Family-service agencies report that even people with incomes of $10,000 a year come to them for advice on handling money. Significantly, not the low but the moderate- and medium-income families are the most frequent borrowers. About half those in the $4,000-to-$10,000 bracket, and even one of three with incomes over $10,000, owe installment debts."

There is much more evidence that personal money management has become a highly complex chore, that credit buying has become a way of life, but most people are not concerned with mounds of documentation, unless they are seeking company in their economic misery. Their real concern is with their own finances, with how they could acquire their share of business and industry's rich harvest of products and services, and still educate their children and have enough money left for retirement.

A large segment of the population is becoming increasingly money management conscious, if the popularity of a plethora of newspaper and magazine articles and books on the subject is acceptable evidence. The personal finance feature that appears twice weekly in *The New York Times* draws up to 150 letters a week, and one particular column offering reprints at 50 cents each of a reference list of free or low-cost money management literature attracted more than 500 requests from readers.

More tangibly reflective of the increasing public awareness of the need for financial guidance, and perhaps of their own disciplinary limitations, has been the growth in popularity of payroll-deduction savings plans. Many employers service deduction plans for employes wishing to make systematic deposits in bank or credit union accounts, to buy savings bonds or, in a few cases, to invest in mutual funds.

In the investment field, it is notable that the number of contractual plan accounts, under which investors accumulate mutual fund shares on a regular "installment" basis, has soared in the last dozen years from less than 70,000 to more than a million, or one in every six mutual fund accounts. Further, since 1953 the New York Stock Exchange's Monthly Investment Plan (M.I.P.) has conveyed more than $300 million of small-investors' capital to market. Under that plan, as little as $40 may be invested quarterly through a stock exchange member concern.

Aware that financially distressed people, at the very least, cannot perform their duties efficiently, some employers have sought to provide money-management counseling and education. The Department of Defense, for one, has established extensive personal affairs programs for members of the Armed Forces. These range from rehabilitation of the financially disabled to "preventive" education of the solvent servicemen.

The urgent need for sensible money mangement by everyone hopeful of achieving long-term goals is underscored by the continuing danger of inflation. Over the last 20 years, this hidden enemy has chewed away a big chunk of the dollar's purchasing power, causing prices to rise more than 70 per cent, according to Federal statistics. An item that cost $1 in 1945 now costs more than $1.70. The annual rate of increase in the consumer price index has slowed in the last decade to an average of about 1.67 per cent. But even this "creeping inflation" can have stunning effect. An average price-index gain of 1.5 per cent a year over the next 20 years would put 1986 prices 30 per cent above current levels, a forecast that many economists think conservative.

What effect would that have on the retirement plans of today's men and women of 40 to 45? What effect would it have on the educational plans of today's parents for their infant children? The answer could be a confident "perhaps none," if these persons plan to reinforce their financial programing over the years with sound savings and investment plans that offer a hedge against inflation.

Historically, deflationary periods, in which prices decline, have limited offsetting effect. For example, prices have nearly doubled since 1929, despite the Great Depression of the 1930's.

Realistic Budgeting Plans

The word "budgeting" makes some people cringe; they confuse it with penny-pinching. It would be worth while for them to heed the following advice of Jerome B. Cohen, professor of economics at the City University of New York, and co-author, with Arthur W. Hanson, of *Personal Finance:** "Budgeting isn't bookkeeping. It is financial planning, and people ought to regard it as such. If you try to keep an exact record of every penny you spend, you give up budgeting. That's not its purpose. The purpose is to enable you to look ahead, not to keep track of the past."

* Homewood, Ill.: Richard D. Irwin, Inc., 1964 (3d ed.).

To avoid the distressing, argument-generating practice of tracing each expenditure down to the last cent, budgeters should overlook small unaccountable items. The occasional "mysterious disappearance" of a few dollars is not unusual, and an attempt to trace them down is useless bookkeeping.

While budgeting is not the chore it has been made out to be, it does demand discipline. It often means forgoing some immediate pleasure (commanding a display of that high degree of maturity) because the cash at hand has been earmarked for a future bill or the achievement of a major goal. The reward is not only the accomplishment of those otherwise unattainable goals but also an increased measure of financial security and, perhaps, family harmony. The spending controls inherent in a sound budget will allow the saving, or at least intelligent spending, of increases in income or of bonuses and other windfalls. Too often this "new" money is lost in the tangle of patternless spending, of paycheck-to-paycheck living.

Most money-management guides suggest essentially the same steps in formulating a financial program, which should be a family affair. In general, they are:

1. Set goals. Establish realistic short-term and long-term objectives—a car next year, a child's college education in 10 years, retirement in 25 years—and estimate the sum to be set aside regularly to achieve them. These will be incentives for the maintenance of a budget.

2. Estimate total income for the year, including savings' interest, stock dividends, veterans' pensions and money from all other sources. When income is irregular, as is the case for some salesmen and professional men, a yearly minimum should be estimated and then divided into equal parts over selected budget periods, weekly, biweekly or monthly.

3. Spread fixed expenses. The year's total for large periodic bills, such as those for taxes, rent or mortgage payments, utilities and heating fuel, insurance, union or association dues, installment payments on loans or purchases, and school tuition should be divided by the number of budget periods, facilitating regular saving in a reserve fund, possibly a separate savings account. Diversion of needed cash and the last-minute scramble to pay large bills that should have been expected would be eliminated.

4. Estimate flexible expenses: clothing, furniture and equipment,

charitable contributions, medical care, recreation, gifts, entertainment and an emergency fund, which, among other things, would make up for a wrong guess on medical costs. This total, too, should be spread evenly over the budget periods.

5. Estimate regular living expenses. These would include personal allowances, food, household supplies and help, laundry, dry cleaning, automobile maintenance and other transportation, newspapers and magazines, postage and entertainment at home. To arrive at these estimates, it may be necessary to record actual expenses for several weeks or longer.

6. Plan repayment of old bills. Include any loans from friends or relatives, as well as installment debts, in fixed expenses. If there are such bills, they should be spread, where possible, over future budget periods for repayment as soon as feasible to maintain good credit (if not social and family) relations, as well as to reduce indebtedness.

A tentative budget should now be drawn. Total expenses, about the same for each budget period, are then matched against income. The final step is to bring the program into balance. One's impulse, at the sight of this tentative budget, may be to drop the whole project as hopeless and complicated—especially if proposed spending exceeds income. But a little more family discussion and mental gyration will result in a workable budget. The rewards are too rich to stop now.

A surplus of income over expenses would be savings toward future goals. If the surplus is too small, or if it is indeed a deficit, expense items must be trimmed wherever possible. In an extreme situation, a person may need, at least temporarily, to increase his income by seeking extra work. If it is a family plan, each member should work to develop cost-cutting or income-producing plans. Children may take on chores that had been done by hired help. The mother may find ways to reduce food costs. All could help whittle down flexible expenses. Certain fixed expenses may be temporarily trimmed.

Financial planning *is* a family affair because each member has a stake in it, each shares in the rewards. But aside from the achievement of economic goals, there are other, more subtle rewards. Sound money-management planning helps to create an objective attitude toward money, helps to instill wisdom in its use as a medium of exchange for current and future needs and pleasures. Further, it generates confidence and resourcefulness in the handling of finances, and educates each family member in home economics. And, of course, "togetherness" in the solution of financial problems can bring the family closer together in other ways.

An essential incentive to cooperative financial planning is a personal allowance for each family member, whatever the age. It will be educational for the young and prideful for all members to manage their personal budgets. In addition to the sum for such necessities as carfare, lunches, clothing, grooming, reading material, club fees, and so on, there should be an amount, however small, for recreation and personal pleasures. Once the allowances have been granted, there should be no demand for an accounting. Gross mismanagement should be treated with compassion and understanding, especially in the case of children, but the individual should be allowed to work out his own money problem, whenever possible. Consistent bailing out of debt spawns irresponsibility.

There are so-called model budgets that may serve as guidelines, but, basically, a budget is a personal thing. It should be tailored to a particular individual or family. Geographic differences may have their effect on the amounts allotted for such items as food and shelter. Moreover, from household to household, there may be differences in objectives, in living standards, in the values placed on certain expenditures, such as entertainment, education, the home. Thus, if a budgeter finds his program too constrictive to accommodate his recreational interests, he should adjust it to allow more money for those interests. If offsetting reductions in other budgetary items cannot be made, the total program may be slowed. Self indulgence? Perhaps, but that would be far better than scrapping the whole budget in frustration, thereby threatening the family's financial future.

In this light, it is imperative that a budget be flexible to allow for changes in financial status, family size, or in attitude or interest. In many instances, actual spending may dictate changes in allotments. For example, one couple suddenly became aware of their evolutionary rise in living standard when they saw the youngest of their three children in a "hand-me-down" coat that looked "cheap." The wife exclaimed, "That was all we could afford when we bought that coat," and then noted she generally had been spending more on clothing than their budget allowed. This sent them to the ledger, where they made extensive and long-overdue budgetary revisions that were reflective of the sizable improvement in the family's income. For one thing, they planned to divert to investments a portion of their cash savings set aside for emergency needs. It was far in excess of six months' net income, a generous emergency-fund minimum.

A Family Balance Sheet

An individual or family may borrow a corporate technique in measuring a personal financial program's effectiveness by periodically drawing up a balance sheet.

Such a procedure of determining, perhaps yearly, one's net worth; that is, the value of all assets less liabilities, will graphically illustrate the progress of the budgeter toward his economic goals. In effect, balance sheets, compared and filed from year to year, are a family's financial biography. A decline in net worth, or even a decline in the rate of growth, serves as a warning that remedial budgetary action must be taken.

The balance sheet is the "still picture" of finance, showing the net worth of an individual or a corporation on a given day. It might be different the day before or the day after because of such factors as depreciation and market fluctuation. In drawing up a personal balance sheet, an individual would list all assets (things he owns) and their market value or cost less depreciation, and then list all liabilities (what he owes). The difference between the sums of the two lists would be his net worth, or his net indebtedness.

An individual's or family's assets might include:

- Cash on hand and in checking and savings accounts.
- Automobiles at market or trade-in value.
- House and other real estate at market value.
- Home furnishings, such as furniture, appliances and outdoor equipment at market value or cost less depreciation.
- Personal property such as clothing, jewelry, a boat and sports equipment at market value or cost less depreciation.
- The cash value in life insurance policies, pension plans, and annuity contracts.
- Stocks and corporate and government bonds at current market value.
- Money loaned to others.

The liabilities might include:

- Automobile loan.
- Unpaid mortgage on house and other real estate.
- Bills due on charge accounts, installment purchases.
- Other loans, such as from individuals, banks or on a life insurance policy's cash value.

A budgeter may measure his economic momentum by comparing his net worth from year to year. However, a satisfactory rate of growth in total net worth is not enough. He must make certain that the growth in specific assets applicable to family goals is adequate to achieve them.

Banks may be willing to accommodate requests for balance-sheet forms, which they generally use to measure the financial substance of potential borrowers.

Working Wives

Wives take jobs for a variety of reasons, ranging from economic necessity to the desire for a career. It must be borne in mind that their net incomes may be surprisingly small, after the payment of taxes, job-related expenses and the price of freedom from many household chores. The extra-cost items may include an extensive wardrobe, a second car and commutation, lunches, child care and perhaps part-time household help. Income taxes would be at a higher than normal rate, since the wife's income, when added to the husband's, would put the family in a higher bracket.

The net gain from a wife's employment should be determined. However, even if the family would not be one cent ahead, it would be worth having the wife work if she would be happiest doing so. What price family discontent and disharmony?

Young married couples would be wisest not to depend too heavily on the bride's income for the obvious reason that it might leave off when pregnancy begins, or shortly thereafter.

2

WHERE DOES THE MONEY GO?

A family's living standard and financial stability may be dictated more by the way it spends its money than by the size of its income. This may be a truism but it becomes increasingly evident and significant as consumers acquire greater amounts of discretionary income—money left over after basic living expenses are paid—and as business and industrial innovators entice them with ever wider varieties of goods and services.

It is further substantiated by the broadening of consumers' horizons. With the national standard of living at a record level, Americans have allowed their materialistic appetites to expand and, simultaneously, they have broadened their goals for the further betterment of their own lives and those of their children. Many of today's necessities were yesterday's luxuries, if they existed at all. Greater emphasis is being put on education, and the more education a person has, the more money he demands; the more money he earns, the greater his desire for goods and services. This serves to stimulate the economy, and as the economy continues strong it employs still more people, swelling the army of ambitious consumers. And the cycle continues to whirl—or so it is hoped.

But the unsophisticated consumer in this society of abundance has a problem of selection. If he is typical, he does not have enough money to indulge himself in all the material pleasures that tempt him, and still meet all his responsibilities and achieve all his goals. Therefore, he and his family must draw up a realistic financial program based on a standard of living appropriate to his income and geared to goals that have probability of achievement. To be successful he must forgo certain goods, services and indulgences for the sake of more vital needs. And, equally important, he must get maximum mileage out of his dollar.

Getting more for his money means becoming a knowledgeable consumer. President Johnson emphasized this need early in 1964, when he appointed Mrs. Esther Peterson to the new post of Special Assistant to the President for Consumer Affairs. Mrs. Peterson has said: "I don't believe that the Government should be a mother and take consumers by the hand and go into the market place and tell them what is good for them and what isn't. But I do think it is the business of Government to be sure consumers are informed."

Mrs. Peterson's efforts complement those of many Government agencies that, directly and indirectly, are protectors and guides of the consumer, and they are doing a good job in many areas. But in the final analysis it is the consumer himself who must take prime responsibility for the management and spending of his money. To that end, he must crystallize his and his family's values—their way of life; for the economic aspects of those values will suggest the family's daily spending pattern and its long-term goals.

Thus, the family that puts special value on a particular area, such as home entertainment, education or travel, will spend proportionately more in that area than other families of comparable income. To keep the books balanced, less money will be spent in other budgetary areas, and this is the seemingly obvious point that may elude the family that has not pinpointed its values and goals.

Because a family's values and goals can be elusive, the first step, in family conference, might be the listing of each member's need or desire for goods and services. Objective review of each item, its function, and whether it could be replaced generally reduces the list and gives guidance in ranking remaining items in order of importance. A logical pattern emerges, and this should be compared with what the family is spending, which may require the recording of all purchases for a month or more.

The consumer with his values and goals clear in his mind will have less tendency to go astray in his buying. But the suggestion of an analysis of all contemplated purchases is not to be interpreted as a purely utilitarian approach to buying. It is important that purchases reflect, where possible, the consumer's desires and attitudes, as well as his needs.

Within budgetary limits, an item may be bought simply because a person likes it, or because its ownership makes him feel "important." Such occasional pleasures tend to assure that the family's total financial program will be maintained. The buying list that has been drawn up can serve as a shopping guide. It would be most helpful if the personal and physical requirements that each item must meet are stipulated. That would reduce shopping time and effort. Fewer items will have to be exchanged because of color, size, shape or any other specific aspect that could be predetermined.

Potential buyers of most products and services must comparison shop before making a decision, being guided by value received, as well as by price. This, of course, would apply primarily to relatively large purchases, or to the first of a series of regular purchases of the same product or service. What may be considered a low price may not be worth a sacrifice in quality or service, but a top price may provide more quality and service than is required. If all factors but price are equal among competitors, then the lowest price offers the biggest bargain. However, if a company sets a low price by dispensing with services or quality factors that a particular buyer decides he could do without, then that company's deal is his bargain.

The level of quality itself is a buying consideration. Buying an item of greater or lower quality than is necessary for its function can be wasteful. A man's business suit, for example, will be subject to longer and greater use than a growing child's coat, so the family should buy the best quality suit it could afford; but the family could compromise on the quality of the child's coat, unless it is to be passed on to other children.

One of the best buying tools is one a family can provide for itself: a consumer-guidance file and library. It would include newspaper and magazine clippings, books, pamphlets, product labels and other materials that guide the consumer in the selection of food, clothing, furniture, high-fidelity equipment, houses and the countless other things a family ultimately will want or need. A family may subscribe to such consumer-oriented publications as *Consumer Bulletin* (published by Consumer's Research, Inc., of New York) or *Consumer Reports* (Consumer's Union of the United States, Inc., in Mount Vernon, New York). These magazines, along with other consumer references, are available in many libraries.

Choice of stores will be based on personal preference, convenience, extent of selection of desired merchandise, price levels and the extent of service provided. Some people, for example, prefer to forgo price discounts at self-service centers in favor of special services offered by other stores. When possible, it is generally best to shop during a store's slack hours, because customers get more time and help in those periods. As to long-range timing, planning ahead makes it possible to take advantage of seasonal sales, for example, clothing and linens in January, furniture and furs in August and so on. Seasonal and other sales are announced in advertisements, which should be followed regularly because they also provide other consumer guidance.

Dr. Leonhard Fuld, the multimillionaire philanthropist who died in 1965 at the age of 82, once made an observation that all consumers might heed. He said: "Here's something you must do. Every month when you pay your bills, be sure to pay something to the most important person in the world—you."

The Pitfalls of Bargain-Hunting

When a product or service is offered at a price that seems too good to be true, there is a good chance that it isn't. Real bargain-price offers are those of reputable sales organizations that periodically offer sales. Some of them occasionally will offer an item at an especially low price—perhaps below cost—in the hope of luring customers into their stores, where they may buy other merchandise at regular prices.

However, according to the Better Business Bureau of Metropolitan New York, consumers also have been barraged with dishonest offers by a number of unethical promoters. Among the many products and services they promote are sewing machines, wall-to-wall carpeting, furniture, vacuum cleaners, automobiles, automatic-transmission overhaul, television set repairs, dance lessons, home furnaces and house siding. Promoters using the "bait-and-switch" technique offer attractively priced merchandise that they do not intend to sell. Their maneuver is to switch the prospective buyer to a "better quality," and more expensive, product by devastatingly pointing out the deficiencies of the initially offered merchandise, its "worthless" guarantee and related features.

The initial offer may be presented in a telephone solicitation, by door-to-door salesmen, by mail or in a "bait" advertisement. The ads generally carry as few qualifying truths as legally necessary in as small print as is available. Other promoters may use the "contest" technique, advising a person that he has won something. To obtain his prize, however, the person generally must buy something else. Some promoters actually conduct contests, but every entrant is a "winner."

The bureau cited the case of a winner of a $50 certificate that allowed her to buy a particular sewing machine model for $169, or another at $199. "The offer may soon be withdrawn, and the price will be $50 more," the salesman said.

"Investigation established that the same machines were available elsewhere at the same prices without the 'valuable' certificate," said the B.B.B., which, like its counterparts across the country, is supported by member companies.

As part of its investigative procedure, the bureau has its field workers pose as consumers. Recent efforts in the home furnishings field have centered on the widely offered "three rooms of wall-to-wall carpeting" for about $100. Carpeting generally is measured in square yards, but these advertisers glibly refer to about 300 "square feet." That would be enough carpeting for three 10-foot-square rooms. The ad may be accurate, but the square-yard-oriented consumer who hears just the numbers can be misled.

That gets the salesman into the customer's home, but once there he starts destroying the product. According to Arthur Startz, vice president of the bureau, a carpet salesman who was unwittingly making a "switch" pitch to a bureau worker, said: "You have to be careful how you vacuum it, because it will run like a woman's stocking. And you're going to have to resand your floors when it's taken up."

A sewing machine salesman, who got in the door with an offer of an $18.50 model, warned the consumer that she should not run the machine for more than 10 minutes at a time, because it "heats up," and suggested that she keep a fire extinguisher handy. He then switched his pitch to a $189 machine that he "just happened to have" in his car.

There are criminal and general business laws prohibiting bait advertising in New York and other states. The Federal Trade Commission also combats interstate bait ads. The laws generally exclude "loss-leader" ads and "trading up" by legitimate companies that point out to the customer the qualities of more expensive products, but do not refuse to sell the advertised product.

The only real protection the consumer has, Mr. Startz says, is sufficient knowledge to be able to say "no" to unethical salesmen. Except in some special situation in which the consumer may have evidence, he generally has no legal recourse once he has signed a purchase agreement. However, to help protect the public, the consumer should report all instances of sales malpractice to the Better Business Bureau, perhaps the state attorney general and, if it is an interstate operation, the Federal Trade Commission. In general, it was said, it takes more than one consumer complaint to establish a strong case.

In its "Guides Against Bait Advertising," the F.T.C. warns consumers to be wary if the salesman refuses to show or demonstrate the product being offered, disparages it, refuses to take orders for delivery within a reasonable period of time, or shows or demonstrates a product that is defective or unusable for the purpose represented in the ad.

The consumer should be prompted by enlightened self-interest to file his complaints, for, after all, he is part of that public he would be helping to protect.

Guarantees and Warranties

Everyone has been assured by a salesman at one time or another that there was no reason for concern about a product's quality or performance, because "it comes with a guarantee." But, what does that mean?

The wise consumer would ask whether the guarantee will cover the entire product or only certain of its parts, and how long that protection will be valid. He must learn what his responsibilities would be under the guarantee, such as whether he must complete and mail the guarantee card that usually accompanies the instruction booklet, and whether he must maintain and operate the product only in certain stipulated ways. Further, he should know, in the event adjustment is required, whether he must return the product to the manufacturer or merely to the seller, and whether he must pay a service or labor charge. The adjustment may involve repair, replacement or a cash refund. If there is an option, is it given to the manufacturer (or seller), the buyer or both?

In essence, a guarantee (or warranty) on any item, be it an electric appliance, clothing, furniture or an automobile, makes certain representations about it that usually are designed to increase sales or limit the maker's or seller's liability. Its protection of the buyer, however, sometimes is narrow, vague or remote. Most consumers, and some retailers and manufacturers as well, use the terms "guarantee" and "warranty" interchangeably. But there is a legal distinction, though it is blurred by extensive misapplication. A warranty normally is issued by a manufacturer, who states in it the extent of his liability for the product he made.

On the other hand, a guarantee may be issued, not by the manufacturer, but perhaps by the assembler, seller or distributor of the product. While the guarantor is not directly or primarily liable for the performance of the product or its parts, he must answer for the failure or default of the manufacturer. In loose terms, he may be likened to the co-signer on a loan, who must pay the debt if the primary borrower doesn't. However, in the case of a guarantee, the consumer would go first to the guarantor, who may have an agreement with the manufacturer to handle this product-service function for him, either independently or as an agent.

Both guarantor and warrantor generally list the obligations and requirements of the consumer in their agreements. The situation is not so clean-cut that the consumer will know that he must deal with the manufacturer if he has a "warranty" or with the retailer if he has a "guarantee." Therefore, at point of purchase, he must make certain that he has in writing exactly who will stand behind the product, and what must be done to get him to do so.

In illustration of the nonconformity, some stores will accept responsibility for some defective products, such as certain electric appliances, and arrange for repairs or replacement, even though they may not be required to do so. Other stores may tell buyers of the very same products to return them to the factory.

Whatever liability limits a company sets in its guarantee or warranty, it cannot deprive a purchaser of the implied guarantees under the general sales laws of his state. In cases of substantial proportions, a lawyer may be engaged to determine whether the best route to satisfaction is application of the legally implicit guarantees or of the company's written agreement.

Another measure of a guarantee is whether adjustment would be on a pro-rata basis and, if so, whether computation would be based on the product's list price or the actual price paid by the consumer. The F.T.C., in its guidelines against deceptive advertising of guarantees, cited an example involving an automobile tire with a list price of $48 and an actual sales price of $24, with a 12-month guarantee. If the tire proved defective after six months, and the adjustment is made on the actual price paid, the customer would have to pay $12, or half his original purchase price, for a new tire. However, if adjustment is based on the list price, he would have to pay 50 per cent of $48, or $24, for a new tire. That being the price he paid in the first place, there would be no effective or equitable guarantee.

Further, when a guarantor says "satisfaction or your money back," the F.T.C. construes it to mean a refund of the full purchase price if the purchaser so desires.

Then there is the "lifetime guarantee." Does that refer to the life of the purchaser, the life of the item bought or the life of the object or device in which the item is installed? Generally speaking, a lifetime guarantee covers the period during which the purchaser or original user owns the product. But rather than assume this, the buyer should determine exactly what is meant.

In the final analysis, a guarantee is only as good as the company behind it. But sometimes even reputable companies make the consumer's job tough, intentionally or otherwise. For example, if a defective product must be returned to a manufacturer in a distant city, how many people are going to put themselves through the trouble of packing it and then lugging it to the post office?

Some Major Money Demands: Food and Automobiles

While there are many important consumer-spending areas, two stand out as consistent claimants of their regular shares of a family's income—food and automobiles. Their persistence makes them worthy of special consideration.

CUTTING FOOD COSTS. A 50-pound sack of potatoes can be bought for $2 from a roadside stand in the farm district on eastern Long

Island. Tomatoes, peaches and other fruits and vegetables can be bought at equally attractive prices, far below the cost in local food stores. That sounds great, and some experts might urge families to stock up and to can, freeze or otherwise preserve those foods that would spoil. The saving, they say, would be substantial. And that sounds great, too—at least in theory. But, how many city dwellers, for example, have the space or facilities for such a project? How many housewives—urban or suburban, employed outside the home or not—have the time to "put up" a couple of bushels of tomatoes or process other foods? And how many know how?

Food costs are high, accounting for 26 per cent of the average urban family's income, but buying from the farm is not the most logical way for most people to reduce those costs. Families with sizable home-freezers can take a step in the cost-cutting direction by buying a variety of meats and processed frozen foods in relatively large quantities.

There are food industry officials, to judge by their advertising campaigns, who would dispute the contention that food costs are high. They would point out that food accounted for 31.4 per cent of outlays from the average family's income in 1950, and an even greater proportion before World War II. But that is because incomes have risen faster than food prices. Actually, Americans, on the average, are spending more than twice as many food dollars as they did 25 years ago. This reflects not only the rise in costs, but also the great increase in built-in services provided by the food industry.

About three-quarters of the foods bought today are processed, many of them partially or fully prepared, according to "Your Food Dollar," a publication of the Household Finance Corporation's Money Management Institute in Chicago.

A National Conference Board study showed that, in 1962, the average American consumed more than three and one-half times more frozen vegetables and three times more frozen fruits and juices than he did in 1948. His annual consumption of fresh citrus fruits was reduced by nearly half in the period, during which his consumption of many other fresh foods also declined.

The amount a family allots for food varies with its income, location, personal tastes, special dietary requirements, amount of entertaining and general way of life. Some guidance is offered by the

United States Department of Agriculture, which estimated the weekly food costs of family units under low-cost, moderate and liberal cost plans.

For example, a husband and wife between the ages of 20 and 34 might spend $14.40 a week, $19.60 or $22.10, depending on the cost level they chose. A couple between the ages of 55 and 74 might spend $12.80, $17.60 or $19.70, with food requirements generally being reduced as people grow older. On the other hand, a couple with two preschool children might spend $21.40, $28.50 or $32.50 a week, and a couple with two school-age children might spend $24.80, $33.30 or $37.90 a week, depending on their plans' cost levels.

In general, if food takes 30 per cent or more of a family's budget, the family is spending too much. Taking all factors into consideration, the family should decide how much it can afford for food, and then see whether it stays within that limit. It can do so by using a special food-money purse or by keeping all food-store receipts and subtracting the cost of nonfood items.

It is possible to enjoy wholesome diets at each cost level, because different kinds and types of food of equal nutritional value are available at various prices. Reading a few books on nutrition and following newspaper and magazine articles on food should arm the consumer with sufficient knowledge to make low-cost choices.

In "How to Stretch Your Money," published by Public Affairs Pamphlets of New York, Sidney Margolius suggests that families "use standard grades (B or C) instead of Grade A or so-called fancy qualities. They are the same nutritionally. The chief differences between Grade A and B is appearance."

Pressed for time, relatively few consumers can cope with the preparation of many fresh foods, and fewer have the time or land to grow their own. But in buying processed foods, they would save a good deal of money and expend little more preparation time if they excluded fully prepared items from their shopping lists. Note, however, that there generally is no waste in prepared foods. Potatoes, for example, cost progressively more than the fresh variety if they are canned, instant, mashed or frozen as French fries, patties or puffs, or are stuffed, baked and topped with cheese and frozen.

Advance planning can go a long way toward reducing the cost and sometimes aggravating effort of keeping the family's pantry well stocked in order to put nutritionally balanced meals on the table. An essential part of that planning is to draw up menus for the period between shopping trips. Account should be taken of foods that are in season and are therefore cheaper, and of weekly advertised specials and promotions by stores and food companies.

Taking a cue from the retailer, the housewife should keep a scratch pad handy, noting on it what supplies her "continuing stock inventory" indicates are low. From that scratch pad, and from her advance menus, she can draw up a shopping list. Using a shopping list, and sticking to it, cuts down on costly impulse-buying of unnecessary items, and helps to assure that she will have all she will need for the week's meals.

Where shopping will be done is also a major cost factor. It is obvious that telephoning an order to a local store that will deliver it will cost a lot more than going to a self-service center and carting the food home yourself. But it isn't always as simple as that. Some families have found that, in their particular neighborhoods, it is cheaper to go to the local butcher for meats. He may charge more per pound than the supermarket's meat department, but experience may have shown these consumers that his meats include less waste. Admittedly, this is more the exception than the rule, but some consumers like the independent butcher's meats better anyway.

In shopping in a chain store or supermarket, consumers may consider the store's own brands, which generally are cheaper than national brands. But, as in the case of lesser food grades, experimentation will tell a family whether it is as well satisfied with these products.

Some food stores offer trading stamps as a shopping incentive. The family not interested in bothering with these stamps, which can be exchanged for merchandise, sometimes can get a cash discount equal to the stamps' value, although the discount usually has to be requested.

The shopper should keep a close watch on the clerks at the checkout counter, for, according to *The Progressive Grocer,* a trade magazine, a recent survey showed that cashiers at supermarkets make errors on 26 per cent of the orders they ring up. It is obviously inadvertent, because the cashiers showed a greater tendency to skip items and undercharge than to overcharge.

Where possible, it is generally economical to buy in large quantities, provided the family can use the extra food and has the appropriate storage facilities, be it a pantry, refrigerator or freezer. Incidentally, freezer sections of refrigerators generally are not designed for long-term storage. In buying "large economy sizes," it would be wise to check the difference, if any, in cost per ounce. Whatever reasons food manufacturers and processors give for following the practice, packing fractional weights and having small products rattling around in large boxes can be misleading to the consumer.

TAKING CARE OF YOUR CAR. "A car is like a woman," said a somewhat downtrodden husband recently. "The proper maintenance of either demands lots of time, attention and cash." His marital problems aside, this gentleman never learned the proper care and maintenance of an automobile. This lack of knowledge is the prime cause of his overspending, for the car is not a "lemon," one of those malfunctioning vehicles that has become increasingly rare in this age of production control.

This is not to say that the cost of automobile ownership is nominal. In fact, it is one of the biggest continuing cost factors in a family's budget. But it can be kept at a sensible level. Once an individual or family gets a realistic view of that cost, less the price of other transportation that can be eliminated, it can be decided whether the desire or need for a car warrants the expense.

Overriding factors affecting the cost of auto ownership include the size and type of car, the length of time it is kept and the extent of its use. Other factors include the owner's driving habits, road conditions, climate and prices of fuel and repairs in his area. In illustration, the man buying a big luxury car every year or two, and driving it hard over bad roads in a hot, dusty climate would be spending a lot more than the man buying a compact car every four or five years, keeping it in a garage and driving it carefully on weekends over good roads in a temperate climate.

A car's depreciation is greatest in the first year, but the rate of decline generally is less in each succeeding year. A dealer in a popular, full-size car selling for about $3,000 said, for example, that a person trading his car in for a comparable new one after one year would have to pay about $800, which would then be his depreciation factor. After two years, the cost might be $1,200, or $600 a year, and after three years, about $1,500, or $500 a year. The frequency of trade would depend on the amount and kind of use the car is put to, as well as on the owner's attitude toward owning a recent model. The car should be replaced, experts say, before repair and parts-replacement costs become excessive. The man who uses his car for business, putting on 25,000 hard miles a year, would trade more frequently than the weekend pleasure motorist.

The average motorist, driving 8,000 to 12,000 miles a year, might consider trading every three to five years. A realistic look must be taken at the extent of "necessary" repairs or parts replacements needed before a decision is made to buy a new car. If a car is in good mechanical condition and looks "clean," but needs new tires, chances are that it would be wiser to buy the tires and postpone the much larger investment in a new car. In so doing, the owner would reduce the annual depreciation of his old car by keeping it longer. He could use that extra time to save toward the new one, thus reducing or eliminating the loan he may have contemplated taking to make the purchase.

To estimate the annual depreciation on the family car, one may subtract the current value from the original cost and divide the remainder by the number of years it has been owned. The fixed expenses of auto ownership are the installment payments, if any; the insurance premium, registration and license fees; and the cost of a garage, if it is rented. The price of insurance could perhaps be reduced, if desired, by adding deductibles to the auto's physical damage coverage. For example, collision insurance would be less costly, if he is willing to pay the first $100 of any claim, rather than the first $50, which is the most common deductible amount for this coverage.

In general, it is wisest to study carefully the owner's manual that comes with the car, and to follow its recommendations. If it calls for oil changes and general lubrication every 3,000 miles, under normal driving conditions, it would be wasteful to have this servicing done every 1,000 miles.

In the automotive field, the popular combination deals are the motor tune-up, the spring or fall check-ups. The auto owner may have a feeling of satisfaction, but did the car actually need all that work? If the spark plugs and distributor points were replaced, it just might be that all they needed were cleaning and resetting, or possibly filing in the case of the points.

An owner of a year-old car that "was running just fine," brought it in for routine servicing. He got a $72 bill for a "tune up" along with a $21 charge for a brake adjustment and front-end alignment. "I believe in taking care of a car," he said. "I have it checked every spring and fall, and trade it in when it's been driven 60,000 miles."

His mistake, automotive experts say, is twofold: First, he has his car serviced by the calendar, rather than being guided by the car's performance and actual needs. Second, and to this the motorist agreed, his complete lack of knowledge of mechanics made him susceptible to anything the service man said. In point of fact, the experts said, there was no indication that the car, having traveled little more than 12,000 miles in its year of existence, was in need of such a major tune up.

There is no question that a good mechanic could recommend low-cost preventive work while lubricating or otherwise checking over a car. Thus, care must be taken in the selection of the man to work on a car. He may come recommended by friends, or he may be selected by trial and error.

DEALING WITH CAR DEALERS. "We made a deal on the car I wanted, agreeing on the price they would allow for my old car. I signed a contract and wrote a deposit check. Then the dealer backed down. He wanted more money from me." The angry and indignant executive was recounting a recent sad experience with a new-car dealer. He was doubly disturbed, because it duplicated an encounter with another dealer earlier the same day. He was the twofold victim of the highly questionable and oppressive sales tactics of certain big metropolitan area dealers who, though they may not be representative of the industry, pose a threat to the buying public because of their size. In each case, the executive reached his agreement with a salesman, who had appraised his car and given no indication that the deal was not a final one.

The ready, willing and able buyer then was left alone in a small office for about 40 minutes, after which a man, introducing himself as "the sales manager," told him he would have to pay more than $200 above the agreed price, because his trade-in "needed a lot of work."

In one case, the sales manager reduced the cost of that "lot of work" and later offered to "split the difference." Stressing that the deal was "fair," he said the addition would come to "only a couple of dollars a month," and badgeringly suggested that the customer was trying to take advantage of him.

The sales manager moved in for the kill, assuming perhaps that the customer was weary of waiting and haggling and was anxious to get his hands on the new car. He had grossly misjudged his prospective buyer. For the executive was not ready to be victimized to the extent of buying under a "revised" deal, as other perhaps less sophisticated shoppers might have done. He tore up his deposit check and the contract, which the dealer had not signed, and walked out of the showroom.

"Even if they had gone back to their original deal," he said, "I would not have bought. I couldn't trust them."

The importance of goodwill is lost on such dealers who think only of today's sale. They advance proposals designed to stimulate a prospect's interest, and then work to get back some of what they appeared to have given away. Sometimes, according to the Better Business Bureau of Metropolitan New York, these proposals are carried in "bait" advertisements, which make promises in big print and modify them in fine print. The executive was subjected in both instances to "high-balling," a technique by which a dealer sets a relatively high initial price on a prospect's trade-in. Then, when the prospect is properly worn down, the dealer reduces it, or makes up the difference on the new-car price or the finance charges. A "low-balling" dealer offers a new car at an especially low price, and then attempts to "sweeten" the deal with costly extras. Or, as in the preceding illustration, he attempts to make up his profit on the other primary elements in the "package"—the trade-in or the financing.

In the course of negotiation all dealers may manipulate these elements to make their packages competitive, but a line sharply divides the many reputable dealers from the few disreputable ones. Honest dealers are unhappy with these black sheep, a dealer said, because "they're ruining our business." The unethical dealers strive to confuse and trap buyers, according to the B.B.B. and several auto men who asked that their names not be used. The calculating dealers may have several men taking turns at working on a client, who reaches the point where he doesn't know who said what to whom.

To allow more time for the sales pitch, the dealer may "lose" the customer's car or its key, which may not be "found" for hours, sometimes not until the customer has agreed to buy. Many people finally give in to this frustrating, fatiguing and sometimes intimidating pressure of overtalking, of mathematical calculation of deal after deal, of lonely waiting. In extremes, they may even unthinkingly sign blank purchase or time-payment contracts, which unscrupulous dealers then "pack" with extra charges.

All this often happens in a small office, which may exert a pressure of its own. Using an interoffice communications system, some dealers are said to eavesdrop on conversations of customers and their companions, who unsuspectingly talk freely among themselves about what they are willing or able to spend. Of course, one must not assume that this is practiced by every agency having private offices for its salesmen. Many dealers, in all good conscience, have set up such offices for the benefit of customers, who often must reveal personal information in arranging to buy a car. Little privacy is afforded by the salesmen's desks lined against a showroom wall.

"Unhorsing" a customer is a variation of the high-balling theme. The dealer tells the customer he thinks he could sell his old car for him in a few days at a particular price, and the new-car deal is written up on the basis of that price. When the customer returns, however, he may find that his car has to be sold for considerably less, but he still is committed to the new-car purchase.

In another variation, a customer may buy a car for delivery in several weeks, during which time he tells friends all about the new car. However, when he returns, he may be told that his trade-in allowance has been reduced because "the used-car market is down," or because his old car's condition has deteriorated. Ashamed to face his friends without the new car, he may agree to a revised deal.

Tradition has it that auto buying involves some degree of "horse trading." Perhaps because urban dwellers are extremely price-conscious, close bargaining—and intensive price competition among dealers—is most prevalent in metropolitan areas, which account for a big part of national auto sales. This sales concentration has created the big-volume dealer. Thus, while less desirable agencies are in the minority, they command critical attention because of their broad impact on the public. They may sell from 1,000 to 5,000 new cars a year, while small-town dealers may sell only a few hundred, or as few as 25.

With the exception of a few manufacturer-owned or subsidized agencies in major cities, franchised dealers are independent operators. Car makers note this when the sharp-practices issue is raised, but they have made some effort to eliminate it. Some critics have labeled much of that effort as "lip service."

There is little discounting in small towns, and most customers have not come to expect it. A dealer, operating in a limited area among people he often knows personally, seeks to build repeat business on service. Many metropolitan dealers do this—some quite successfully—but they complain that slim profits, high overhead and a dearth of experienced mechanics make the task difficult. Many of their regular customers have been recruited from the stream of "comparison shoppers" who roam from dealer to dealer.

Salesmen are pressured by their bosses to do a better job on financing. Aside from a commission on the sale of insurance, which usually covers only physical damage to the financed car, the dealer also gets a share of the finance, or service, charge. Time-payment charges are legally different from interest on a loan, though their effect is the same.

The New York State limit, though most dealers reportedly charge less, is 7 per cent of the total owed for each year of the repayment period on a new car, and up to 13 per cent on a used car. Those would be equivalent to true annual interest rates of at least 14 and 26 per cent. At 7 per cent, $2,000 due over three years would increase by 21 per cent, or $420. However, the dealer would have an arrangement with a finance company or a bank, which would assume the financing at perhaps a 4.5 per cent advance discount per year, for a total cost of $270. The dealer would keep the $150 difference.

As one dealer put it, "The man who can least afford it pays the highest rate, because his credit is poor." It is this man who often is attracted also to the "no-money-down" deal, in which a high-interest personal finance company loan provides the "cash" down payment. While an automobile is a big purchase for most anyone, to this man, who must meet a personal loan bill and an auto installment each month, the car becomes his whole life.

Most shoppers can avoid the pitfalls of auto buying by selecting a reputable dealer. This may be done through friends or, with a particular dealer in mind, through the Better Business Bureau, which will check on the company in its file of 250,000 and report its findings. There may be a "pattern of consumer complaints." The shopper's next line of defense is to remain alert, never losing track of his own auto and never signing forms without knowing their contents. In evaluating a deal he should consider all its parts. What is the price of the new car, less the trade, if there is one? What is the actual financing cost? Would it be wiser to borrow the money from a bank or credit union and negotiate a cash deal for the car?

If a shopper feels he has been wronged, he may appeal to the manufacturer and the Better Business Bureau. After investigation, the bureau may seek an adjustment from the dealer, and, if the case warrants, may refer it to the appropriate law-enforcement agency. Of course, the shopper may also consider consulting a lawyer.

AUTO RENTAL GUIDELINES. A number of individuals and families, particularly city dwellers, don't own cars, but want them for weekends, vacations or entire seasons. Then there are families who need or want a second or third car for short periods. Some persons planning to buy an automobile may want to rent a model of their choice to put it through a more thorough trial than a demonstration ride would allow. The simple answer in all instances is to go to an auto rental company. The tough corollary questions are: Which company, and what is a fair price?

In the United States, there are hundreds of auto rental (short-term) and leasing (long-term) companies, and almost as many rate schedules. In Manhattan, for example, such concerns take up about 14 pages in the classified telephone directory.

"Competition is fierce," the head of one company said, "and that means bargains for the public." But a "bargain" is only as good as the comparative value received. Putting price aside for the moment, one should review the auto rental services and benefits that are considered essential, and those that may or may not be of special importance to him. Essential factors are the vehicle's reliability and the extent of insurance coverage provided. Most reputable companies trade in their cars after they have been driven about 20,000 miles, notwithstanding a major concern's implicit suggestion in its advertising that it is unique in this practice.

It is a sensible practice, an industry executive said, giving customers some assurance of safety and holding down a company's maintenance costs (and complaints), which generally climb after a car has been driven 20,000 miles by many motorists, some of whom may treat the auto roughly. Furthermore, by the time a rental car has been driven that far, the new models are out, and promotion-minded companies want to offer new cars. A customer should be wary of the concern offering "late-model cars," unless he is convinced that they are in top condition. A discount sometimes is offered as an incentive to rental of cars more than a year old.

The measure of reliability goes beyond the age and condition of the rented car. The best of autos can develop problems. What happens to the customer stuck on the road? A national company, or a regional one, if the breakdown occurs in its area, may have an office close by. If so, the company, upon notification, may arrange for quick repairs or, if necessary, provide a replacement car. If no office is near, the company, upon notification by long-distance phone or wire, may authorize repairs, and the customer would have to await their completion. The cost of notification should be deducted from the rental bill. The concern of a customer over this service should be guided in large part by the range of his travel and the value he puts on his time. If he plans to cover a large area, he may want a company with a maximum number of offices in that area.

As to insurance, most companies provide up to $100,000 of indemnification for one person injured in an accident and up to a total of $300,000 for all persons injured in one accident. Protection against property damage generally is at least $25,000. Some concerns provide more coverage. Collision insurance, protecting against damage to the rented car, also is included, but with a $100-deductible clause, making the customer liable for that initial amount in damages. Some companies also have a $25-deductible clause on the fire and theft coverage. Customers may eliminate those deductibles, usually by paying an additional $1 a day or $5 a week, and less on longer-term leasing.

But there are a few more insurance questions that must be asked by the man about to rent a car. Will the insurance remain effective if there are other drivers, and, if so, must they be over the age of 21 or 25? Also, would the coverage be voided if an accident occurred outside a particular geographic area or if it was determined that the driver exceeded the speed limit or violated some other law? Is the customer responsible for the theft of a car he forgot to lock?

Among the factors that a customer may or may not deem important are the following:

- The right to pick up a car in one place and return it at another, either within a metropolitan area or, in the case of large companies, sometimes nationally. There may be a charge for this service.
- Immediate availability of cars.
- Variety and types of cars available, for example, compacts, convertibles, station wagons, and luxury and sports cars.
- Delivery service, for which there often is a charge.
- Advance reservations. These generally are available, but may be more difficult or expensive to arrange—with telephone calls or telegrams—over great distances, unless the company has offices in the customer's city and at his travel destination.

Once a shopper has considered all other auto-rental factors, as they relate to his needs, then he may evaluate cost, as it relates to those factors.

Costs vary within a community, primarily for competitive reasons, and nationally, chiefly because of market differences. For example, in New York City, charges are higher over weekends than on weekdays, because weekend demand is greater. But the reverse is true in many other areas. San Francisco reportedly is unusual in that rates are about the same, weekday or weekend, because of a consistency of demand.

The rate may be a fixed amount for a given period, plus a charge for each mile driven, in which case the company pays all fuel bills. If the mileage charge is reduced or eliminated, the customer buys the gas and oil, and this could mean a saving if he expects to drive extensively. His fuel cost could range from 2 to 3 cents, depending on the size of the car and its equipment. In New York, the weekday rate for a standard-size sedan may range from $7 a day and 7 cents a mile to $8 and 12 cents a mile, depending on whether the company is a discounter or not. A weekend special—Friday afternoon to Monday morning—might range from $25.95 and 10 cents a mile to $27 and 11 cents a mile.

Rental of a compact car can mean savings of $1 or more a day and 1 to 2 cents a mile, and a still smaller foreign car affords an even greater saving. Savings also are available in the form of free parking, employer discounts, part-time rates, and vacation and other specials.

3

LIVING TODAY ON TOMORROW'S INCOME

The market place for the poor is "a commercial jungle in which exploitation and fraud are the norm rather than the exception."

That harsh-sounding observation was made by Dr. David Caplovitz of Columbia University, author of *The Poor Pay More*. He was addressing a Consumer Action Conference, sponsored by the Office of Economic Opportunity and the President's Committee on Consumer Interests, in Washington in August, 1965. The professor was discussing the plight of the poor, who, in "their vulnerability to 'easy credit,' " are often staggered by "the excessive burden of debt foisted upon them by high-pressure salesmen."

But, while the problem is especially severe among the poor, it also has had devastating effect on many families in relatively more affluent segments of the population. Families of moderate and so-called middle incomes may be just as vulnerable to the high-pressure salesman. Further, they may be more tempted to satisfy their material appetites because of a relatively recent phenomenon: Increasing numbers of people have greater amounts of discretionary income, that is, money above the amount required for basic living needs. Our surging economy is geared to pay-as-you-go living on installment plans, charge accounts and phenomenally ubiquitous credit cards.

"About 65 per cent of all new cars and 75 per cent of the used cars purchased in this country are bought and paid for through some type of installment sales contract," says the International Consumer Credit Association of St. Louis. "And about 85 per cent of other durables, such as furniture and appliances, are bought through this method of consumer credit."

Often it is indiscriminate spending and a lack of credit-buying knowledge that lead a person of moderate or greater income into economic plight. The obvious antidotes are advance planning and credit education. Sidney Margolius reports in "A Guide to Consumer Credit," published by Public Affairs Pamphlets of New York: "Today, the average family has obligated about 13 per cent of its after-tax income for installment payments. Since about half the families have no such debts, those who do obviously owe more than 13 per cent—perhaps 25 per cent or more."

Many high-charge creditors are willing to extend a greater proportion of credit than that. The debtor is left with no safety margin. For example, a construction worker with a wife, three children and another child expected, recently complained that he could not meet his monthly debt repayments of $171.50, though he worked steadily. The crushing blow, after having bought furniture and a car on time, was the loan required to meet a family emergency.

Loans: Interest rates, personal and auto loans, life insurance policy loans, savings banks and savings and loan associations, industrial banks and industrial loan companies, pawnbrokers, high-cost loans, the debtors' rights

Most money management experts agree that a person should not borrow unless he absolutely must. The loan should be for a family necessity, to meet an emergency or perhaps to buy a car that is essential to his work. Once a person has decided he must finance his purchase, he should shop just as carefully for credit as he does for the required goods or service. Whenever possible, it is generally wisest to take a separate loan, because some lenders charge much less than others, and because the cash buyer can more readily "bargain" over price or take advantage of discounts and sales.

To compare credit or loan sources, one must determine true annual *interest cost or loan charges.* As a rule of thumb, when a flat charge for each $100 of loan is levied for each year of repayment, the annual cost is twice that charge. Thus, if it costs $6 a year to borrow $100, the true annual interest rate is about 12 per cent. When the loan charge is a percentage each month of the unpaid balance, the true annual interest charge is 12 times the monthly rate. For example, if the monthly rate is 1½ per cent of the unpaid balance, the true annual interest rate is 18 per cent. However, if the monthly rate is a percentage of the original loan, then the true annual interest rate is about twice that, some 36 per cent, because the average unpaid balance over the year of regular payment is only half the original loan.

Personal and auto loans are available from banks across the country at $4.50 to $6 per $100, plus 25 to 50 cents for insurance that automatically repays the debt if the debtor dies, bringing the true annual loan charge to from 9½ to 13 per cent. Credit unions charge from three-fourths of 1 per cent to 1 per cent a month (sometimes including insurance) on the unpaid balance, putting the true interest rate at about 9 to 12 per cent a year. Depending on the geographic location, true annual interest charges can range from 18 to 42 per cent at small loan companies, 12 to 34 per cent on car loans arranged through auto dealers or finance companies, and 18 to 20 per cent or more on installment purchases of appliances through retailers.

Life insurance policy loans are attractive because the true interest rate is as stated—generally 5 per cent; but, unless steps are taken, insurance is reduced by the loan. The true interest rate is the stated rate also on home mortgages, which are not under discussion here (see Chapter 4). A long-time homeowner requiring a large sum, however, might consider refinancing his house.

Needless to say, one should keep away from those illegal lenders known as loan sharks, who generally charge incredibly exorbitant rates.

In some states, *savings banks and savings and loan associations* are permitted to grant personal loans, but generally only against savings accounts. In most cases, a person may borrow an amount equal to up to the full value of his savings-bank account, or up to 90 per cent of his association account. He would pay a greater rate of interest on his loan than he would receive on his savings. The incentive to borrow rather than withdraw savings may be that there would not be a great enough compulsion to replenish the account. It also may make good sense to borrow rather than withdraw, if a savings-dividend or interest-payment date is near. For the payment lost on withdrawal of the money too soon might be greater than the charge on a short-term loan.

Many people may scoff at the thought of going to a *pawnbroker*.

While those with good credit standing can do better, others could do worse in states like New York, where pawnshops are closely regulated. A pawnbroker makes short-term, expeditious loans on personal property left with him. Among items that may be pledged as security are jewelry, watches, furs, silver, cameras, radios, musical instruments, optical goods, typewriters and men's clothing. State laws vary widely, and so do interest charges, which may range from 2 to 10 per cent a month (true annual interest of 24 to 120 per cent). The borrower may redeem the merchandise by repaying the loan, with interest, or sometimes may renew the loan by paying the back interest. The loan is repayable in a lump sum, not installments. The borrower need not pay anything, but he would forfeit his property, which ultimately would be sold at auction. He usually would be entitled to the excess, if any, of the resale price above the loan amount, interest and auction fee.

There are times when a person must settle for a *high-cost loan* he vitally needs, because his credit standing is not good enough for cheaper loan sources. It is axiomatic that the more liberal the credit extension the greater the interest and finance charges.

But, in his desperation, *the debtor must not neglect to protect his rights.* The states have laws governing credit sales, but they will not protect the consumer automatically. He must take the responsibility, too, for knowing what the law requires and seeing that those requirements are met. In New York, for example, he may obtain a copy of "Know Your Rights When You Buy on Time," a booklet of the New York State Banking Department, 100 Church Street, New York, N. Y., 10007. He may also direct complaints to that agency, or the comparable one in his state, as well as to the Better Business Bureau and his lawyer.

The cardinal credit-buying rule is to read the contract carefully before signing it. It must comply with the law. It must be filled in completely, lest the seller later pad it with unwarranted charges. Its figures must be itemized, so that the buyer knows exactly what he is paying for. In general, it makes sense not to take the salesman's word for anything.

A debtor who finds he cannot keep up the payments should tell his creditors immediately and, together, they may work out a solution. Repossession of the property, which the creditor often can accomplish without a court order, does not free the debtor from future payment. In fact, legal and other fees may be added to the unpaid balance.

Most lenders appear to be advocates of borrowing only for essential reasons. One company, for example, recommends that people should "never borrow money needlessly." But the same company heavily promotes vacation loans. Some people may argue that vacations are "essential," but their benefits may be more than offset by the burden of having to pay for them later.

Installment Buying: Conditional sale, chattel mortgage, bailment lease contracts, oppressive contract clauses, rebates

The installment-purchase spiral has reached a level at which almost anything can be bought now and paid for later, be it clothing, a dishwasher, a car, an ocean cruise or a plane trip. When the credit is obtained from the seller of the product or service, it is called "installment-sale credit." However, a buyer may obtain an "installment cash loan" from a lending agency and pay cash for his purchase. The buyer who arranges for financing with the retailer often ends up repaying a lending agency, too, because many retailers either sell their installment-sales contracts to a sales finance company or have an open agreement with one. The retailers do this either because they have insufficient lending capital, or because they can use their money more profitably elsewhere.

The seller of merchandise, or the finance company holding the installment contract, generally seeks to protect himself against the buyer's general creditors or against "innocent third-party purchasers" of the merchandise from the original buyer. Unless the seller takes certain legal steps, those other parties would have first claim on the merchandise, should the buyer fail or sell.

How the seller protects himself should be of special interest to installment buyers. He normally seeks his shelter in one of several types of contracts: the conditional sale, the chattel mortgage or, less frequently, the bailment lease. Buyers should make it a point to read these contracts before signing them, questioning the seller or finance company on all doubtful areas, so that they know exactly what their obligations are. The starkly real contract terms take over where the salesman's promises leave off.

Most installment contracts are of the *conditional sales type,* under which title to the merchandise remains with the seller until he has received payment in full. If payments are not made on schedule, the merchandise may be repossessed. Depending on state law, the payments that had been made may be regarded as rent for use of the merchandise, or may be partly refunded to the buyer. But the likelihood is slim that the buyer in default would get much, if any, of his money back, even in states that provide the legal apparatus, patterned on the Uniform Conditional Sales Act, that would make it possible. In general, the procedure in those states calls for the sale at auction of the repossessed property by the seller or finance company. He is obliged to return to the buyer any money remaining after he has taken the unpaid balance on the defaulted installment debt and the expenses of repossessing and selling the property. It sometimes is difficult for the debtor to learn what the resale price was and whether the auction was honest. If the proceeds of the resale are insufficient to cover the unpaid balance of the installment debt, the seller or finance company may decide to take legal action to obtain a judgment against the debtor for that deficient amount. The installment buyer thus would find himself owing more money on merchandise he no longer owns.

He would be in a similar situation under most conditional contracts, if the property were lost, destroyed or damaged. For, while the title would remain with the seller until the debt is canceled, the responsibility remains with the buyer, who would be obliged to continue his payments. However, since there is a chance that he would be unable to do so, the seller usually protects himself with insurance on the property, which the buyer pays for.

In most states, a *chattel mortgage contract,* when used to secure an installment debt, gives the seller of the merchandise a proportionate interest in it. This enables him to ask in court to have the property sold at a sheriff's or marshal's sale for his benefit, if the debtor defaults.

Under the relatively little-used *bailment lease,* title to the property bought on an installment plan remains with the seller, and may be purchased by the buyer for a nominal sum, usually waived by the seller, after the last payment has been made. If the buyer defaults in his payments, the seller takes back the merchandise, and has no obligation to return any part of the payments already made, since legally they were paid for use of the property while the buyer had it in his possession.

As noted, the credit buyer's first rule of self-protection is to read the contract before signing it. He must make certain that all blanks are filled in so that the seller cannot "pack" it with additional charges, be they for unwarranted "services" or unwanted merchandise. The buyer should be alert to such *oppressive contract clauses* as the following:

1. *Wage assignment*. This clause may give the creditor power to collect all or part of the buyer's wages, if an installment payment is missed. This legal process, known as "garnishment" or "garnisheeing wages," obliges employers to withhold all or part of the debtor's wages until the debt is paid. Some employers discharge workers whose wages are garnisheed. The percentage of a person's wages that may be taken by a creditor is limited in some states, such as New York, which sets a 10 per cent ceiling.

2. *The add-on clause*. This often is included in a contract to cover a series of installment purchases, such as for furniture, and makes earlier purchases security for new ones. If the buyer defaults on his new payments, he may lose not only the new merchandise, but also the earlier items on which he had completed payment.

3. *The acceleration clause*. With this, all installment payments are immediately due and payable, should the buyer default in one payment, for whatever reason. Unable to pay the total unpaid balance, the debtor sees his merchandise carted away for resale, which may not absolve him of all future liability.

4. *The "balloon" clause*. A contract containing this stipulates a final payment that is substantially larger than the preceding installments. Discovering this too late, the buyer may lose his property after having paid a good part of its price, or be forced to refinance, often at still more disadvantageous terms.

In addition, there may be obscure or hidden clauses that obligate the buyer to pay for something he neither wants nor needs. Hidden costs also can pass unnoticed, if all charges are not itemized. The buyer should demand this, so that he knows what he is paying for.

An important point for a buyer to remember is that, even if there is dissatisfaction with the product, he is obliged to meet the installment payments stipulated in his contract, particularly if the debt is with a finance company or bank. Under certain circumstances, he may be released from his obligation if the credit was issued by the seller, or if the finance agency had been directly involved in and responsible for the original transaction. Similarly, the buyer generally must turn for fulfillment of a guarantee or warranty to the manufacturer, seller, contractor or whoever issued it, but not to the bank or finance company.

If the buyer decides to prepay all or part of his debt, he may or may not get back part of the finance charge, depending on his state's laws. In about half the states, the amount of *rebate* is regulated, but in the others, it depends on the seller's or lender's policy. In any case, the debtor does not get back as much as he expected.

Lenders in regulated states and reputable lenders elsewhere generally apply the formula known as the "rule of 78," or the "sum of the digits." The "78" is the sum of the digits from 12 back to 1, and would be applicable to a 12-month contract. In the first month, the lender would have earned 12/78 of the total finance charge, in the second month an additional 11/78, in the third month an additional 10/78, and so on. Over the first six months, he would have earned a total of 57/78 of the total finance charge. In any month that the debtor prepaid, his rebate would be the number of 78ths that the lender had not earned.

For example, if the finance charge, after allowable deductions, is $82.50 and the account is paid off in six months, 57/78 of the finance charge, or $60.28, would have been earned by the finance company. The balance of 21/78, or $22.22, would be payable as a rebate to the prepaying debtor. On a 24-month contract, the formula changes. The sum of the digits from 24 back to 1 is 300. The lender earns 24/300 of the total finance charge in the first month, 23/300 the second, and so on.

Credit Plans: Regular charge accounts, budget accounts and revolving charge accounts, 90-day charge accounts, installment sale credit

Customers at most stores can charge their purchases or buy on some form of credit plan. Major stores, such as large specialty shops and department stores, may have their own charge plans, while smaller outlets may participate in charge and credit programs sponsored by banks or other independent finance organizations.

The *regular charge account,* or "open account," generally calls for payment of bills shortly after the end of the month in which credit purchases are made. Retailers who extend this "charge-it" privilege usually require no down payment and make no separate or direct charge for the credit. However, the cost of the credit is included in the purchase price, and therefore also is paid by the cash customers.

Stores also offer *budget accounts* and *revolving charge accounts.* A budget account permits the credit buyer to pay his charge bill over an extended period, such as three to six months. A revolving charge account is basically a line of credit. The customer can make purchases up to a given maximum and agrees to pay what he owes in monthly installments. Whenever the monthly installments reduce the balance due on the account to below the maximum allowed, the buyer again can make purchases up to that maximum. If the entire amount is paid when due, there are no further charges. However, if only a portion of the amount is paid each month, there is a charge, generally computed at the rate of 1½ per cent a month (18 per cent true annual interest rate) on the unpaid balance up to $500, and 1 per cent a month on the excess above $500. Many stores impose a comparable charge on budget account balances and on regular charge account balances that are not paid within 30 days after monthly statements are rendered.

Some men's and women's specialty stores have *90-day charge accounts,* under which payments are divided into three equal monthly installments and no interest usually is charged. Many department stores also extend this service on certain large purchases, such as of furniture.

In addition to the accounts described, retailers also may extend *installment sale credit* on purchases of relatively high-priced goods, such as major appliances and furniture. Department stores, mail order houses, automobile dealers, appliance stores and most other retailers usually make a separate charge for installment sale credit. The charge may be called "interest charge," "finance charge," "financing charge," "carrying charge" or by some other name. The rate can vary widely. For example, if geared to the monthly unpaid balance it may range from 1½ to 3½ per cent a month of that reducing balance. That would put the range of true annual interest rates at from 18 to 42 per cent.

The Credit Card

The great American charge-it or credit card phenomenon shows no signs of slackening. It is not only a phenomenon, but a potential problem, since hundreds of millions of dollars are involved. Is it being abused? Are people getting seriously in debt through the use of easy credit? There are no easy answers, but the questions persist.

There are general-purpose credit cards on which charges may be made simply by presenting them at any affiliated restaurant, hotel, motel, airline or store. Credit cards may be used for such items as wigs, fireplace equipment, nursery stock and garden supplies, pets and accessories for pets, model railroads, gear for horseback riding and clothing for fat men. In Honolulu, tourists can use their credit cards to see divers for black coral. If you can name it, you usually can charge it. In addition to the general-purpose cards, there are millions of gasoline and auto service cards issued by major oil companies, telephone credit cards, air-travel cards and other "specialized" credit cards. Even these are broadening in scope. For example, several companies are offering to sell insurance and other unrelated products and services to their credit-card holders.

It is not too difficult for an applicant to obtain a credit card. If he applies for a general-purpose card, he generally must have an income of at least $7,500 a year. As is the case for most credit applicants, he must also undergo a credit investigation. His initial fee of $8 to $10 will pay part of its cost, after which he must pay a nominal annual fee. The credit organizations make their money primarily from the deductions of 4 to 7 per cent on the restaurant and other bills they pay on behalf of cardholders. These restaurants and other organizations pass this charge on to all their customers in the form of higher prices. That, perhaps, is why some rather high-priced eating places are known as "expense-account" restaurants.

Credit cards, like department store and other charge cards, make it easy for people to fall into a pattern of overspending, of living beyond their means. It is easy to forget that cards are like cash, and that the day of reckoning never is too far off. The guiding rule, therefore, is to treat credit cards like cash.

Losing a credit card is like losing a signed blank check, and that risk is faced by more than 20 million Americans who carry one or more charge cards. There is no problem if the loss or theft is detected immediately, and the issuer of the credit or charge-account card is promptly notified in writing, provided that the card has not been fraudulently used in that brief period between the loss and the written notification.

But sometimes, days, weeks and even months might pass before the infrequent user of credit cards discovers the loss of one. The greater the time lapse between loss and notification, the greater the risk of misuse. The spending spree of a thief or unscrupulous finder of a card could be quite extensive if it lasted only a day or two, but it could be monumental if it was of longer duration. Leading credit cards are internationally recognized and it is conceivable that a thief could use one of them abroad, after having charged the air fare to his destination. All this could happen in only a couple of days, thanks to the jet age.

Who pays the thief's bills? If they were run up before the card issuer had received notification (it usually must be in writing) of its loss, the rightful owner of the card would have to pay, according to most card issuers and a number of court decisions.

An outstanding exception is a California appeals court's decision in favor of a cardholder who had been sued for $1,622.99 in charges made by a thief before the issuer had been notified. The case, the Diners' Club, Inc., v. Whited, is discussed by Howard S. Irvin in an article in *The North Carolina Law Review* (Vol. 43, 1965). Mr. Irvin notes that the appeals court reversed a lower court decision, "holding that, although the terms of the issue-holder contract seemed to call for absolute liability for all purchases made with the card before notice, the issuer and the merchants nevertheless owed a duty of reasonable care to see that 'irregular charges [were] not unnecessarily incurred.' "

Of further significance, he says, is the fact that the court followed a rule set forth in a previous case, Union Oil Company v. Lull: "That the issuer suing a holder on the liability provision has the burden of proving that both it and the merchant involved used due care in accepting the charges." He concedes that the merchant might not be able to recall his actions, even if "due care" had been taken, and that the location of witnesses might be difficult and costly. But, he says, it "would be even harsher to put this burden of proof on the holder."

The holder was not present when the unauthorized charge purchases were made, and "it would be impossible in most instances for him to prove that due care was not used."

Mr. Irvin added that "it appears that the result reached in the Diners' Club case is the fairest. If neither the issuer, holder nor merchant has been negligent, and if the parties have used due care in carrying out their various duties, or if only the holder had been negligent, the contractual liability clause between the issuer and the holder should be given full force and the holder should be liable for the unauthorized purchases."

While the conscientious person who loses a credit card might take encouragement from the California decision, he still may be held liable for unauthorized charges made before he has properly notified the card issuer. What can a card carrier do to protect himself? Two things: take special care in the use of credit cards and consider the possibility of passing the risk, for a fee, to one of the many insurance companies that have recently marketed credit card coverage. Among the "due-care" guideposts are the following:

- Promptly notify the issuer of a card of its loss. Immediately telephone or wire the company to show good intentions and follow up with the mandatory letter bearing the holder's signature. Upon its receipt, the company will take responsibility for stopping all unauthorized charges, and issue a new card.
- Never lend a credit card, unless willing to take complete responsibility.
- Destroy all old cards and any unsolicited cards received in the mail that are not going to be used.
- Make certain that a card is returned after each purchase, and replaced in pocket or purse.

A variety of credit card insurance coverages are available to the individual and the business organization, though the discussion will be restricted to the individual. The protection may be bought separately or added to another policy that had been issued by the same company. Some insurers will add the coverage to most personal policies they have issued, be they homeowner's, household fire, casualty or marine policies.

In general, credit card losses will be paid if the insured has taken proper precautions and has complied with the card-issuer's loss provisions, the primary one being immediate written notification. But the coverage often is broader, in that it also protects the policyholder against losses caused by forgery or alteration of checks. Aside from the named insured, the coverage often extends to such other residents of his household as his spouse and persons under age 21 who are in his care.

Because of the variation in credit card insurance rates and policy provisions, the shopper should make sure he knows what he is buying.

One company offering credit card coverage, which includes check protection and may be added to another policy or bought separately, charges the individual $2 a year for each $1,000 of coverage. The three-year rate is the usual 2.7 times the one-year rate, or $5.40 per $1,000. The highest protection amount bought thus far was said to be $10,000 and the average was about $2,500.

A number of other companies sell credit card coverage only in combination with a depositor's forgery bond or a family forgery bond. In essence the depositor's forgery bond protects the insured against loss through forgery, raising or altering of his checks. The family forgery bond provides that protection, along with protection against losses from acceptance of checks that prove to have been forged, raised or altered. It also provides some protection against counterfeit currency.

The three-year cost of the depositor's forgery and credit card coverage is $10 for $1,000, $16 for $2,500, $22 for $5,000 and so on, up to $49 for $100,000 and $3 for each additional $25,000. The three-year cost of the broader family forgery and credit card coverage would be $29 for $1,000, $39 for $2,500, $54 for $5,000 and so on, up to $172 for $100,000 and $17 for each additional $25,000.

When Debts Accumulate: Financial counseling, consolidation loans, the Bankruptcy Act

Financial ills are much like medical problems—the earlier they are detected, the less painful the remedy and the more complete the cure.

That sounds good, but people still get into financial trouble because of economic reverses, family emergencies or bad money management. What can be done when trouble develops depends on the extent of the difficulty. A family that suddenly finds itself straining to keep income even with expenses usually should not have to go outside the home for a solution. A review of its budget should indicate where cuts can be made. If the family has no formal budget, one should be drawn up immediately. The task may not be so easy for the family faced with large medical or other "crisis" bills. It would be even more difficult for the family with sharply reduced income or with over-extended credit.

When indebtedness threatens the ability to meet basic living expenses, the best thing to do is to seek counsel outside the home. A qualified outsider may objectively recommend solutions, and perhaps help to expedite them. In extreme cases, it may be necessary to seek relief under the Federal Bankruptcy Act.

Once a reputable counselor has been selected, the family should be completely candid with him. He cannot do an effective job without all of the facts. *Financial counseling sources* include family-service organizations, credit unions, some banks and lawyers. Some families use a reputable accountant, whose exposure to varied personal and business situations make him well qualified. Others may have the benefit of a nonprofit credit counseling service in their community.

A counselor may help a family to prepare a budget and learn how to live with it. If debt repayment remains burdensome, he may negotiate with creditors for an easier repayment plan without penalty. Or, he may arrange for a long-term *consolidation loan* that would cancel most, if not all, other debts, which may carry high-interest charges. The large loan's long term would allow a repayment schedule that would better fit into a family's budget. One should weigh carefully a decision to commit himself to a debt-consolidation loan without the guidance of an impartial expert. There are so-called financial advisers who advertise their promise to "help you pay your bills," but they frequently do not provide all the services that their promise implies, and their consolidation loans often are exorbitantly expensive.

A man must turn to the *Bankruptcy Act* if he cannot obtain a consolidation loan or is so inundated with debt that all roads to solvency are blocked. Under the Act, he may file a petition of bankruptcy or, if qualified, seek the shelter of Chapter XIII, the wage earner's plan. That plan protects wages and essential property of a debtor wanting to avoid straight bankruptcy by repaying debts from future earnings.

Whether rooted in puritanism, pride or ego, the general attitude toward bankruptcy is negative and a man may find that difficult to live with. But there are other than social aspects to be considered. Secured debts must be paid or the merchandise returned. Co-signed loans become the debts of the co-signers. The cost of going into bankruptcy may reach $300 or more. Moreover, one who has taken this step may have difficulty in obtaining a job, especially if it requires bonding. However, several studies indicate that former bankrupts do not always have difficulty in obtaining credit.

A majority of a debtor's creditors must approve his filing of the Chapter XIII petition, at which time all interest charges usually stop. Secured loans, particularly mortgages on real estate, were not intended to be included, according to several interpretations, but they often are. In those cases, interest on such loans may be allowed, as an incentive to lenders who could otherwise repossess the property. Unsecured lenders may not need such incentives since they have the most to lose. A Chapter XIII petitioner also may spend $300 or more in fees. Efforts reportedly are being made in many areas to limit a lawyer's fee to between $150 and $200. In addition, there are filing fees of about $15 and a trustee's fee of up to 5 per cent of the debts, plus expenses.

The debtor makes his required payments, spread over three years, to the trustee, who then pays the creditors, thus making the Federal Government a collection agency. An employer may agree to deduct the payment from a debtor's salary and forward it to the trustee.

"The discouraging and alarming fact is that there is no uniformity of application of Chapter XIII," Linn K. Twinem, chairman of the American Bar Association's consumer-bankruptcy committee, said. "We believe it should be more widely used, from the viewpoint of the debtor, the community, society and the total economy." Several observers attributed the limited application of Chapter XIII to the attitudes of lawyers and bankruptcy referees, who are appointed by Federal judges. Many referees, it was said, either do not believe in Chapter XIII—especially older referees—or do not want to take the burden of administering such a long, drawn-out process. Lawyers may feel the same way, one observer said. "On a straight bankruptcy, they can earn up to $300 or more, almost in a matter of minutes."

More than 90 per cent of the 171,000 bankruptcy petitions filed in the fiscal year that ended June 30, 1965, were in the nonbusiness category, Mr. Twinem noted, "and there are indications of another 10 per cent increase in the total number this year." In fiscal 1963, some $850 million in debts were involved in bankrupt estates. In fiscal 1964, the total was $1.11 billion. "A good part of that money could have been returned to the economy under XIII," Mr. Twinem declared, "while at the same time sparing many debtors from the bankruptcy stigma." He rejected arguments that Chapter XIII continues the debtor's oppressive burden, noting that repayments are tailored to his needs, and if this cannot be done, the petition is denied.

Creditors, according to the lawyer, "have become quite sympathetic toward this approach." In the last several years, they have encouraged XIII, he said, and have helped set up community credit counseling services, which parallel Chapter XIII in function, but operate outside of the courts. A service in Phoenix, Arizona, one of the oldest, distributes $1 million a year in debtors' repayments. There are more in many other cities. Some are being established in the East, including New Jersey and New York. Studies independently conducted in the last year by four universities—Michigan State, Utah, Ohio and Arizona—Mr. Twinem said, reported the same general conclusion: 25 to 50 per cent of those who filed personal bankruptcy petitions could have repaid their debts under Chapter XIII.

4

A PLACE TO LIVE

The way people live, their interests, needs and desires, their incomes and spending patterns, determines where they should make their homes. Some serious introspective thinking, financial calculation and family discussion should precede decisions to choose the city or suburb, to rent or to buy.

A certain mobility, a freedom and flexibility of action may be enjoyed by single people, childless couples or those with grown children. With the exception of newlyweds, these people usually have no major economic obligations looming before them, and they often can afford the extra cost of "ideal" living quarters.

Families, especially large ones with young children, generally are more restricted, by additional space needs and by the children's educational, recreational and other requirements. The purchase of a house, even at some distance from the breadwinner's place of employment, is sometimes the only economically feasible way to meet space needs. But even these families should weigh all other factors before making a move. For example, close proximity to place of employment may be important, if, because of temperament or schedule, working family members would find it difficult to commute long distances. Further, excessive commuting time could make the father's working day so long that he loses touch with his family, setting the stage for further problems.

Then there are a family's special interests. A family whose members' primary interests carry them outside the home would be less concerned with its physical aspects than would a family that enjoys entertaining and looks pridefully to its "castle." Theater buffs, urban-university students (perhaps working family members at the graduate level) and others with city-oriented interests and associations should weigh carefully any decision that would take them out of their sphere. But the country life is made to order for others who would be stifled by the city. Handicraft hobbyists and do-it-yourself enthusiasts, for instance, would find their reward in pleasure and economy as homeowners, a role that others might detest. A shift to suburbia also would be ideal for nature lovers or those who would enjoy what small-community life has to offer.

Choosing a Home: Houses, cooperative apartments, condominiums

For some individuals and families, rental of shelter is ideal. They shun the immobility or responsibilities of home ownership. They can move when the lease expires. There is no initial investment, aside from possible payment of advance rent as security to the landlord.

Potential home buyers may use rented quarters as a base of observation of a neighborhood or town. Should they find the area unsuitable or undesirable, they can move. That would be much less difficult and expensive than selling a house.

Apartment living may be appealing because of the limited responsibility, the ability to come and go as one pleases, even for extended periods, without concern for the building's maintenance. Rental of a house, on the other hand, affords greater living and storage space, as well as the pleasures of a yard and garden, but it also means taking on some of the owner's responsibilities.

A tenant must determine at the outset of house rental exactly what his responsibilities are, whether he is expected to pay heating and other operating costs, maintain the house and grounds, put up storm windows and screens, shovel snow and perform other chores. If so, the rental fee should reflect that, possibly making it economically feasible for the tenant to have some of the work done by hired hands.

The buyer has three basic choices: *a house, a cooperative apartment,* or a *condominium unit*. The last is most like ownership, for the condominium buyer takes title to his apartment, while the cooperative dweller buys stock ownership in the cooperative, a nonprofit corporation, and the right to occupy a specific apartment.

A condominium dweller, whose vote in the operation of the building is proportionate to the size of his apartment, is taxed separately on his unit. He is responsible only for mortgage indebtedness and taxes on his property and for his proportionate share of the expenses of operating the common property—such as the halls, elevators, heating equipment—in which he has a share. He has no mortgage indebtedness, tax or other liability for his neighbors' property, and generally may sell his unit to whomever he chooses. However, like a co-op, the unit usually must be offered to the condominium first.

Conversely, a co-op resident, who has only one vote regardless of the size of his apartment, pays his proportionate share of taxes, mortgage and operating costs on the entire co-op in his monthly "rent." He is dependent on the solvency of the entire co-op, and should he want to sell, he must have the potential purchaser approved by the co-op's board of directors. It should be noted that co-ops, especially middle-income developments subsidized through tax abatements, have become increasingly popular in metropolitan areas. The demand for relatively low-cost housing reduces to a minimum the risk of tenant-owner default and of resulting failure of the cooperative corporation. Advocates of cooperatives say that a tenant-owner's proportionate monthly maintenance and loan-payment charges—further reduced by deduction from taxable income of his share of interest and real estate tax paid—are considerably less than rent for a comparable apartment.

Advocates of home ownership note that mortgage repayment is a form of enforced saving that steadily increases a family's equity, or ownership, in a house. That investment could be further enhanced, they say, by an increase in property value. Long-time homeowners often find it economical to raise cash for a child's education or some other vital need by refinancing their homes, in which they have built a large equity. Homeowners, too, may deduct property taxes and mortgage interest from taxable income. Home ownership generally is considerably less costly than rental of a comparable dwelling, but comparison of home ownership with apartment rental can be misleading. A friend recently compared the rental cost of his attractive four and one-half room apartment with a "small house"—six rooms, garage and grounds. Taking into account the down payment and the allotment for mortgage payments, taxes, heating, utilities, insurance and general upkeep, the house appeared more costly, but it provided much more than the apartment. In the long run, the house might actually prove less expensive, allowing for the tax advantage, equity build-up and expected property-value increase.

Because the economic advantage of home ownership is generally long term, it would be wisest for families expecting to move frequently —perhaps every five years—to rent their homes. This would eliminate the annoyance and often substantial expense of buying and selling houses.

The Price of Shelter: Budgeting for a home

The amount that can be spent on housing will vary, even among families of the same income, for budgets are highly individual. A large family, for example, normally cannot allocate as great a percentage of income for shelter as can a small family, even though its demands may be greater. But there are other variable budgetary factors. The emphasis a family or individual places on other expenditures, such as for education, vacations, entertainment, recreation or automobiles, will affect the shelter allotment. Certain of these other expenses may be trimmed, but too sharp an adjustment may stir discontent and possible family discord. The new house, or the better apartment, would lose its warmth if it is resentfully regarded as unworthy of the sacrifice.

Setting the maximum allowable monthly outlay for housing, therefore, requires review and possible revision of the family's entire financial program, including determination of how much cash there is for moving costs and, if a home is to be bought, for a down payment, legal fees and other acquisition costs. Thus, a family would decide how much it might deviate from the prescribed guidelines. Money management experts suggest that the average monthly cost of shelter should equal a week's after-tax income, and that the purchase price of a house should equal from two to two and one-half times gross annual income. To remain within sensible limits, some families settle for a smaller, less-expensive house that later could be expanded, such as a Cape Cod with expansion attic.

The mechanics of arriving at the monthly shelter cost that would most comfortably fit into a family's financial program involves the listing on a monthly basis of all budgetary items except current housing costs. These would include savings toward specific goals, food and clothing, utilities, medical care, insurance, recreation, automobile costs, contributions, installment payments, personal allowances, vacations and all other items. Subtracting this total from average monthly after-tax income will show the shelter cost permitted by the present budget. A family deciding it is not enough would look to other cost items that may be reduced without greatly distressing any member.

While monthly rent usually is fixed, at least for the duration of a lease, home-ownership costs are somewhat variable and include: mortgage payments; property taxes; property insurance; utilities, including gas, electricity, telephone and water; heating fuel; general upkeep, including repairs, redecoration, remodeling and the cost of help that may be hired to maintain the house and grounds.

As a budgeting device, property taxes and insurance costs often are paid with monthly mortgage payments to the bank, which in turn pays them for the owner as they come due. To determine the monthly average cost of some of the items, it may be necessary to obtain the annual estimated cost and divide by 12. Making realistic cost estimates usually requires consultation with a bank's home-financing specialist or a reputable real estate broker or lawyer.

The adviser can also guide a family on the price it can afford to pay for a house. After estimating what portion of its monthly housing allotment may be assigned to the mortgage payment, he determines the size and term of the loan that can be carried by the monthly payment. As will be later discussed, that amount varies with interest rate, type of mortgage and number of repayment years. However, in consultation with the family, he would suggest the type best suited to its needs and qualifications. Adding the estimated mortgage loan to the down payment would give the approximate price a family may comfortably pay for a house.

To arrive at the amount available for the down payment, as well as for moving expense and other initial costs related to home purchase, a family must first total all its savings and the market value of securities it owns, if any. From this must be subtracted funds earmarked for other important family goals and an amount to meet the cost of illness or other emergencies to the extent that such costs are not covered by insurance.

Initial expenses above the down payment are not inconsequential. A buyer of a $34,000 house in Bergen County, New Jersey, complained: "I put $9,000 down on the house, and I expect to get that back if I decide to sell. But then it cost me another $1,133 that I'll never see again." Getting down to less affluent terms, the American Bankers Association estimates that these charges—the closing costs —might come to about $500 on a $20,000 house bought with the aid of a $12,000 mortgage loan. The exact amount would vary with the location.

Costs related to buying a house and obtaining a mortgage, with approximate ranges for a $20,000 to $40,000 house, may include:

Survey	$ 35 to $200
Title fee	$ 75 to $200
Mortgage tax	$100 to $200
Recording fees	$ 5 to $ 20
Buyer's lawyer	$ 50 to $400
Bank's lawyer	$ 75 to $150
Repairs required for mortgage	Open
Engineer (making inspection for buyer)	$ 35 to $ 55
Advance real estate taxes	Up to ½ year
Advance insurance premium	Up to 3 years

When a buyer takes over an existing mortgage on the house, he may save as much as $200 in closing costs. Furthermore, the loan may carry lower than prevailing interest rates.

A home buyer also must allow for moving expenses, for costs of cleaning furniture, rugs and drapes; redecorating or remodeling the new home, and acquiring new indoor and outdoor furniture, appliances and gardening equipment.

The closing fees, moving expenses and other "extras" involved in home purchase may cause the potential home buyer some concern. But better he know about them now, when he can prepare for them, than later when they would be a painful surprise.

A Good Lawyer

Perhaps the most effective hedge a buyer, seller or builder of a house can have as protection against unforeseen expenses—and heartache—is a good lawyer, preferably a general practitioner who has had considerable experience with real estate in the particular area.

Frequently, without benefit of lawyers, buyer and seller enter into what they believe to be an informal agreement, whereby the buyer makes a nominal deposit of perhaps $100 and both sign a brief memorandum noting sale of the property. These agreements may have the effect of a contract, while providing for none of the terms and conditions the parties' lawyers would have insisted upon. Many thousands of dollars may be jeopardized by such a step.

A buyer without a lawyer may find himself in serious trouble. He cannot depend on the bank's lawyer, whose job is to protect the bank. What protects the bank may not protect the purchaser. Many title exceptions unacceptable to a buyer's lawyer would be passed over by the bank's lawyer. For example, a bank holding a 60 per cent mortgage would not be bothered by encroachments of a neighbor, who uses the driveway or has had a fence on the property long enough to establish a claim, because a resulting reduction in property value would not endanger the bank's dollar interest.

The buyer's lawyer would seek an adjustment with the seller of a pending assessment. He would make certain that the streets in front of the house have been accepted by the local government as satisfactory and that the local government will maintain them. He would seek a guarantee from the builder as to the roof, appliances, landscaping and so on. If a builder wants to postpone landscaping because of winter weather, the lawyer would see that money is set aside to cover the job in the spring.

A seller needs a lawyer to advise him whether to assign his mortgage or to require the purchaser to get his own mortgage money. When a Veterans Administration mortgage—the so-called G.I. mortgage—is turned over to someone else, the original borrower can be held liable, if the purchaser loses the house through foreclosure proceedings. However, a Federal Housing Administration or conventional mortgage may be transferred in a manner that will free the seller from further accountability.

The lawyer also may remove from a deed clauses that hold the seller responsible for future assessments or for damages in the event that an encroachment or a property restriction comes up years later.

In short, the lawyer earns his money by taking some of the worry, unhappiness and risk out of a housing transaction, which, at best, is complex.

A lawyer's fee of one per cent of purchase price is not uncommon, though it may run considerably below that in some communities. A person should discuss the fee with a lawyer before retaining him. The lawyer is unlikely to bring the matter up himself, according to a Missouri Bar Association survey.

The Choice of Neighborhood

Once it has been decided whether to rent or buy, to live in apartment or house, in city or suburb, the next step is to choose the neighborhood or community best suited to the needs, interests and pocketbook of the individual or family.

There are two approaches to the choice of neighborhood. The first is to investigate an entire area and select one or two suitable neighborhoods in which to concentrate the search. The second is to evaluate neighborhoods as housing opportunities arise in a generally acceptable total area. By elimination, this, too, usually results in confinement of the hunt to a few neighborhoods.

A neighborhood may be evaluated visually, through conversations with residents and tradesmen and through inquiries at community agencies, such as the school board and the police and fire departments. The prime points of consideration are:

- The appearance of the neighborhood and the residents' general standard of living to be gauged in part by the quality, size and condition of the houses.
- Convenience to good schools, houses of worship, recreational facilities;
- Quality, convenience and cost of transportation;
- Adequacy of police and fire protection;
- Location of commercial, civic or transportation facilities—distant enough to eliminate disturbing noises or unpleasant odors, but close enough to make traveling convenient;
- Zoning regulations and building restrictions enforced effectively enough to assure preservation of the neighborhood's quality.

Proper evaluation of neighborhoods will reveal that each has a character of its own, and the diligent investigator will discover the one within his income that will best suit his own and his family's needs and interests.

There is the question, too, as to whether a family will be accepted and easily assimilated into a neighborhood. If it is a homogeneous neighborhood in terms of economics, attitudes and interests, a new family that is "different" may not fit in. The question of prejudice is a serious one that a member of a minority group unfortunately must consider. There are many neighborhoods that have been integrated successfully, but the grim truth is that this has not always been the case. While the laws in many areas give a family the right to live wherever it chooses, it must weigh carefully whether its members, particularly its children, could bear the pressures and emotional stresses that could be exerted by a united front of bigots. The family's cause may be just, but it must recognize that the price can be high.

The Right Home: Rentals, resale houses, building, prefabricated houses

It often takes time to find suitable housing in the right location. But the time will be well spent if the result is a home the family enjoys. In general, shelter shoppers should let friends and relatives know what type of housing they want and where, and should follow newspapers' classified ads, perhaps running one of their own, and register with a reputable real estate agent. Any rental vacancy should be compared, when possible, with comparable apartments or houses in terms of convenience, quality and cost. Families interested in cooperative apartments should match prospective purchases with comparable rental quarters to determine whether the monthly cost differential warrants the initial investment.

The home buyer's task is broader, for he has the choice of *building* his own house on property he has purchased, *buying* a new one or an existing one (generally referred to as a *resale house*).

One of the preliminaries to building or buying a home is deciding how much house the family needs, how many rooms, what arrangement is best and what architectural style suits the family's preferences. A helpful guide to such decisions is the plentiful supply of magazines with articles on home design. Reference works are also available in libraries. Consideration should be given to the special features each family deems important: an extra bathroom, a study, a playroom, a fireplace, a two-car garage. It should be borne in mind, however, that such features are costly, and that there are few housing bargains, though bargains are as widely rumored as are "terrific automobile deals." As a compromise, certain preferred features may be obtained at the expense of less-desired ones—a fireplace, for example, compensating for the lack of an extra bathroom.

Also useful to preliminary planning are visits to home construction and equipment exhibitions, to model homes of real estate developers and to other houses up for sale. The choice of a new or "resale" house may be dictated by what is available in the particular area selected. Whether new or used, each house has its advantages and drawbacks.

A prime advantage of the new house is its easier financing. It often can be bought with a cash down payment of 5 per cent of the purchase price, or less. In the sale of an "old" house, the mortgage lender might require a down payment of as much as one-fifth or one-third of the purchase price, and might limit the number of repayment years, perhaps to 20 compared with 30 or more for a new house.

Starting out with a new house gives a family a good feeling. Everything is bright, modern, fresh and clean from the beginning, often with decorating and other features completed to the buyer's taste. If properly inspected and bought from a reputable builder who stands behind his work, the house will not carry the threat of large repair bills as might an old house. But a new house will require certain other major expenditures for landscaping, screens and, if the climate mandates, storm windows. Furthermore, patience during the "break-in" period, when such "bugs" as sticking doors and windows and temperamental heating systems appear, is a necessary virtue for any family buying a new house.

An older home, on the other hand, often has a weathered charm, and a spaciousness and sturdiness of construction unavailable in a new home in the same price range. It may have a good lawn, attractive landscaping, screens, storm windows and other features a new-home buyer would have to add on his own. If the house is in an established neighborhood with adequate schools and little room to grow, property taxes are not likely to take the sudden leaps typical of many new communities.

Older houses, however, often are available at attractive prices precisely because they need painting, decorating and modernization. But it would not be wise to grab up a "bargain" if the prospective purchaser does not have the cash or the inclination to cope with this refacing job, or if the cost of the work puts the price of the house above that of a comparable new one. An old house is not a bargain either if it is in a deteriorating neighborhood, or if the combined cost would price it above the average of comparable houses in the area, for in such cases the owner would never get his money back on resale.

The risk of costly repair of defects might not become apparent until an older home has been lived in for a while. Such risk can be reduced, and the cost of modernization perhaps eliminated, with selection of a resale house under 10 years old, preferably about five. Hopefully, the first owner would have had time to develop his landscaping, to install additional equipment, and to solve most "new-house problems," yet the house would not be so old as to require major repairs or modernization.

But any house is a "blind item" to the novice. Therefore, whether the house under consideration is new or used, it is imperative that the prospective buyer have it inspected by an expert. The shopper may evaluate its appearance, size, room arrangement and other visual features, but the expert can detect construction defects, and measure the quality, adequacy and condition of electrical wiring, the heating system, plumbing, roofing, insulation, paint and other factors. A specialist also should be engaged to inspect for termites and the extent of any resulting wood rot. The inspector could be a qualified builder, engineer, architect or real estate appraiser.

An expert's fee, like a lawyer's fee, is a sound investment. Not only will he tell the prospective buyer what is wrong—and what is right—with the house, but he also often will estimate the cost of recommended repairs and modernization. The cost of repairs he discovers might justify a request for a downward revision of the selling price, which, if won, would still make purchase economically feasible.

An alternate route to home ownership, one that promises to fulfill a family's every wish and desire, is the custom *building* of a house. Expert guidance is as much needed by the family building a home as it is by the home buyer. Too often, families inexperienced at reading blueprints are surprised and disappointed with the finished house. Time and professional consultation should be the major ingredients of planning and study of blueprints. It costs little at this stage to make changes, which may be offset in cost, if necessary, by economies in other design areas. But changes in the course of construction can be prohibitively expensive.

Some people find it practical to engage an architect to design and oversee construction of a home for a fee of up to 15 per cent of building costs. That may sound like a lot of money, but a good architect could more than offset it with design and construction savings. A man who serves as his own general contractor, dealing himself with subcontractors on various phases of construction, frequently finds that his inexperience and lack of building knowledge costs him a good deal of money and mental anguish.

Another procedure is the purchase of a standard plan, possibly through a magazine or from a building-supply dealer, and the engagement of a contractor to build from the plan. The plan should be professionally checked for compliance with local building regulations and adaptability to the selected site. Some builders and contractors offer a selection of plans and include the cost in the price of the house. If the house is to be part of a housing development, the overall price also will include the land.

Still another procedure is the purchase of a *prefabricated or factory-built house,* and the hiring of a contractor to erect part or all of the house. Manufactured houses may be bought at various stages of completion. The amount of work assigned to the builder and the degree of completeness of the prefab will depend on the buyer's inclination and ability to assume the do-it-yourself role, allowing a considerable saving.

Before the prefab or building plan is bought, or the custom design formulated, the site must be selected, unless it is part of a package deal. The buyer can evaluate the neighborhood and the visual qualities of the lot, but the architect or builder and an appraiser must be consulted before a final decision is made. The architect will evaluate the plot as a building site, pointing out factors that will influence the design and construction of the house. In size and shape, the house must be appropriate to the lot and to other houses in the neighborhood. The appraiser or mortgage lender will measure the lot's market value and the part it can play in the home-financing plan. Fully paid for, the lot perhaps can serve as the down payment.

A family that decides to build should have an extra cushion of cash to cover those almost inevitable "unexpected expenses." It should, furthermore, be long on patience because the process of building can be protracted and nerve-racking. To minimize unexpected expenses, the family should maintain records of all costs and commitments, nail down the exact fees to be charged by specialists and others engaged and, with a lawyer's aid, ascertain that all costs are stipulated in contracts. A family must know beforehand all costs of home acquisition and ownership. That knowledge is its best assurance that the enjoyment of its home will not be stifled by economic pressures.

The Right Financing Plan: Mortgages, interest rates, F.H.A. and V.A. loans, second mortgages, refinancing, mortgage-redemption insurance

A *mortgage,* like the house itself, must suit a family's needs and qualifications. As much care must be taken, therefore, in shopping for the right mortgage as for the right home.

The lender, known as the mortgagee, advances to the mortgagor, or borrower, the cash he needs to buy the house or for other purposes, if he already owns the house. In return, the borrower pledges the house and property as collateral and agrees to repay the loan, with interest, in regular installments, usually monthly, over a specific number of years—commonly 20, 25, or 30, sometimes more and sometimes less. The borrower also promises to maintain adequate fire insurance on the house (the lender holds the original copy of the policy), to pay all taxes and to keep the property in good order.

At this point, the home buyer already has determined the maximum he can spend for housing—his down payment and monthly shelter allotment, including the monthly mortgage payment. However, the amount of mortgage loan that can be obtained is predicated on many other factors, including the family's credit standing, the type of mortgage, conventional or government-backed, and the age of the house, which usually establishes the percentage of loan allowed against the total cost. Other relevant factors are the rate of interest and the number of repayment years. Wise shopping is important, because these factors may vary from lender to lender. Mortgage lenders include commercial banks, savings banks, savings and loan associations (known in some states as cooperative banks and homestead associations), life insurance companies and mortgage bankers.

Interest rates in the current mortgage-money market range to more than 6 per cent, placing the majority of mortgages among the most attractive of consumer loans, in the eyes of lending institutions. The fixed monthly payments will have been calculated to amortize the loan and to pay the interest over the term of the mortgage. The interest is based on the unpaid loan balance; as that balance is reduced, the portion of the monthly payment devoted to interest will be reduced, allowing progressively more for loan repayment. Thus, early payments are made up primarily of interest due, but the final payment is all amortization, and it cancels the debt.

The following is illustrative of the monthly charge for each $1,000 borrowed at various interest rates and repayment periods:

Interest rate	*15 years*	*20 years*	*25 years*	*30 years*
5%	$7.91	$6.60	$5.85	$5.37
5¼	8.04	6.74	6.00	5.53
5½	8.18	6.88	6.15	5.68
5¾	8.31	7.03	6.30	5.84
6	8.44	7.17	6.45	6.00

As will be noted, the longer the mortgage term or payment period the lower the monthly outlay, but the greater the total interest paid. For example, interest charges at 5½ per cent on a $20,000 mortgage would total $13,018.60 if repaid over 20 years, and $16,846 if repaid over 25 years. The $3,827.40 saving in interest charges afforded by the shorter term may be appealing, but the difference in monthly payments may not, especially if the bigger payment strains the budget or puts the house out of reach. Over a period of 20 years, the monthly bill would be $137.60, or 20 times $6.88, compared with $123, or 20 times $6.15, over 25 years.

It makes better sense to settle for the mortgage deal providing a payment that fits comfortably into a family's budget. Later on, if the family finds it has surplus cash—above the needs for other financial obligations and goals—prepayments may be made on the mortgage, reducing the term and total interest charge. With this in mind, it is advisable to seek the privilege of prepayment without penalty when negotiating the mortgage agreement. Even if there is some penalty, however, it usually still is advantageous to prepay.

Government-insured mortgages, issued by banks and other private institutions and backed by the Veterans Administration or the Federal Housing Administration, carry interest rates of 6 per cent where they are available. They generally allow larger loans for longer periods. F.H.A. mortgages carry an additional one-half per cent as a mortgage-insurance premium, some of which usually is returned when the mortgage is paid up. Prepayment may be made without penalty or limitation on *V.A. loans,* and without penalty for prepayment of up to 15 per cent of the original loan in any one year on

F.H.A. loans. The discounting of Government-backed loans is precluded by law where it involves payment of the discount by the borrower to the lender, but there is no restriction on such payment by the seller or builder of the house. Under discounting, a cash payment is made to the lender of a percentage of the toal mortgage loan, in addition to the usual closing costs, at the time it is issued.

Most mortgages today are of the so-called conventional type, issued by individuals or private lending institutions. They carry higher interest rates—predominantly 6 per cent or more—but usually can be obtained in far less time than can a Federally insured loan, and with much less paper work. However, the F.H.A. reportedly is striving to process applications more expeditiously.

Except under special circumstances, the obtaining of a *second mortgage* to buy a house (in addition to the primary one) is not recommended. A second mortgage, which the primary mortgagee usually must approve, generally carries high interest and service charges. The additional monthly payments are usually more than a budget can endure, especially in the case of a family needing a second mortgage.

Is it a good idea to have an open-end clause in the mortgage agreement. With it, the homeowner wishing to raise cash in later years for remodeling or a child's education may do so by asking the lender to advance it, enlarging the unpaid balance under the terms of the original mortgage, thus extending his repayment period. If his credit is good and his property has retained value, and if the lender feels other conditions, including current interest rates, warrant it, the request will be granted. The total debt, new and old, generally cannot exceed the amount of the original mortgage loan. *Mortgage refinancing* is most advantageous for large loans, in which long-term repayment and relatively small refinancing charges, if any, are decisive factors.

It would be economically impossible for most families to continue living in their homes, should the breadwinner die prematurely, unless he had made some insurance provision. One such provision is the *mortgage-redemption policy,* a form of life insurance obtainable at relatively low cost. The least expensive of these is a term policy declining in coverage as the unpaid balance of the mortgage loan is reduced.

5

AN INSTANT ESTATE: LIFE INSURANCE

A man must work for his potential earnings year by year. If he should die, the money stops. And his family, if it is typical, might have to live frugally in the event of his death, unless he had made provisions for life insurance, for an "instant estate."

Such an estate, generally not attainable without life insurance, could mark the difference between continued achievement and economic death to a man's survivors. It could help put bread, and sometimes a little cake, on their table and an adequate roof over their heads; it may assure college educations for the children and grant a widow the dignity of financial independence. Most important, this estate stands like a silent sentinel from the moment a life insurance applicant has been accepted by a company and has paid his first premium.

All promotional and merchandising efforts aside, provision of this economic protection is the basic function of life insurance, and nothing else does it better. It should be bought with this in mind; all its other features—savings, investment qualities, retirement benefits—are secondary. Taken out of a policy's context, such factors generally are not competitively strong enough to motivate the astute consumer who is not interested in additional life insurance.

But are people always aware when they should buy more life insurance? Salesmen often are rebuffed, not always without justification, with the sometimes annoyed, sometimes angry exclamation, "I have enough life insurance!" What *is* enough?

It has been said that a man should have four to five times his annual income covered by life insurance, but such a generalization cannot be accepted as a valid guide. Life insurance cannot be measured in dollar amounts, but in terms of what it must accomplish in a family's estate-planning program. Insurance, with other resources of the insured and his family, should provide the money his dependents would need upon his death. Other sources of support may include savings, investments, Social Security and Veterans Administration benefits, and death benefits provided by some employers, some unions, and professional and fraternal associations.

The variable personal factors—the prime ones being a man's income and resources, the size of his family, their ages and objectives—make it mandatory that a life insurance plan be highly individualized, tailored to the particular needs of the insured and his family.

The Right Amount of Insurance: Formulating an estate plan

Once a family has established its financial program, it can get down to serious estate planning. It must determine long- and short-term economic needs that would obtain in the event the prime income producer dies; it must estimate the sufficiency of available resources in filling those needs. The function of life insurance in estate planning is to close the gaps left by those other resources.

Emphasis will be placed on insurance of the father's life because he generally is the primary income producer. (The advisability of insuring the wife and children will be discussed later.) After an estate plan has been formulated, the family immediately should fill as much of the resulting insurance need as sensible budgeting will allow. The master plan can serve as a future guide in meeting other insurance needs as the breadwinner's income increases. It is important that the plan remain flexible, allowing for upward or downward revision, as family circumstances change.

The major components of an estate plan, which would consider all financial resources, are:

1. *Immediate cash for death expenses.* This sum, unhappily referred to in insurance terminology as the "clean-up fund," would pay the increasingly high cost of dying—medical and funeral expenses, debts, taxes and estate-settlement fees, including those of a lawyer. The medical, hospital and other costs of a final illness or fatal accident may be substantially in excess of accident and health insurance

coverage. A $2,000 allocation for these expenses is minimal, and should be increased if a family's circumstances warrant it.

2. *Readjustment fund.* Time for readjustment must be allowed a family faced with the economic, as well as the psychological, problems resulting from the death of the father and chief income producer. Important decisions must be made, and making them in haste could prove costly. Should the house be sold? Should a family business be sold? Should the widow or older children seek work, and if so, do they need special training? At best, a family generally must look forward to a reduction in its living standards. The readjustment fund would grant them the time to prepare for it, to catch their breath in a trying emotional period. Ideally, the fund should equal at least six months to a year of the husband's income, less taxes and what would have been his expenses.

3. *A mortgage fund.* If the family owns its home, allowance for full repayment of the mortgage would provide the family with relatively low-cost housing, if it chose to remain in its home. If it decided to sell, elimination of high monthly mortgage payments would relieve the pressure to sell quickly and possibly at a loss. Furthermore, the entire sale price would be available to apply to other needs. Certain low-cost life insurance policies are designed for this purpose.

4. *Family income.* Because the greatest income need occurs when the children are young, an actual budget showing minimal family needs should be drawn subject to periodic review. Then it should be determined how much of the budget would be covered by existing assets and potential benefits, such as Social Security and benefits available to many dependent survivors of Armed Forces veterans.

If all other resources prove insufficient, life insurance must take up the slack. Insurance may be in the form of a lump-sum benefit, that is, immediate cash that could be invested, providing supplemental income while preserving the principal for later needs. Or it may be in the form of monthly income paid by the insurance company. As we later shall see, there are family-income plans that may be added to basic policies at relatively small cost, paying a monthly check to a family in the crucial years while the children are growing up.

5. *An emergency fund.* An emergency fund would meet an unexpected crisis, such as a major illness. Without it, the well-planned but perhaps restricted financial program of a widow may be disrupted.

Generally, $1,000 or less would suffice, but the size and health of the family are key factors.

6. *Income for the wife.* Such income would begin when the children are on their own, and would be reduced in proportion to the widow's reduction in financial responsibility to them. She may not need any extra income at this point if she has remarried or gone to work, but it must be remembered that the employment market and income potential for middle-aged women with only nominal experience has never been large. Social Security benefits normally would have stopped when the youngest child turned 18, and could not resume until the widow turns 60. Even then, she would be aided by supplemental income.

7. *Special funds.* The objective of special funds may be to meet a future goal, such as the financing of college educations for the children. Naturally, the fulfillment of such goals comes after basic needs such as food and shelter have been satisfied.

A family should not be discouraged by the magnitude of the estate plan that these components would suggest. While few families have the assets, or the means to buy the necessary life insurance, to establish a complete estate program, the very exercise of formulating one will stimulate constructive thinking about what can be done to make the family's way easier should the father die. And, most important, this preparatory thinking and discussion can be accomplished now, without the emotional pressure death exerts on a family.

Many families are surprised at how much can be accomplished. A family at least would have a head start in its new way of life without father, if it could be assured of only three components: immediate cash for death expenses, a readjustment fund and a mortgage fund. Knowing it might be so restricted, the family can begin considering now what it might do to supplement income or accomplish particular goals. The mother and older children, for example, might think about what type of work they could do to increase earnings. The whole family might consider how the children could get through college, despite the lack of funds. What would their chances be of acquiring scholarships, student loans and part-time jobs? With the total estate plan spread before them, the family could plan to meet other of its requirements, in order of importance, as income improves.

An estate plan makes clear that life insurance needs generally cannot be represented by one round sum. There are short- and long-term needs, lump sum and monthly payment requirements. The exception is the case, sometimes recommended, in which the widow immediately would receive the cash proceeds of all insurance policies. But, even in this instance, the amount would have been established by the estate plan, not any rule-of-thumb formula. That sum, together with other cash and invested assets, could be invested in sound securities, perhaps high-yield bonds, a mutual fund stressing income and preservation of capital or, under supervision, quality stocks. The investment income would be supplemented in the important family years by Social Security and other benefits. When college or other special projects arise, a part of the principal could be used.

Under the right circumstances, this plan could be most advantageous, but many factors must be considered before it can be accepted. The widow must be capable of handling a large sum of money. It might be prearranged that she invest in specific bonds or mutual funds, or that she put the funds into the hands of a reputable investment counseling firm.

For some segments of the estate plan, it might appear necessary to take more insurance than would otherwise be necessary, but this would be offset in the long run by a reduction in insurance requirements of later segments. For example, the commuted, or immediate cash, value of a family-income plan providing $100 monthly for 20 years would provide perhaps only two-thirds of that income if invested at 5 per cent. Therefore, if the full $100 monthly income is needed, it would be necessary to buy 50 per cent greater coverage to obtain enough of a commuted value to yield $100 monthly. But, at the end of the 20 years, the family would still have the cash that provided that income. It would then be able to apply it to other needs, such as college for the children or income for the widow in her middle and later years, otherwise to be met by additional insurance, or not met at all.

Insurance for a Wife

"Insure my wife? Are you out of your mind? I'm the provider for my family. If anything should happen to her, God forbid, I'll still be the provider."

That angry comment may astound many of today's young husbands and fathers, but it was, in fact, the almost verbatim declaration some 35 years ago of a then-young, and proud, family patriarch. He was not unlike his contemporaries, and little changed from his predecessors, who failed to recognize that the replacement of a wife's services as housekeeper and mother, in the event of her death, would cost money. Not fully mindful of the function of life insurance, they generally had policies on their own lives that would barely have covered medical, burial and other final expenses, let alone pay their families' bills during a brief adjustment period.

But lack of understanding of life insurance can hardly be given as the prime reason for the attitude of past generations toward policies on their wives. If they had enjoyed the material advantages of today's family heads, they, too, would have had willing "teachers" at their doors, policy applications in hand. Instead, with little or no insurance on either parent, the death of one often meant break-up of the family unit, or premature assumption of too-burdensome responsibility by the oldest child.

The way to greater security is easier for modern parents, thanks to enlarged incomes, more extensive educations and the aid of Social Security, employe-group insurance and other benefits. Their greater awareness has made them more conscious of the need for insuring the wife and mother. But the primary question always stands: Does the father have adequate insurance on his own life?

If the answer is "yes," it then must be determined how much insurance would be needed to ease the economic burden of a wife's death. This would be accomplished by measuring each area or aspect of resulting economic loss and deciding whether it could be comfortably absorbed by the family's income and assets. According to experts, the replacement cost might range from $1,200 to a startling $10,000 a year, depending on the family's economic status and the ages and degree of dependency of the children.

In the case of a wife who contributes to the family's income, it may be considered vital to its financial program to replace at least a part of her earnings with insurance proceeds should she die. Wives in about a third of the nation's households have outside employment.

No one likes to put a dollar value on a loved one, but the husband's loss of income-tax privileges at his wife's death may be large enough to warrant coverage. In general, this would apply to a widower without dependent children, for he would lose his wife's $600 personal exemption and the advantages of filing joint returns. A widower with dependent children would be allowed deductions from taxable income of up to $600 for the care of one child and up to $900 for the care of two, provided they are under 13 or permanently disabled. The reduced tax rates for a "head of household" make up in part for the loss of joint-return privileges.

Another potential economic lose to a family without a mother is in Social Security benefits. This should be of great concern, since these disability, survivor and retirement benefits usually are an important part of a family's financial program. If a widower with dependent children becomes permanently disabled or dies, benefits to his family may be reduced because of the wife's absence. Meanwhile, their budgetary needs would be swelled by the cost of replacing her essential services. At a widower's retirement, the total Social Security benefit also would be reduced by the amount his wife would have received. In fact, his monthly check would be slashed by a third, for his wife would have received a monthly sum equal to half his retirement benefit. Potential benefit losses would be calculated for a family at its local Social Security Administration office.

Wealthy families would be concerned with what ultimate effect a wife's death would have on estate taxes. A major estate tax advantage would be lost, for a surviving wife can claim a "marital deduction." This would exempt up to 50 per cent of her late husband's estate from taxes, provided that proper financial and legal precautions had been taken. To illustrate, a $120,000 estate left by a widower may be subject to an estate tax of about $10,000. If there were a surviving wife, there would have been no tax liability, provided that the estate had been properly prepared. On the other hand, if a wife outlives her husband and is left with a large estate, the tax burden at her death might be sizable because certain advantages would be unavailable. Protection against this contingency also may be desired.

After all applicable areas of potential economic loss from the wife's premature death have been surveyed, the family must tally the "bill." The answer will be a lump sum, including an amount for final medical and funeral expenses, and possibly supplemental monthly income for the children's dependent years. After estimating how much can be absorbed by income, savings, investments and other assets, the family must decide how much its budget can spare for life insurance to cover the rest.

Because that allotment usually is small, it may not be possible to do all that a family's survey recommends. To get the most protection for the money, it should concentrate on policies such as term and whole life, which stress protection more than savings. There also are combination family policies that provide low-cost protection for the wife and children, while putting primary insurance emphasis on the father.

Insurance for Children

It was not too long ago that the birth of a child to the average family meant the almost automatic purchase of a small life insurance policy, perhaps for $250 or $500 of protection, from the peripatetic, premium-collecting debit man. For a few coins a week, parents had the satisfaction of knowing they were doing "the right thing" by their offspring. With an eye to the policy's cash-value build-up, many bought it more as an enforced-savings device, as a "start" for their child, than as death protection. But, more often than not, the sum of that death protection, as small as it may have been, would have been heavily depended upon should the ultimate tragedy have stricken the economically pinched family. There was only one thing wrong: The father, or breadwinner, had little more insurance, if any at all, on his own life.

There is some truth to the saying that, the more things change, the more they remain the same. For, in the vast majority of cases today, fathers carrying insurance on their children's lives do not have enough on their own. People may have larger incomes, but they are spending more, for the simple life is no longer simple. And this generally means that household heads must leave larger estates if they want their families to continue living at more than a subsistence level (by today's standards) and to achieve educational and other goals. However, even when the father is adequately insured, it is not always wise to buy insurance on the child's life. Buying additional insurance on the father's life instead will satisfy many reasons for wanting juvenile insurance, while providing additional advantages. At a father's death, insurance on his child's life naturally does not pay off. In fact, the child's policy may be discontinued, unless the mother can continue paying the premiums, or the contract includes a "payor benefit." That benefit, obtained at extra cost, waives further premium payments if the payor dies before the child is 21. Insurance on the child's life, therefore, may mature or be paid up in time to provide cash for his college education or to finance some other special planned-for objectives. But cash may be needed before that. An emergency may force surrender of the child's policy for its immediate cash value—a fraction of its ultimate value.

On the other hand, proceeds from a policy on the father are immediately available at his death. Even if the contract stipulates that the money be paid by the insurance company at some future date, such as when the child is ready for college, arrangements for emergency withdrawals would be possible before then. Furthermore, the money, that is, the entire face amount of the father's policy, would be earning interest while in the custody of the insurance company.

It has been argued that the insurance must be on the child's life if the father is uninsurable. However, if the true goal is savings, not protection, why buy a policy? What good would a paid-up college fund be, for example, at a child's premature death? It would be far better to put the insurance-premium money into other much more productive investment and savings vehicles. If "enforced savings" is the attraction, a man could use the payroll-deduction device to buy bonds or make automatic deposits in a credit union or bank account, or he could enter into a contractual plan that "obligates" him to invest monthly in a mutual fund, or he could utilize any of the other enforced-savings devices available. He and his child would be ahead.

Parents naturally must place insurance on the child if they wish to cover medical and funeral expenses, which, in the case of a child's death, may run from a few hundred dollars to more than $1,000. The low-cost coverage afforded by a combination family-plan policy would be adequate for this purpose.

The policy also must be on the child if it is the parents' (or grandparents') wish to start him on a permanent life insurance program that he may take over when he is earning his own way. This idea is advocated in some quarters because the child may be uninsurable for health or occupational reasons when he is older, and because his yearly cost when he takes over could be up to nearly $5 less per $1,000 of protection than the going rate at his attained age. The older the buyer, the higher the insurance rates.

Opponents argue that the adult cost of a policy bought in childhood is less only to the extent of its accumulated cash value. In short, if the cash value of an old policy is 20 per cent of the face, or protection, amount, then the cost is about 20 per cent less than the price a new policy would have cost. Therefore, that early premium money, they say, could have been more wisely invested, providing the child with an even bigger gift.

The insurance industry, with some interest in instilling the virtues of their products in the minds of people early in their lives, has designed a number of policies specifically for parents and other relatives susceptible to the idea of starting a child's insurance program early. The concept is somewhat akin to establishment of a dowry, for the child-grown-older can present to his or her spouse a budding life insurance program as a wedding gift, which they may build as they wend their way through life. The concept also is said to help educate a child in the ways of prudent money management.

One of the special contracts is the "jumping juvenile," which usually is sold in units that provide $1,000 of protection to age 21, and then automatically increase fivefold, with no premium increase or medical examination. The expanded policy is attractively priced; the under-21 cost per year is high, giving nominal protection for the money.

The Brighter Side

Complete estate planning should take into consideration the economic factors of continued life, as well as of premature death. And both efforts are complementary, for the assets being built up under threat of early death may be utilized in retirement, supplementing a pension and Social Security benefits. Those policies in the life insurance program that are permanent may be surrendered, if not needed, and their cash values received in lump sums or as supplemental income, or they may be converted into paid-up or extended-term policies, eliminating future premium payments. This adds some positive thinking to an otherwise somber task.

A Reputable Insurance Counselor

Once the role of life insurance in a family's program has been delineated, it must be determined how far its budgetary allotment for insurance will let it go. A good deal depends on selection of the "right" policies. A young man may pay as little as $5 a year for $1,000 of protection, or as much as $45, depending on the type of contract involved. If he needs a great deal of protection, the most expensive contract wouldn't do. But would the least expensive one be a wise choice?

A reputable agent could help to provide the answers, of course, but, before seeing him, it would be wise to be as knowledgeable as possible in the ways of life insurance. This would not only allow intelligent discussion, but also would make it possible to evaluate him as a counselor. Bad insurance advice may cost a man a lot of money, but it could cause his family a lot of grief should he die.

The "products" of a good life insurance company are like building blocks for the creative insurance man to use in building a program to satisfy a customer's needs within the limits of his budget. The customer, armed with basic insurance knowledge, could judge fairly well whether the agent is capable of doing this.

Be wary if the agent is persuasively promoting high-priced policies that have "tremendous savings that you could use in retirement" but that provide only a fraction of the protection needed now. Be wary if he urges that an existing policy be dropped in favor of his, a practice (called "twisting") that usually is costly. He shouldn't fool the astute shopper, whose knowledge is his protective wall against pressure selling, or emotional spellbinding ("You owe it to your loved ones to invest in this policy.") or the immortality route ("With this policy, your presence will be felt long after you have passed on"). Alerted, the buyer will suspect that the agent's real interest is in his own pocketbook, for high-priced policies bring high commissions. Reputable agents do not resort to such measures. They know that, in the long view, honest consultation and quality service pay off far more handsomely than "short-cut" sales tactics. Buyers to them are not one-shot deals but clients who will need more insurance as their families and incomes grow, and who have friends who may want to buy insurance from "a reputable agent."

Choosing an insurance agent requires the care taken in choosing a lawyer. If a salesman does not come recommended by respected acquaintances, then he should be able to provide references, and his company should be a sound one with a name the buyer recognizes. A buyer should not do Brother-in-law Harry a favor at the expense of his family if it is apparent that Harry is unqualified or is selling insurance "until the right opportunity comes along."

Policies should not generally be bought by mail. Aside from the fact that there is no personal counseling in such cases, the company may not be licensed to sell in the buyer's state, minimizing the benefit of the state's protection and maximizing the cost of litigation in the event of dispute.

The Language of Life Insurance

Before discussing the types of insurance available, it would be best to define some of the most frequently used terms. Among them are:

Beneficiary: The person named in the policy to receive the money when the insured person dies.

Cash value: The money a policyholder gets back if he gives up his "permanent" policy.

Contingent beneficiary: The person named in the policy to receive the money when the insured person dies, if the beneficiary has died. Several contingent beneficiaries may be named, and the first surviving one down the list would get the money.

Dividend: Refund of premium overpayment on a participating policy. Being a refund and not a profit, it is not taxable. It cannot be guaranteed, because it depends on the insurance company's operating results.

Double indemnity: A policy provision, added at extra cost, providing for payment of twice the policy's face amount if death is accidental. Some companies offer triple indemnity under certain circumstances.

Face amount: The sum, stated on the face of the policy, that will be paid on death of the insured or at maturity of the contract.

Grace period: Usually 31 days after the premium due date, during which an overdue premium may be paid without penalty. The policy remains in force.

Industrial life insurance: Insurance sold in amounts under $1,000, and more usually under $500, by debit men, or insurance agents with sales territories, who personally collect the premiums weekly or monthly. The coverage, which has declined in popularity, got its name because it was born a century ago, in the early days of the industrial revolution, and was sold mainly to factory workers. It is expensive because of high administrative costs, and therefore provides little protection for the dollar. A $250 policy could cost a young man 25 cents a week, or $13 dollars a year, which could buy up to perhaps $2,000 of other types of insurance.

Insured: The person on whose life a policy is issued.

Level-premium insurance: The cost of such insurance is distributed evenly over the period during which premiums are paid. The premium remaining the same year to year, it is more than the actual cost of protection in the earlier years of the policy and less in the later years, when the chance of death is statistically greater. The overpayments in the early years build up the reserve, or cash value, which, in effect, is included in the face amount paid on death.

Maturity: When the face value becomes payable.

Mutual life insurance company: A nonprofit corporation that technically is owned by its policyholders, though they generally are not encouraged to attend annual meetings, do not elect directors and officers and have little or no say about their company's operation. These companies usually issue participating policies.

Nonparticipating policy: A contract on which the premium is calculated to cover the anticipated cost of insurance protection and related expenses, allowing for a profit. No dividends are paid. "Non-par" policies are issued by profit-motivated stockholder-owned life companies, many of which also sell participating policies for reasons noted below.

Paid-up insurance or paid-up policy: Insurance on which all required premium payments have been made. As distinguished from a policy that has matured, a paid-up contract cannot be surrendered for the full face amount, but rather for its cash value, which may be as much as two-thirds of the face amount. By contrast, a paid-up endowment is "mature," paying the face amount.

Participating policy: A contract on which the premium is calculated to allow some margin over the anticipated cost of protection and expenses. Usually after the first year or two, the policyholder receives partial refunds of those overcharges in the form of so-called dividends. The device evolved in the days when devastating plagues and inaccurate mortality tables made claims-payment prediction difficult. It has been continued, however, because the unrefunded overpayments in the first year or two help to pay the high cost of acquiring business, because the overpayment-and-refund cycle provides an insurance company with more investment capital, and because people like to receive "dividends."

Policy: The contract with the insurance company.

Policy loan: A loan made by an insurance company to a policyholder, with his policy's cash value as security. The insurance protection is reduced by the amount of the loan until repaid. The most prevalent interest rate is an attractive 5 per cent a year.

Premium: The regular amount paid for the insurance.

Premium loan: A policy loan made to pay the premium.

Settlement option: One of the ways in which the policyholder or beneficiary may choose to have the policy proceeds paid. This may be in a lump sum or under several income plans.

Waiver of premium: A provision, added at extra cost, that will keep a policy in force without further payment of premiums. It usually applies when the payor becomes totally and permanently disabled, as defined in the policy, before age 65.

The Four Basic Types of Life Insurance: Term, whole or straight life, limited payment life, endowment

As to the kinds of insurance available, hundreds, perhaps thousands, of policies are being offered by the merchandising-conscious insurance industry. But, in fact, they all are based on one or more of only four basic types of life insurance: term, whole or straight life, limited payment life and the endowment.

All four naturally provide death protection, but their premium rates vary widely, essentially because of variations in the "savings" feature. Those savings are the cash values that build up in permanent, level-premium policies. It is axiomatic that the faster that build-up and the greater a policy's ultimate cash value the higher the premium and, therefore, the smaller the amount of life insurance received for each dollar paid.

Term insurance generally has no cash-value build-up, so it usually has the lowest premium. Whole life costs more, but it slowly builds in cash value over a lifetime of premium payments and protection, as its name implies. Limited payment life provides lifetime protection but costs still more, because it accumulates cash values at a faster rate—within a "limited" premium-payment period of perhaps 10, 20 or 30 years or to age 65.

Endowments are predominantly savings vehicles and, therefore, are most expensive. The cash value builds up to the face, or protection, amount of the policy within a specified number of years, perhaps 20 or 30, or at a particular age of the buyer, such as 65. This near-100 per cent cash value is in sharp contrast with the cash values of whole or limited payment life, which generally grow to little more than 60 per cent of the face amount.

Cash values may be a form of savings; they certainly are counted among a man's assets, but they cannot be taken unless he gives up his policy. Short of surrendering the policy, he may borrow against its cash value, at interest. If he dies, the cash value is part of, not additional to, the face-amount paid to his beneficiary. The beneficiary would, in effect, get only the cash value, when it exceeds the insurance amount, as it might in such policies as the costly retirement-income contract.

In a sense, cash values center on the insured's gamble against dying. For, if he lives, he can enjoy their benefits, perhaps incorporating them in his retirement program. If he were assured that he would never get to use them, and such assurance to an insurable and therefore healthy man is highly unlikely, the additional payments toward this "savings" feature would be a waste. By their very nature, such savings are enforced, and this might be an attraction to people who could not otherwise put money aside consistently.

An analysis of a permanent policy shows why the cash value cannot be taken without surrendering the policy. It also shows how it can allow a level premium, that is, payment of the same amount of money in each year of its premium payment period, whether that be 10 or 20 years or a lifetime. As the reserve, or cash value, of a policy builds up over the years, less and less "pure" insurance protection is needed to make up the difference between the cash value and the face amount, or guaranteed payment on death.

In the early payment years, when the insured is young and statistically less likely to die, and when the policy's cash value is small, he is paying more than enough to buy the proportionately large amount of insurance needed to make up the face amount. In the later years, however, when the insured's statistical chance of death is greater and the cost of insurance is correspondingly greater, he can still pay the same premium as in earlier years, because less insurance is needed to make up the difference between the now-enlarged cash value and the face amount. A paid-up policy may have a cash value of only 60 per cent of the face amount, but that reserve is invested by the insurance company, with other policy reserves, to yield enough—and sometimes more than enough—to pay for the insurance needed to make up the 40 per cent difference.

The permanent policy has been described as a combination of a savings account and decreasing face amount term (pure) insurance, which, as its name suggests, reduces in insurance value each year. Strong opponents of permanent insurance argue that the savings account is disadvantageous, and that the insured would do better by buying his own decreasing term insurance and investing the savings portion more profitably in other savings or investment media. This "buy-term-and-invest-the-difference" philosophy later will be more fully discussed.

More conservative dissenters see a place for permanent insurance in a life insurance program. In the early family years, when the children are young and insurance needs greatest, a man can stretch his insurance dollars by building a tower of term protection on a foundation of permanent insurance. In the later years, when responsibilities and insurance needs generally are reduced, the man can retain all or part of his permanent insurance. Its level premium will assure him of a relatively low insurance bill in that period when his income may be reduced. Those permanent policies he does not need may be surrendered, with the reserve providing cash or supplemental income.

Let us now examine more closely the four basic types of coverage.

Term life insurance, like fire or automobile insurance, provides protection for a specified period of time, and the buyer gets nothing back when it expires. It may pay dividends, if it is a higher-premium participating policy, but there is no cash-value build-up. If there is, the policy is not truly term insurance, which is supposed to be pure protection, with no "savings" feature. The exception may be the long-term, level-premium term policy, which may have some cash surrender value in the early years, at least in theory.

In general, term is written for one, five or 10 years, but some companies offer it for longer periods or to a particular age, sometimes as advanced as 65. It may be bought in separate policies or in combination with other life insurance. The premium rates are low at early ages, but climb steeply for older buyers. However, as death protection —forgetting for the moment the cash values and other promoted features of so-called permanent policies—term insurance always demands a smaller cash outlay than any other form of individual insurance available when the term is bought.

This is apparent in a review of the range in typical yearly cost of $1,000 of life insurance for men at different ages. The following figures were provided by the Institute of Life Insurance. They show the cost per $1,000 of coverage provided by a nonparticipating policy and, in parenthesis, by a participating policy, which pays dividends.

Age at Purchase	Term (5-year renewable and convertible)	Whole Life	Limited Payment Life (paid up in 20 years)	Endowment (20 years)
20	$ 8.30	$ 15.00	$ 23.80	$ 47.05
	(10.30)	(18.00)	(28.15)	(49.95)
25	8.35	16.80	26.15	47.20
	(10.55)	(20.10)	(30.75)	(50.30)
30	8.70	19.10	28.95	47.50
	(10.95)	(22.70)	(33.80)	(50.90)
35	9.80	22.05	32.25	48.10
	(11.80)	(26.00)	(37.40)	(51.90)
40	11.50	26.00	36.15	49.20
	(13.85)	(30.25)	(41.75)	(53.60)
45	14.10	31.00	40.85	51.10
	(17.20)	(35.75)	(46.95)	(56.20)
50	18.95	37.05	46.55	54.00
	(22.70)	(42.90)	(53.45)	(60.20)

The cost per $1,000 of protection generally is reduced when larger policies, $10,000 or more, are brought, giving the effect of a quantity discount. Because of greater longevity, women usually pay less, their rates generally being those of men three years younger.

Term insurance rates increase steadily at each notch on the age scale, because increasing age brings statistically greater risk of death. The premium rates for term policies of longer than one-year duration remain the same, and are an approximate average of the rates that would have been charged, if the policies had been rated year by year.

Two term-policy provisions worth considering, though they add slightly to the cost, are the right to renew the policy or to convert it to permanent insurance, both without having to take a medical examination. A man can know that he will be able to maintain his insurance program, usually to age 65, even if his health deteriorates in the meantime, making him otherwise uninsurable.

One of the most flexible of term insurance forms is decreasing term, which can be bought separately or as part of a permanent policy. The maximum coverage it offers at the beginning of its long protection period, up to 25 years or more, or to a particular age, gradually reduces to zero by its expiration date. The annual cost remains constant. Thus, this is useful to families desiring to have the steadily decreasing unpaid balance on a home mortgage or other major loan paid off at death, or to leave the family with supplemental funds for the children's growing years, which steadily reduce in number.

Whole life is the most popular of the permanent, cash-value accumulation, level-premium policies. It is known by many names, including straight and ordinary life, though any policy of $1,000 or more on an individual life, with premiums payable annually or oftener, technically is ordinary life. Whole life provides lifetime protection in exchange for lifetime payment of premiums. The premium rate, though greater than for term insurance, is lowest of any permanent insurance, thus providing the most permanent protection for the dollar.

Whole life is the bread-and-butter contract of most insurance companies, which often adorn it with impressive-sounding names. The most ludicrous of these is "endowment at 95," which means that the insured himself would receive the face amount, if he is alive at age 95. This would be true of any whole-life policy, since it would mature, or pay off the face amount, when the insured dies, actually or statistically. For insurance purposes, statistical death is up around age 95. Many companies offer whole life, whatever they may call it, at slightly reduced rates in larger policies, usually $10,000 or larger face amounts. They are passing on savings in administrative costs afforded by issuing and servicing one large policy rather than several small ones.

Limited payment life differs from whole life only in that higher premiums are paid over a specific period, usually 20 or 30 years or to a specific age, such as 65. As a result, the cash-value build-up is faster. The idea of being done with premium payments in a relatively few years may be attractive, but this type of policy provides less protection for the premium dollar and would be disadvantageous to families needing the most protection for their limited insurance allotments. However, it has appeal for people, such as professional athletes and entertainers, whose incomes may be especially high over a relatively small number of years.

Endowments, as has been noted, are essentially savings policies and are expensive. They are written for a given period of time, perhaps 20 or 30 years, or to a particular age, the most common 65. If the insured dies in that period, his beneficiary receives the face amount; if he lives to its end, he gets it. This idea, too, appeals to many people, but the same disadvantages of the limited payment plan are present in greater degree, because endowments are so much more costly.

If a man dies in the nineteenth year of a 20-year limited payment policy or, worse yet, of a 20-year endowment, his beneficiary would get only the face amount. His large "savings" would be helping to make up that face amount, about 95 per cent of it in the case of the endowment, and more than half in the case of the limited payment policy. Think how much less-expensive insurance, such as whole life, might have been bought with the money spent on either of these expensive policies. Or less costly insurance in the same amount might have been bought and the cost difference saved or invested for the benefit of the insured or survivors.

Even more expensive than the endowment to age 65 is the retirement-income policy, a savings contract that ceases being an insurance policy once the cash value exceeds the face amount. At death, the face amount or the cash value, whichever is greater, is payable to the beneficiary. The retirement policy differs from the endowment in that, at maturity, usually age 65, it pays a monthly income, rather than a lump sum.

Life Insurance Packages: Family income, family maintenance, family, extra protection, preferred risk, modified life

Combinations of the four basic forms of life insurance turn up in packages being offered by insurers, and some of them are quite attractive. But it must be remembered that the only bargain in life insurance is the policy that best meets a man's needs within his ability to pay for it. Pricing is somewhat competitive, but not so much so that there is a wide spread among companies in the prices of comparable products. And, because prices and basic products are somewhat standardized, any insurer generally can make up the combinations, or "packages" that other insurance companies are offering.

One of the most popular combination contracts is the *family-income policy,* because it provides supplemental income to a family in the important and most expensive years when the children are growing up. The policy is a combination of decreasing term insurance and basic permanent coverage, usually whole life. Once the decreasing-term portion has expired, the cost reduces to that of the basic permanent policy, which the insured may retain. The most typical family-income period covered is 20 years. Such a policy, therefore, would provide that, if the insured died within 20 years after buying the policy, his beneficiary would receive $10 a month in "family income" for each $1,000 of the policy's face amount for the balance of the 20 years. That would be 1 per cent a month of the policy's face amount, but 1½ or 2 per cent also are offered by some companies at additional cost. In addition, the beneficiary also would receive the policy's face amount, in cash or additional income, at the insured's death or at the end of the family-income period, depending on the contract.

It may be decided to take the commuted (immediate cash) value of the family-income plan at the insured's death, rather than the monthly payments. If the decision is to be left to the beneficiary, the insured might have to include that option in the policy if it isn't already there. The commuted value would be the remaining insurance amount of the decreasing-term portion of the contract. For example, that would be nearly $16,000 in the first year of a $10,000 whole-life policy carrying a 20-year family-income rider providing $100, or 1 per cent of the face amount of the basic policy, in monthly payments during the family-income period. Therefore, the beneficiary would immediately receive nearly $26,000, including the commuted value of the family income and the $10,000 of basic coverage. In the tenth year, the commuted value would drop to less than $10,000, reducing the total immediate cash payment to less than $20,000.

A variation on the family-income policy is the *family-maintenance policy*. The difference is that the total family-income period begins with the insured's death. For example, if 20 years of payments are stipulated, the 20-year-income period would begin after the insured died, provided that he died within 20 years after he bought the policy. If a man bought this type of policy in 1966 and died in 1976, his family would receive a monthly income until 1996. By comparison, if he had bought a family-income policy instead, the monthly payments would have stopped in 1986, or 20 years after purchase. The family-maintenance policy's obvious advantage makes it more expensive.

Not to be confused with the family-income or family-maintenance policies is the *family policy,* which insures the whole family. Usually issued in $5,000 units, the father would have whole-life insurance protection in that amount, the wife would be covered by $1,000 or $1,250 of term insurance and each of the children would have $1,000 of term protection. This is especially economical for large families, for each child is automatically covered 15 days after birth at no added cost. Of course, a family must watch these and any other special features, for each one costs money, and those extras can cut deeply enough into a family's insurance allotment to leave the father underinsured.

Then there are *extra-protection policies*—a rare breed—that also combine term and whole life. The extra protection, which usually continues to age 60 or 65, may be $1,000, $2,000 or sometimes $3,000 of term insurance added to each $1,000 of basic whole-life coverage. This extra coverage provides less protection for the extra-premium dollar than does the family-income feature, but it can be carried for a longer period.

Preferred risk policies, when available, are an attractive lure to people in excellent health, who are in the safest of jobs and can buy at least $10,000 or $25,000 of insurance. The policies, usually standard whole-life contracts, are available to these qualified people at appreciable rate reductions.

The *modified life* policy is for the person, such as the young physician or other professional, who cannot pay now for all the family protection he needs, but expects his income to improve sufficiently within a few years. The policy provides low-cost term insurance for perhaps three to five years, after which it automatically converts to a whole-life policy, with the premium rate rising accordingly.

The Cost of Life Insurance: Annual net cost versus long-term cost

The net cost of a policy is, essentially, what a person pays, less what he gets back, if anything. His return may be in the form of dividends on participating policies or, upon surrender of the policy, its cash value, or both. A controversy has raged for years among insurance and securities men over how one might arrive at the true net cost. Old-line insurers, in general, stress permanent policies, though they have been putting increased emphasis on combination policies that include term insurance to satisfy family needs at reasonable cost. Securities men, particularly mutual fund advocates, along with some new insurers, recommend the cheapest form of pure insurance, or term, and investment of the extra money that would have been spent on more expensive policies. At best, there are complications in calculating net cost, but it would be worth a man's while to try it. His findings would be a helpful guide in filling his insurance needs.

The *annual net cost* is easy. It is the premium paid, less dividends, if any. But determining the true long-term, or surrender, net cost is not so easy. The procedure usually is illustrated in a 20-year projection. From the total premium due is deducted anticipated dividends, if any, and the 20-year cash or surrender value, which is stipulated in the policy. The answer is presented as the policy's 20-year net cost.

But that is not the complete answer, the dissenters say. The true net cost, they maintain, would be the earnings potential of the premium payments had they been invested elsewhere. Those other investments might be systematic deposits in a savings account or be regular purchases of stocks, mutual fund shares, corporate or Federal bonds. The earnings from these savings and investments generally would be subject to income taxes, and this must be taken into account. However, there are tax-exempt local and state government bonds, which would be especially attractive to persons in high-income brackets. A tax-free yield of 4 per cent might be the equivalent to them of up to 8 per cent or more in taxable income.

This approach might appear academic to the family man who is not in an economic position to choose between investments and essential life insurance protection. And how many men are? Furthermore, any purchase, whether it be of life insurance or a car or a magazine subscription, could generate discussion of what the purchase price might have earned if invested or put into a bank, and the conclusion perhaps rightfully would be that the actual cost of the product or service was the price plus its "lost" earnings.

Like any other product or service, life insurance costs money. If the *long-term net cost* of a policy is low, or if there is even a small profit to its owner, then the policy in all probability has a high premium rate per $1,000 of coverage and a relatively rapid and large cash-value build-up. Thus, the policy owner's apparent long-term net cost is low, primarily because he is providing the insurance company with investment capital (the cash value), and the income the company earns on that capital is the insured's additional cost. If, by investing that capital himself, he could generate greater income than can the insurer then his insurance cost is greater by that difference in investment yield.

Advocates of the "buy-term-and-invest-the-difference" concept say their plan puts the insured way ahead of the game. And, under the right circumstances, it can. Essentially, under the classic version of the plan, a man would buy term insurance, including a good deal of decreasing face amount term, all of which would provide initial protection equal to his total life insurance need. Then he would determine the cost difference between that protection and the more conventional coverage including a lot of higher premium permanent insurance. In each premium payment period, he would invest that difference, building his own cash values, which, according to the advocates, ultimately would more than offset the decline in insurance protection afforded by the decreasing term policies.

As the man grew older (perhaps in his mid-40's), he would convert a sufficient amount of the term insurance to permanent policies, so as to stabilize his annual outlay for the basic protection he will need for the rest of his life. This basic protection might be to cover death expenses, lifetime income for the wife and an emergency fund.

But, under what circumstances would it be wise to buy term and invest the difference? First, the man must be highly disciplined; he must be capable of systematically investing the "difference" as if he were meeting regular bills. Too often a man has started the program, and then found other uses for the money he should have been investing. Second, the man must be capable of selecting the right savings or investment vehicle, or of seeking out the right advisers. Third, and finally, the man's economic position and life insurance program must be such that they warrant consideration of such a program. In the extreme, a man who can just barely afford term insurance to meet at least a part of his insurance needs has no time to worry about the "difference." The insurance buyer must achieve that delicate balance between being underinsured and being "insurance poor." More often than not, his objective doesn't go beyond trying to match the amount of insurance his budget will sensibly allow with the amount of insurance his personal survey indicates he needs.

To go as far as possible toward filling as much of the life insurance requirement as their budgets will allow, many families find that they must rely heavily on term insurance in its various forms. A typical family might buy whole life, the least expensive permanent insurance, to provide lifetime protection against the continuing economic risks of death. These may be the immediate death expenses, income for the wife's later years and an emergency fund.

The needs of shorter duration may be satisfied with term, much of which can be bought at lowest cost in combination with the permanent insurance. These needs are felt in the family's growing years—family income, mortgage protection, special funds for college and other goals. Because these needs generally reduce with the passage of time and possibly with the growth of a family's other assets, many of them can be met with minimal cash outlay by decreasing face amount term. As has been noted, this is available separately or as part of such other policies as the family-income and family-maintenance contracts.

Extra Protection Against Accidental Death: The double-indemnity provision, flight insurance

People are attracted to such low-ticket items as the *double-indemnity provision* and *flight insurance*. They are bought almost automatically. The first makes the death payment twice (sometimes it is triple) the policy's face amount if death is accidental, and the second pays off if the insured dies in a commercial flight. But are they worth the price? Is the additional insurance needed? If the added protection is needed, the man and his family had better take another look at their insurance program. There is no sound reason why a man's family would need a bigger estate if he were to die accidentally rather than from natural causes. The money might better be spent on expanding the family's basic program. The real appeal of such purchasing may be to man's instinct for gambling, latent or otherwise.

Life Insurance Premiums: Service charges, late payment, cancellation of a policy

Premiums may be paid annually, semiannually or, if the total bill is large enough, monthly. The greater the frequency of payments, the greater the extra-service cost—up to 10 per cent or more of the basic annual premium. It is best, therefore, to pay each policy on an annual basis. If there are several policies, each annual payment may be spaced so that the total cost of all life insurance doesn't hit a family in one brief period.

The family can save for itself the extra money that a company must charge to spread a policy's premium payments over the year by doing the same thing themselves. They can set aside an appropriate amount in each budgetary period, weekly, monthly or whatever, and have the total premium ready when it is due.

Should a premium due date be missed, there is a grace period of up to 31 days in which to make it up. If the insured is unable to do so, and the policy is of a permanent type, he may take a premium loan against the cash value. Some policies have an automatic premium loan provision, and it can be added to others at no extra cost.

If the policy owner feels he cannot continue the payments, or does not want to, he has a choice of three "nonforfeiture values" under a permanent policy. He may take the cash value (the amount for the year of surrender is stipulated in the contract) in cash or as income under various short-term or lifetime arrangements. He could take a paid-up permanent policy providing less insurance than the original contract, its size depending on how much the net cash value will buy in a single payment at the insured's attained age. Or, he could take extended term insurance in the amount of the original policy for as long a period as the net cash value can buy.

The Dividend Options

Dividends on participating policies may be taken in cash, used to reduce premiums due, left with the insurance company to accumulate at interest, or used to buy additional paid-up life insurance. Some companies have a "fifth dividend option," under which one-year term may be bought each year, and was designed primarily to offset policy loans made on the minimum-deposit purchase plan. Under that plan, advantageous only to people in high tax brackets, policy loans are kept at the level of the increasing cash value, and the proceeds are used toward payment of the premium.

To keep annual cash outlay as low as possible, a family would find it most practical to take dividends as credit in the payment of premiums. They could be taken when needed, if left with the company at interest, but it must be determined whether the interest rate is competitive with that of banks, savings and loan associations and other thrift institutions.

The Beneficiary: Primary and contingent beneficiaries, changing the beneficiary

To minimize the risk of neglecting to change the named beneficiary as family status changes, an insured may use wording that would cover most contingencies. For example, a man may name his wife as primary beneficiary, and then name a number of contingent beneficiaries, each of whom—if she died—would be eligible in turn to receive the money if the primary beneficiary and the contingent beneficiaries named before him all died before the insured did. The first contingent beneficiary may be the insured's children, named as a group, who would share the proceeds. Some policies automatically include children as contingent beneficiaries. It is safest to specifically name an adopted child; and if the insured wants only the children of his present marriage and not of a previous marriage to benefit, he must so specify. Additional contingent beneficiaries may be other relatives or close friends, or perhaps a favorite charity. The policy owner may reserve the right to change the beneficiary, but it may be wiser, if not necessary, under certain circumstances to make the decision irrevocable. It makes good sense to get the advice of a lawyer and tax expert. If there are no living beneficiaries at the insured's death, the proceeds would go into his estate.

Insurance Payments

As stated in the policy, the proceeds may be paid immediately in one lump sum, or provide income under one of the following settlement options:

1. The money may be left with the insurance company until taken by the beneficiary who in the meantime would receive regular checks for the interest it earns. This option, except under special circumstances, would not be advisable, unless the interest rate was competitive with that paid by banks and other institutions. The option is useful to the family that needs time to select the best option.

2. Monthly installments of any denomination could be paid until the insurance proceeds and interest have been exhausted.

3. Monthly income may be paid over a desired number of months or years, using up principal and interest in that period.

4. Monthly income for life. Obviously the amount paid monthly on a given policy will be smaller if the beneficiary is young and likely to collect for a long time, and larger if he is older. Reduced lifetime income may be taken in exchange for a guarantee by the insurance company of a minimum number of payment years, "10-years certain" or "20-years certain," for example. If the beneficiary dies during this period, a named contingent beneficiary would receive the income for the balance of the period, or its cash equivalent.

In any case, if the insurance company has agreed to pay interest on principal or monthly installments for a specified period, or until the money is exhausted, and the beneficiary dies, the balance of the payments due, or the principal in the case of the interest-payment option, will be paid to the next contingent beneficiary. It no contingent beneficiaries have been named or none is living, the unpaid proceeds will go to the insured's estate.

The insured may choose the pay-out plan, or leave the decision to the beneficiary.

Group Insurance

Any person generally should take advantage of the opportunity to obtain group insurance at his place of employment, through an association or other organization, because it usually is the lowest-priced, usually term, protection available. Essentially, it is cheap because the insurance company has nominal administrative cost. A large number of people are protected under one master policy, which is issued by the insurance company in a single sale, and which is paid for in single large sums by the employer or sponsoring organization, who does most of the individual bookkeeping. The cost advantage is especially great for older people in the group, for the price per $1,000 of coverage is an average for the group, geared to a median age.

Advantages to all are that there is usually no medical examination required, and that the employer often pays part or all of the premium. While the coverage generally terminates shortly after an employe quits or retires, he usually has the option to convert the coverage to an individual permanent policy without a medical examination. Some plans allow employes to carry at least a small portion of their group life insurance into retirement.

Credit Life Insurance

Here is another advantage of group life insurance, for most credit insurance is written on a group basis. This low-cost protection assures payment of the unpaid balance of a loan or installment debt at the borrower's death, or sometimes in the event of his total and permanent disability. This leaves his family free of indebtedness. The insurance generally is obtainable through the lender or installment seller. While the rates generally are modest, the consumer must remain alert, demanding to be shown in the sales or loan contract just what the insurance coverage and cost are. There have been reports of instances, not widespread, in which borrowers have been overcharged. If the borrower cannot compare insurance costs but is suspicious, he should turn to his state's insurance department.

Insuring the Uninsurable: Persons with health defects, hazardous occupations

Many persons who cannot obtain standard life insurance at standard rates because of health defects or because their occupations are considered hazardous may buy it at higher premium rates. The amount of the surcharge varies with the reason for the rejection as a normal insurance risk. An encouraging trend has become apparent in recent times, in which the insurers are becoming more liberal in their dealings with these substandard risks.

If a person desirous of obtaining life insurance thinks he may be rated as a substandard risk because of some ailment or physical defect, he should first check with his private physician. If the condition is temporary or can be corrected, it would be wise for him to wait, unless the insurance need is pressing and an unreasonable period of time might pass before the condition was eliminated. A major reason is that, if a substandard-risk policy is bought and the insured then eliminated the reason for the substandard rating, it often is difficult and time-consuming to have the policy rerated as standard. Furthermore, if, upon medical examination, an applicant for life insurance is rejected, the findings of that examination are available to all other life insurers. This may make it difficult at some future time to buy a policy, even though the deficiency may have been corrected.

G.I. Insurance

Armed Forces veterans who have not taken full advantage of their opportunities to buy or convert to a permanent form Government life insurance should contact their local Veterans Administration offices for the latest information on whether they might recover that fumble. Any person who needs life insurance should utilize this privilege to the fullest because the policies generally are the best insurance bargain available. The maximum obtainable is $10,000.

Probably the best bargains were offered to veterans who had served in World War II or before April 25, 1951. The rates are low and the dividends generous, because the Government decided not to use premium funds to pay operating costs and benefits on the lives of servicemen who died in service or later from service-connected disabilities. Further, casualties were fewer than anticipated and insured were in top health. All Federal insurance is cheaper because there are no sales commissions or other business-acquisition expenses.

Korean War veterans and all others who served for at least 31 days in the period from June 25, 1950, to January 1, 1957, were allowed to obtain attractively rated life insurance after service under the Servicemen's Indemnity and Insurance Acts of 1951. World War I veterans may still obtain up to $10,000 of United States Government Life Insurance if they are in good health.

There are features beyond low cost that make a veteran's life insurance policy far more valuable than he might suspect. For example, all policies but those with a policy number that starts with "K" have a disability waiver of premium clause, eliminating future payments by a totally and permanently disabled policyholder. The "K" policy automatically "matures," when the insured becomes totally and permanently disabled. The policy may remain in force at full face amount, or the insured may elect to take monthly payments, which would slowly reduce the death benefit.

Other than "K" policy owners may obtain a total-disability provision at nominal extra cost. This provides for benefits of $5.75 (on U.S.G.L.I.) and $10 (on N.S.L.I policies) a month for each $1,000 of insurance in force, if the insured becomes totally disabled before age 65. These benefits do not reduce the face amount of insurance protection.

After a column on veterans' insurance had appeared in *The New York Times,* a Cincinnati reader wrote to the author, asking whether he should retain or cash-in his paid-up G.I. insurance. The 50-year-old veteran bought the $10,000-face-amount, 20-payment policy in 1945 at age 30 and it now has a cash value of $6,100.

The deciding considerations are essentially the same, whether the policy is a Federal or a commercial one. Since, in effect, the particular policy's $6,100 in cash value would be included in the $10,000 payment at the insured's death (as is the case with any permanent policy's cash value), the insurance portion is only $3,900. Thus, the individual must decide whether his insurance needs warrant his keeping the $6,100 on deposit for the sake of obtaining the additional protection. If not, he must then decide whether he can invest the $6,100 more profitably, and chances are he can.

6

SECURITY ON THE INSTALLMENT PLAN: RETIREMENT

The achievement of economic security in retirement is within the grasp of more Americans than ever before, and their number is growing each year. This is a product of our affluent society; as we reap the rewards of our ever-burgeoning economy, we are better able to raise the living standards of all Americans, particularly the aged.

Periodically liberalized Social Security benefits and larger numbers of employe-pension plans provide a degree of security that was only dreamed of a generation ago. To some, these benefit and pension payments seem sufficient and more than they had hoped to attain. To others, they are the foundation on which to build a complete financial program for retirement. However, if one is to build on that foundation, total family-financial planning is essential. For the task of supplementing basic benefits, though made easier, still requires additional insurance, savings, investments and other assets.

Social Security: Financing the program, Primary Insurance Benefit

The Social Security identification card in a man's wallet is one of his most valuable documents, particularly if he is married. For it could be worth thousands of dollars in benefits to him and his family. The substance and flexibility of those benefits becomes apparent in a study of the uses to which a family man might put his card. Cash benefits will be paid, upon application, to the family in the event of his total disability, untimely death or ultimate retirement. They may provide the only means of support in time of family stress or in old age, or serve as the basis for estate and retirement planning. In addition, as discussed in Chapter 7, the Social Security Act's Medicare program would provide free hospitalization insurance and low-cost medical insurance for the man and his wife when each turns 65. Use of Social Security benefits as a base for financial planning is a major selling point of the life insurance industry.

FINANCING THE PROGRAM. The Social Security program is financed with a tax on the first $6,600 in annual earnings of each insured person. The amount of tax paid by a worker is matched by his employer. The tax rate paid by self-employed persons is about one and one-half times the employe's rate. Included in the tax rate is a portion to finance separately the hospitalization insurance part of the Medicare program. That separate rate was set at 35/100 of 1 per cent for 1966, and, like the basic Social Security tax, will be increased periodically, to 8/10 of 1 per cent by 1987. The combined Social Security and Medicare tax rate for employes and employers and for the self-employed are as follows:

Year	Employer/Employe	Self-Employed
1966	4.20%	6.15%
1967–68	4.40	6.40
1969–72	4.90	7.10
1973–75	5.40	7.55
1976–79	5.45	7.60
1980–86	5.55	7.70
1987 and after	5.65	7.80

PRIMARY INSURANCE BENEFIT. An insured worker's Primary Insurance Benefit is the key to all calculations of cash Social Security benefits. It is the amount he would receive each month if disabled or retired. His dependents or survivors would receive percentages of that amount. The basic benefit can range from a minimum of $44 a month to a maximum, if calculated at the end of 1965, of $132.70 for a man or $135.90 for a working woman. Under the law, as liberalized in 1965, the maximum possible benefit will grow to $168 for men retiring in 2004 or later, and for women retiring in 2001 or later. The total in benefits received by an insured person's family may not exceed $309.20. This, too, will grow, to an ultimate $368.

Calculation of the primary benefit is based on the worker's average monthly Social Security-taxable income in the years worked after 1950. The person may exclude a low-income year for the computation year. In addition, a man may exclude five other low-income years, and a woman may exclude eight other low-income years. This is to her advantage, for the more low-income years eliminated, the higher the average monthly income. It is especially true in view of the fact that the maximum earnings creditable for Social Security benefit computation is lower for past years. It is $3,600 for 1951 through 1954, $4,200 for 1955 through 1958, $4,800 for 1959 through 1965, and $6,600 beginning in 1966.

Those increases explain the difference in primary benefits of a man and a woman who turned 65 and retired at the end of 1965. By projection, it also explains why the maximum benefit will steadily increase. Here is how it worked in the cases of the man and woman whom we will assume both earned the Social Security-taxable maximum or more since 1950: Of the 15 years worked after 1950, the man may exclude six years, one for his computation year and the five others. Of the nine remaining creditable years, he would be credited with the $4,800 maximum for each year since 1959, but with only the $4,200 allowable maximum in 1957 and 1958. This would put his average monthly wage, for benefit calculation purposes, at $388, and his monthly benefit at $132.70. However, the woman in the same situation need only select her best six years. If these were the last six years, she would be credited with the maximum $4,800 in each year. Therefore, her average monthly wage, for benefit calculation, would be $400, putting her benefit at $135.90

The benefit formula is 62.97 per cent of the first $110 of the average monthly wage, plus 22.9 per cent of the next $290 and 21.4 per cent of the excess over $400. Under a creditable-earnings ceiling of $4,800 a year, the maximum average monthly wage was $400 (1/12 of $4,800). However, with a rise in that ceiling to $6,600, the maximum average monthly wage will climb to an ultimate maximum of $550 for the person with the maximum creditable earnings in all calculation years. Applying the formula to that sum would yield a primary insurance benefit of $168 a month.

Special Social Security Benefits: Retirement, survivors' and disability benefits, benefits for women

Next we will discuss the Social Security benefits that would become available on retirement, total disablement or death of an insured person. Like the preceding discourses, it will show the scope and basic structure of the Federal program, but the reader should take special note of two points: First, the benefits are not automatic; they must be applied for at a Social Security Administration office. Second, the Social Security Act's complexity makes it imperative that an individual visit a local administration office for a detailed explanation and analysis of his particular situation.

RETIREMENT BENEFITS. Most people associate Social Security with retirement.

A fully insured man or woman may retire at age 65, and receive his or her full monthly primary insurance benefit. Either may retire as early as age 62, but benefits would be reduced permanently by 5/9 of 1 per cent for each month they are paid before age 65. With the total family benefit maximum as the ceiling, the retired person's dependent spouse and children each would be entitled to benefits equal to half the retired worker's primary benefit.

To receive benefits, a child must be totally disabled, or under age 18 or, if a full-time student, under 22. The dependent spouse must be 65 to receive her full benefit, or at least 62 to receive a reduced benefit. A retired worker who is under age 72 may earn up to $1,500 a year and still receive benefits every month. If he earns more, 50 cents in benefits will be withheld for each $1 of earnings between $1,500 and $2,700. Above that, $1 in benefits will be withheld for each $1 earned. However, if in any month he earned no more than $125, he would receive his full benefit for that month no matter how much he earned the rest of the year. If he is 72 or older, there is no limit as to the amount he may earn and still receive full benefits.

"Earnings" would be pay for work of any kind, whether or not covered by the Social Security law, and all net income from self-employment. Income from savings, investments, pensions and insurance does not affect retirement or survivors' benefits under Social Security. Also excluded would be royalty income, if it is being received on copyrights or patents that the retired person obtained before reaching age 65. The additional earnings of a person who works after applying for retirement benefits may increase the amount of his monthly benefit. He will not have to apply to have his benefit refigured, because the Social Security Administration will be doing it automatically with electronic computers.

SURVIVORS' BENEFITS. Upon the death of a Social Security insured worker, a lump sum of three times his monthly primary benefit, but no more than $255, will be paid to the surviving spouse after application has been filed for benefits. The benefits would be based on the amount his primary benefit would have been, and it is calculated as if he was age 65 at death. Within the total family benefit maximum, his widow and first child each would receive three-quarters of the primary benefit amount, and each additional child would be entitled to half. Within the maximum, his dependent parents also would be entitled to benefit payments. No benefits would be available to the widow, if she is under age 60 and not caring for a child under age 18. At 60, she may receive reduced "widow's benefits," permanently cut by 5/9 of 1 per cent for each month they are received before age 62. By not taking benefits until age 62, she would be entitled to the full benefit, which is 82.5 per cent of her late husband's primary benefit.

To illustrate, if the husband's primary benefit would have been $100 a month, his widow's full benefit at age 62 would be $82.50 a month. It would be permanently reduced to $76.90, if her payments had begun a year earlier, or to $71.50 if they had begun two years earlier, at age 60.

A child would receive benefit payments until age 18, or until 22, if he is a full-time student. A child who becomes totally disabled before age 18 would be entitled to lifetime benefits.

DISABILITY BENEFITS. To qualify for disability benefits, a worker must be deemed to be "totally disabled" and unable to pursue "substantial gainful activity" for a continuous period of at least a year. His benefits would be the same as if he had reached age 65, for they are calculated on his earnings record in the same way. Each of his qualified dependents would receive an amount equal to half his primary monthly benefit. The entitlement would extend to children on the same basis as for survivors' benefits. The worker's wife, or former wife under certain circumstances, also would receive benefits if she has at least one child under 18 in her care, or if she is age 62 or older. Total family benefits are subject to the maximum family limit.

Following the letter of the law, it might be adjudged that a disabled executive was capable of performing at least a messenger's or office-boy's job. However, persons close to the Social Security Administration gave assurance that all factors would be taken into account, including a person's educational and other qualifications, as well as the types of work available in his area. "Our most important rule," a Social Security executive said, "is that we must judge each case on its own specifications and merits." There is no nationally uniform definition of "total disability." Subject to final approval by the Social Security Administration's division of disability in Baltimore, cases are decided by the administration's so-called "state agencies." Each agency relates its decisions to its particular state's laws and employment conditions.

Once a worker has qualified for disability benefits, he and his family will begin receiving benefits in his sixth month of disability. Should he become well enough to return to work, he would be allowed nine months to regain occupational stature, during which he would continue to receive benefit payments. The payments would end after the nine-month period. They would be resumed, with no waiting period, however, if the worker again was forced to stop working because of his disability.

A worker who loses his eyesight gets somewhat more liberal treatment under the disability-insurance provisions. If he is between the ages of 55 and 65 and unable to engage in his usual occupation because of his blindness, he would be eligible for benefits. He need not qualify for any other "substantial gainful activity," but he would not receive benefits in any month in which he pursued such an activity. Requirements for fully insured status are reduced for workers under age 31 who lose their sight, and further reduced for workers under age 24.

There may be a reduction in Social Security disability benefits for a worker receiving workmen's compensation payments. The reduction would be to the extent that combined total benefits to him and his family exceeded 80 per cent of his average monthly Social Security-taxable income during all his working years since 1951, or during the best five years, whichever is to his advantage. There is a so-called "freeze" on a disabled worker's earnings record during his period of disability, so that the level of benefits in future claims will be preserved. Thus, in calculating, for example, the retirement benefits of a worker who had received disability benefits for two years, those unemployed years would not be counted in arriving at his average monthly Social Security-taxable income during working years.

There are several ways in which the Social Security Administration maintains watchful control over a person receiving disability benefits. Addition of earnings credit to his Social Security account would be one indication that the "totally disabled" person was actually working. Another indication might be his income tax return filed with the Internal Revenue Service. In addition, the administration's local staffs conduct yearly check-ups. They communicate with the beneficiary, in person when possible, asking whether there has been any change in his condition, whether he is working, when he last saw his physician and so on. All disability-benefit applicants must agree to at least visit or cooperate with a state rehabiliation agency that communicates with him. Under the new legislation, state rehabilitation agencies will be reimbursed from Social Security trust funds for the cost of services provided to workers or children entitled to disability benefits. In case of disability, a worker, or someone in his behalf, should apply for benefits as soon as it is apparent that the disability will continue for a long period.

BENEFITS FOR WOMEN. A few of the Social Security Act's advantages to women have been discussed, but there are others. For example, the widow who works and has her own Social Security account number, may exercise retirement options other than the ones described above, if it is to her advantage. She may begin receiving benefits as early as age 60 under her late husband's account, and, at age 65, may choose to receive benefits under her own account.

Here is how it might work: A 62-year-old widow is advised that monthly payments on her own account would be $100 at age 65, or reduced by 20 per cent, to $80, if she decided to begin receiving benefits immediately. Her husband, she is told, would have been entitled to $100 monthly on his own account, and her widow's benefit at age 62, therefore, would be $82.50, or $2.50 more than her own account would provide at that age. Under the law, she may apply for the higher widow's benefit of $82.50 a month at age 62, and then shift to her own account at 65, increasing her monthly income to $100. With modification, this advantage extends to the working woman who chooses, as is a widow's right, to begin receiving reduced widow's benefits before age 62. When she shifted to her own account at age 65, her payments would be reduced permanently by the difference between the monthly widow's benefit she received at the early age and the amount she would have received had she waited until age 62.

One might take the case of the widow who would be entitled to $82.50 a month at age 62 under her husband's account, and $100 a month at 65. If she chose to retire at age 60, her widow's benefit would have been reduced to $71.50, or $11 less than the "full benefit" at 62. At 65, when she shifted to her own account, her payment would be reduced by the $11 difference, to $89 a month.

Moving to another area, a divorced woman could qualify for a wife's or widow's benefits, if she had been married to the worker for at least 20 years and she was receiving half her support from him, was receiving "substantial contributions" from him under a written agreement, or was entitled to them under a court order. A woman could receive benefit payments as a "surviving divorced mother," if she has in her care a child who is under age or disabled. Old-age payments to a widow or dependent widower would not be discontinued in the event of remarriage. The amount, however, would be reduced to 50 per cent of the amount the deceased worker would have received. That 50 per cent would apply also to a widow who had begun receiving reduced payments before age 62. Dependent widowers normally cannot receive old-age benefits before 62.

The more liberal attitude of Congress toward women, it has been said, is based on the rationale that women would have less of an opportunity than men to remain employed, particularly in later years.

Annuities: Straight life annuity, life annuity with installments certain, installment refund annuity, cash-refund annuity, joint and survivor annuity, variable annuities

When conversation turns to retirement income, someone generally mentions annuities. The word is a comfortable one, because it conjures up images of economic security. But many persons, caught up in life's maze of activities and responsibilities, are somewhat vague about these complicated contracts and how they work. Some confuse annuities with life insurance policies, because both are generally sold by insurance companies—sometimes in combination.

In essence, a life insurance contract promises to pay a man's beneficiaries a certain sum at his death, while an annuity contract promises to pay him an income for as long as he lives. But there are many variations on these themes. Bought separately, an annuity may be paid for with a lump sum or in installments over a period of years. Income may begin immediately after the contract has been fully paid for, or it may be deferred for a number of years, perhaps until the annuitant, or the contract buyer, has reached retirement age. If the purchaser dies before his annuity income starts, his beneficiary usually receives the amount he put into it or its cash value at his death, whichever is greater. By surrendering the contract before income begins, the owner himself would get the money.

Some holders erroneously refer to their life policies as annuities, while others rightfully do so, and this is a major point of confusion. Those who are right own combination contracts, usually called retirement-income policies. Such a policy provides immediate death protection, but its cash value builds up rapidly, ultimately far exceeding the insurance amount, in which case the beneficiary would receive the cash value. For example, a 30-year-old man might pay about $340 a year for a policy that provided immediate death protection of $10,-000 and, if he lives, a monthly income of $100 beginning at age 65. At that point, the premium payments stop, the insurance factor ends and the contract's cash value may be around $18,000. Depending on the income option taken, there may still be a death benefit for a period.

There are other factors that cause confusion of life contracts with annuities. A beneficiary may elect to take the proceeds of a life policy as income, or an insured person who lives to retirement may choose to surrender his permanent life insurance policy, and take its cash value as income. In both instances, the effect is to buy a single-premium annuity with the life policy's proceeds. The annuity purchaser is trading his principal for lifetime income, the size of which is based primarily on the price, his age and the mortality table. In essence, the table reflects average life expectancy for a particular age group, making the lifetime-income guarantee possible. Payments that do not go to those who die prematurely can go to those who live beyond the average number of years. Women must pay more for annuities, because they generally live longer than men and therefore are likely to receive the incomes for longer periods. In contrast, women usually pay less for insurance, because at most any given age, their chance of death is less than for men.

There are several ways in which annuity income may be taken, all of which guarantee it for life. The choice depends, in large part, on the annuitant's health, the amount available to buy an annuity, the importance put on size of income and the concern with heirs. The principal methods are as follows:

1. *Straight life annuity*. This provides the maximum income the purchase price will allow, but it stops at death, whether that occurs after one payment or hundreds.
2. *Life annuity with installments certain*. If death occurs within a specified period, perhaps 10 or 20 years, a beneficiary would receive the income for the balance of that period. The longer the "certain" period, the greater the reduction in the size of income.
3. *Installment refund annuity*. If death occurs before total income equals the amount paid in, a beneficiary would continue to receive the income until the total payments reached that amount.
4. *Cash-refund annuity*. This is similar to the preceding option, except that the beneficiary receives the balance of the original investment in a single sum.
5. *Joint and survivor annuity*. Two people, usually husband and wife, receive the income, which continues as long as one of them is alive. This usually provides the smallest income for the investment, especially if one spouse is much younger than the other.

Illustrative single-premium annuity prices released by a major life insurance company indicate the comparative cost of the options. A 65-year-old man buying $100 of immediate monthly income would pay $13,379.40 for a straight life annuity, $15,189.90 for a refund annuity, or $17,422.70 for a joint and survivor annuity, if his wife is his age.

Before deciding on an annuity, a person must estimate the total retirement income he can expect from other sources, such as Social Security, savings, investments and a company pension. The supplemental income would fill the gap, if any, between what these sources would provide and what he needed. No family man should consider an annuity until he has sufficient life insurance. A retirement-income policy, combining both, might look attractive, but its price could buy more than twice as much insurance protection. The most widely sold annuities—and those discussed here—are known as fixed-dollar annuities. They promise a predetermined, unchanging income, which is drawn from a reserve that is invested in bonds and mortgages providing guaranteed return. The reserve is made up of annuity payments.

A relatively new type of annuity that is not yet widely available is the variable annuity. The paid-in funds for this type of contract are invested primarily in the stock market, and the annuitant's income varies with investment results. The objective is to provide a hedge against inflation—market values are expected to rise with the cost of living in the long view.

Among the advantages of the regular fixed annuity are the freedom from investment worry, protection against a depression (income would not be reduced), lifetime-income guarantee and ease in saving for old age by using the "enforced" installment plan. In addition, there is a tax advantage that can be significant to those in high income brackets. The annuity payments earn interest, but income tax is not due on that interest until actually collected, which would be in lower tax-bracket retirement years. Among the disadvantages are that little, if any, of the money put into an annuity can be left to heirs, and that a relatively low return is earned by the investment (the income is part interest, part principal). Further, if inflation cut the dollar's purchasing power, the annuity income would not increase, and once annuity income began, the investment generally could not be withdrawn in an emergency.

Thus, the individual must weigh carefully whether there is advantage to investment in an annuity or in other media, or whether to diversify, achieving a combination protecting in part against deflation. If it is decided to buy an annuity, then it must be determined whether it is wiser to pay for it in installments over the years, or to invest the money elsewhere, perhaps more profitably, and then buy a single-premium annuity.

THE VARIABLE ANNUITY. This weapon against inflationary erosion of retirement income is gaining favor, though it is still not widely available.

That erosion of purchasing power has been severely felt, especially since World War II, by persons dependent on the fixed income of standard annuities. Unlike the standard annuity, the variable does not offer a fixed-dollar income and is not supported by fixed-income investments, such as bonds and mortgages. Instead, payments into a variable annuity are invested primarily in common stocks, and the contract holder's ultimate income is based on the results of those investments.

In general terms, a contract buyer would periodically pay a predetermined premium, for which he would be credited with "units," or shares, the exact number depending on the prevailing share value of the assets in the total fund, made up of payments of all participants in the particular plan. When the annuitant retires, he receives the current value each month of a predetermined number of units. Thus, if he were entitled to payments of 10 units a month, and the unit value in three consecutive months was $10.10, $9.90 and $10.20, his retirement income for those months would be $101, $99 and $102.

Advocates of variable annuities maintain that they allow the incomes of retired people to advance with the economy. To support their arguments, they generally point to the Teachers Insurance and Annuity Association, which, through its companion organization, the College Retirement Equities Fund (CREF), is credited with introducing the first variable annuity in this country in 1952. This plan, available to college teachers and administrators, has served as the model on which later plans have been fashioned. Participants, who now number nearly 150,000, have the option of diverting up to three-quarters of their payments to the variable plan, with the rest going toward a fixed-dollar annuity. The fixed-dollar annuity serves as a deflation hedge in that it guarantees the rate of retirement payment from that segment of the plan. Social Security benefits also provide a deflation hedge, in that they not only are guaranteed, but also have been increased periodically.

The unit value of the College Retirement Equities Fund may change daily as market values of underlying securities fluctuate. However, to provide some stability of income for retired participants, the organization's investment managers adjust the unit pay-out rate once a year on March 31, and it is applied for the 12 months beginning May 1. Thus, participants did not feel the mid-1962 market break until May 1, 1963, when the unit pay-out rate dropped to $22.68 from $26.13. But it went up to $26.48 in 1964, $28.21 in

1965 and $30.43 in 1966. If a professor retired in 1958 with a monthly income of $100 from the guaranteed portion and the value of 10 units from the variable, his fixed income would have remained constant at $100, plus several dollars in dividends, but the variable would have grown from $167.10 to $304.30. Investment results are enhanced by the fact that almost all of the payments collected by the nonprofit CREF are put to work. No sales commissions are paid and operating expenses in 1965 were kept at 0.36 per cent of average assets. Assets totaled $609.05 million on December 31, 1965.

The CREF plan, in its relatively short existence, has proved successful for its participants, but are variable annuities available to employes in other fields or to individuals? The legal battle to market variables has been fierce. As to workers, a small but growing number of employers are offering group variable annuities. Individuals may buy them in some 22 states, but New York is not among them. Regulatory control has been the prime factor in the legal battle. Proponents of the variable, in the main, have been life insurance companies, the most notable of which is the Prudential Insurance Company of America. These companies are state regulated. However, the Federal Securities and Exchange Commission has maintained, with success in the courts, that variable annuities are securities, not insurance policies, likening them to mutual funds. Therefore, it ruled that variables must be regulated under the Investment Company Act of 1940, which, among other things, requires establishment of a separate investment company for the sale and administration of variable annuities. This would also mean loss of certain tax advantages to the insurers. Life insurers defend their role as the rightful administrators of such a contract because of its promise of a lifetime income. The size of that income, in terms of numbers of units paid out, is predicated on an accepted mortality table, such as is used by the life insurance industry.

Private plans such as CREF and other variable annuity contracts under consideration by some banks, mutual funds and other organizations would provide lifetime payments, but could not guarantee them, though the odds against their being able to do so are small. The guarantee is not there, because the risk of a mortality-table error is proportionately shared by all the participants in the plan. The safety valve is in the constant check on the rate of payments and the level of the fund. The few life insurers that sell variables to individuals have bowed to the S.E.C., subjecting themselves to dual regulation. One is the Variable Annuity Life Insurance Company of Washington, which opened the floodgate of litigation when it set up shop in 1955, but is now licensed to sell the controversial contract in some 20 states. CREF is unencumbered by S.E.C. regulation because of its sponsor organization's classification as a nonprofit, tax-exempt educational group whose contracts are not sold to the general public.

But the Federal commission has eased its restrictions on other group plans as well. It reportedly has done so in the belief that a group plan would provide sufficient protection to the public, in that the decision to buy presumably would be in the hands of experts. Such groups might be employe groups of 25 or more members or business and professional bodies whose members seek tax-sheltered benefits allowed under the Self-Employed Individuals Retirement Act of 1962. While such plans are not subject to the 1940 act, they do come under the less stringent Security Act of 1933, which requires registration of contracts with the S.E.C. before their sale and the presentation of a fully informative prospectus to potential buyers. Allowed that latitude, insurers have been pushing sales to employe groups and qualified associations. Individual employers, too, have variable annuity proposals under study. One is New York City, whose municipal employes' pension funds have total assets in excess of $4-billion. A recently completed study of the feasibility of diverting part of that huge fund to a variable annuity plan provides strong ammunition for advocates of such plans. As the rate of use accelerates, more and more management, association and labor-union leaders may be inspired to consider variables.

Further, some of the trusteed plans, which dominate the pension scene, may be encouraged to take that additional step toward variable pay-out, especially those that already have an escalator clause increasing benefit payments as the cost of living rises. Many of the trusteed funds already are heavily invested in common stocks, but the pension pay-out usually is at a fixed benefit rate. It either is paid directly out of the fund or with a conventional annuity bought by the fund at the participant's retirement.

Perhaps sooner than expected, the variable annuity will be presenting another dimension for the employe to measure when evaluating his company's retirement program.

Pension Plans: Company plans, Self-Employed Individual Retirement Act of 1962

It is great when the boss provides—or contributes to—a pension plan, whether it is inspired by social conscience, the persuasive powers of labor leaders or the need to offer employment incentives. But what does a particular pension plan mean to the individual employe? Will its benefits, in combination with Social Security income, be sufficient to provide for his retirement years, or must he seek some means of supplementing it? Or will he be forced to continue working? Further, is its promise of "security" strong enough to bind him to his job? If he contemplates a change, is a prospective employer's plan better or worse? Or is the income increase large enough for him to decide that, with discipline, he could provide his own retirement security?

But the questions don't stop there if an employe is to evaluate his pension plan properly, and such evaluation is essential to sound personal retirement planning. Among other things, he also must know whether the plan includes preretirement disability and death benefits, whether he gets anything if he quits before retirement and whether there would be benefits for his widow if he dies in retirement.

For answers to his questions, a man should go to his employer, or to his union, if that organization administers the plan. A detailed booklet usually is available. He then may compare his plan with others described in library references and in news stories, particularly accounts of labor-contract settlements. To measure the plan's role in his financial program, a man must estimate total benefits and retirement income available from other sources, such as savings, investments, insurance and Social Security.

As a guide, an adequate "average" retirement income, in the view of most experts, should be at least 50 to 60 per cent of a person's final working salary. However, a larger proportion may be required by a person in a low-income bracket, while a man earning a large salary may get by with a smaller percentage of final earnings.

A pension plan may cover all or certain categories of employes in one company, or it may cover members of a certain group, such as a labor union, in which case it may be the product of negotiations with several companies. The advantage of the multiple-employer pension plan is that the individual may move from company to company within an industry without disrupting his pension.

The cost of a pension plan—actuarially calculated to provide promised benefits—might be absorbed by the employer or shared with the worker. Sometimes a company provides a basic plan and offers a voluntary supplemental one, to which the employe would contribute. Payments by the company usually are a percentage of payroll or, for hourly workers under industrywide plans, a certain amount for each hour worked by a covered employe. Payments by an employe usually are a percentage of salary, often limited to that amount above Social Security taxable income, now $6,600 a year.

Under most plans, payments go to a bank or trust company, which invests them primarily in common stocks and corporate bonds, and benefits are paid directly from that trust fund. Other plans are handled by life insurance companies, which provide retired employes with lifetime-income annuities. Still other plans are part-trusteed, part-insured. Several states, including New York, have authorized insurers to offer employers equity funding of pensions, under which pay-in funds may be invested primarily in common stocks. Favorable investment results would reduce the employer's cost and, conversely, unfavorable results would increase it, but benefits would remain unchanged, being provided by annuities bought at each employe's retirement.

Generally, the earlier a person joins a plan the better, in terms of retirement income and other benefits. But many employers impose restrictions. The minimum-age requirement may range from 25 to 35, and the minimum length of service may be set at one year or as long as five. Older employes may be excluded. The method of calculating pensions is included in most plan descriptions and usually is based on length of service or a combination of salary and service.

The service-only formula is extensively applied in industrywide plans and generally provides the same payment to each worker, whatever his salary was. The combination formula may be a percentage of average annual salary in all the plan-participation years, or in the last several, perhaps five or 10. Percentages vary, but it is the final dollar figure that counts. Advocates of percentage formulas note that they provide proportionately greater benefits as salaries rise. The same advantage is cited for employers' fund payments of a percentage of payroll, rather than a fixed amount, for the greater the pay-in the greater the pay-out.

While the average retirement age remains at 65, there is a trend toward earlier retirement. To encourage it in this age of automation and labor abundance, some industries and individual companies are offering full pensions to persons wishing to retire as early as 55 or 60, provided they have met minimum service requirements. More typically, however, a person's pension is sharply reduced by early retirement. Provisions vary widely for persons working beyond normal retirement, ranging from full pension along with salary (in a labor-scarce field) to reduction in pension credit (a penalty for not stepping aside).

A pensioner's income continues until his death, after which his family normally gets nothing save perhaps the amount he may have contributed and not yet received in benefits. However, some plans offer liberalizing options, although they reduce the pension's size. For example, there may be a guarantee that, if the pensioner dies within a certain period, perhaps 10 years, payments would go to a beneficiary for the remainder of that period. Or, the pensioner may elect a "joint and survivor plan," under which his widow would continue to receive the same or a reduced pension at his death.

Employes in a "vested" plan would receive, upon leaving after a certain minimum number of years in the plan, all or part of the employer's contribution in cash or in future retirement benefits. In addition, his payments, if any, would be refunded, with interest. If disability and death benefits are provided, they usually are less than retirement benefits and apply to employes in the plan for a certain period and above a certain age. Disability payments go to a "totally and permanently disabled" man, but definitions of that phrase range from inability to perform his usual work to inability to perform any work. The payments may be further reduced by disability payments received under workmen's compensation or Social Security.

At best, a pension plan is complex, but the time it takes to evaluate it properly is well spent. If it falls far short of the mark, a man may still have time to supplement it, seek improvements or look for another job.

Tax-sheltered retirement plans are allowed under the *Self-Employed Individuals Retirement Act of 1962,* also known as the Keogh-

Smathers Act. Its objective is to give the self-employed the tax advantages enjoyed by corporate employes covered by employer-financed plans. The nation's 9.2 million self-employed include such persons as physicians, lawyers and owners of unincorporated businesses.

In essence, the law permits them to contribute up to 10 per cent each year of income earned from actual work, or $2,500, whichever is less, to their own pension plans or retirement funds. They now may deduct half that amount from taxable income, and, beginning in 1968, all of it. To qualify, they must provide parallel pension arrangements for employes with three or more years of service. Retirement benefits, which a self-employed person must begin drawing from his accumulated fund sometime between the ages of 59½ and 70½, will be taxable to the extent that they are attributable to deductible contributions. The tax rate generally will be lower than that paid by the contributor in his more productive earning years.

If a person terminates his program before he reaches age 59½, however, he has several choices. He may "freeze" the assets already accumulated, utilizing them at retirement, or he may immediately take them, paying an income tax penalty on the previously untaxed portion. The amount would be added to his income for the year in which he received it. He would then pay a higher-bracket tax on it, as income that year, and an additional surcharge of 10 per cent of that tax amount. The penalty is especially harsh to discourage use of the program for tax evasion. The penalty does not apply if a plan is terminated because of death or total disability.

Under the Keogh Act, there are four primary investment vehicles that may be used to finance retirement programs: (1) Annuity contracts of life insurance companies; (2) mutual fund shares, bought through a bank and held in its custody; (3) a special new series of Treasury savings bonds; and (4) trust accounts with banks. The law's complexity makes it essential that a person planning to set up a self-employed retirement program consult an expert, such as a lawyer, accountant, insurance man or a banker.

7

TAKING THE ECONOMIC PAIN OUT OF ILLNESS

A discussion of the problems confronting individuals and families seeking protection against the economic pressures of illness and disability essentially divides into two parts, though there is some overlapping. First, there is the vast number of young and middle-aged persons concerned with maintaining financial insulation against the ills and mishaps that may befall them or their families. Most of these people can build their protective programs around a nucleus of coverage provided by their employers. Then there are the nearly 20 million Americans who are 65 or older, and are, therefore, eligible for the benefits of the Social Security Act's Medicare program. The program, approved by Congress in 1965 and put into operation on July 1, 1966, is rather liberal, but it is far from comprehensive. Thus, it is up to the individual to determine what supplemental coverage he will need.

Basic Coverage: Hospitalization, surgical, general medical, major medical, income protection, comprehensive policies

One of the most essential but baffling tasks of the modern family is selection of the "right" health insurance plan. It is essential because it is the only sensible means the average person has of eliminating, or at least reducing, one of his greatest economic hazards: the high cost of illness. It is baffling because thousands of health policies and plans, most of them legalistic in appearance and content, are aggressively being offered by hundreds of companies. How many policyholders and participants know exactly what protection they own? How many prospective buyers know what they are about to buy?

Most people rely for information on their insurance agent, or on what they read in a company's advertisements and promotional literature. Such trust sometimes is misplaced, for misleading promotional claims can lure people into buying inadequate policies that prove to be exorbitantly costly when accident or illness strikes. For example, promoters of a policy with surgical benefits of "up to $500" may suggest, at least by implication, that their contract is more comprehensive than a higher priced policy providing surgical benefits of up to only $300. But the $500 maximum may be for some rare operation, while payments on more common surgery, such as an appendectomy, may be considerably below those of the $300-maximum policy. Thus, the seemingly more comprehensive $500-maximum policy is cheaper, because its protection is actually less than that of the $300-maximum policy.

Reputable insurance men and companies deplore deceptive advertising and sales practices, and so do alert consumers. The individual buyer can insulate himself against such practices by applying the basic rules of the wise consumer. In this case he would acquire some knowledge of health insurance, read the contract before making his decision, unhesitatingly ask questions about cloudy areas, compare competitive products and forever bear in mind that "you get what you pay for."

Most money management experts believe that the majority of people have inadequate health insurance or the wrong kind, and statistics seem to bear that out. According to the Health Insurance Institute, 77 per cent of the nation's civilian population "had some form of health insurance protection through voluntary insuring organizations in 1963." But the key phrase is "some form," because insurance paid 30.8 per cent of the public's medical-care bill that year, according to The Social Security Bulletin of December, 1964.

Health insurance is available on an individual basis or through a group. In general it is wise to take advantage of group coverage that may be available through an employer, labor union, fraternal group or other organization. That is true even if the company does not pay for all or part of it, because it is cheaper than the coverage bought individually, reflecting the "quantity discount" that results from the insurance company's reduced sales and administrative costs. A group participant should study benefits provided, so that he may decide what, if any, supplemental health insurance coverage he will need. Another major advantage of group coverage is that a person who may not be qualified to buy an individual policy usually is automatically eligible for coverage afforded to other members of his group. If he leaves the group plan, he usually can convert to an individual policy, at higher cost.

In essence, health insurance is protection against hospital and medical expense or against loss of income resulting from sickness or accident. It may provide cash or "service" benefits, or a combination of both. Hospital or medical costs in a cash-benefit, or indemnity, policy, are paid according to the provisions of the contract. Payment may be made to the insured person or to the physician or hospital. Under a service-benefit plan, the insured person is provided with medical and hospital services stipulated in the contract, and payment for those services is made directly to the physician or hospital. The major types of protection, several of which are sometimes combined in one policy, are as follows:

1. *Hospitalization:* Depending on the policy, benefits may meet all or part of hospital charges. There is a maximum limit on the number of days of hospitalization. Cash or indemnity policies may set a daily cash limit for room and board and a maximum sum for other services, such as laboratory, medicines, operating room, anaesthesia and X-ray. Service-benefit contracts generally set limits on benefits, not their cost.

2. *Surgical:* Payments are made according to a schedule in the contract. Fees also may be allowed for visits to the surgeon's office before and after an operation.

3. *General Medical:* Certain nonsurgical costs are covered, such as physician's visits to home or hospital, or the insured's visits to his office. Such benefits vary widely from policy to policy.

4. *Major Medical, or catastrophe:* This eases the economic burden of a protracted illness or serious accident. Most contracts carry a "deductible clause," which can range from $50 to $1,000 and a "co-insurance clause," which stipulates that the company will pay a percentage of the costs above the initial deductible amount. The maximum total benefit may range from $4,000 to $20,000. Thus, the owner of a policy with a $100 deductible clause and a 75 per cent co-

insurance provision would pay the first $100 of a claim and 25 per cent of the bills above that to a maximum total of perhaps $5,000. Bills in excess of that amount would be uninsured.

5. *Income protection:* Such a loss-of-income, accident-and-sickness indemnity, or disability policy provides stipulated cash benefits, usually weekly or monthly, during the period the insured is not working because of illness or accident. There usually is a waiting period before payments begin, and a ceiling on total payments.

A family may find it practical to supplement its basic hospitalization, medical and surgical plan with a major-medical policy. In effect, the basic coverage pays the insured person's deductible and co-insurance amounts due under the major-medical policy. There are *comprehensive policies* that accomplish this by combining basic coverage and major medical. These may be less costly than separate policies would be, for the major-medical section covers a portion of only those expenses above those that are covered by the basic hospitalization-medical part of the contract. Thus, after the basic benefits have been exhausted in a given claim, the insured person's initial out-of-pocket expense would be his major-medical deductible. It may be, perhaps, $150 per claim or $150 per family member in a calendar year. Thereafter, the co-insurance clause would apply, the policy paying perhaps 75 or 80 per cent of additional costs, up to a maximum total.

Differences Among Plans: Noncancellable guaranteed renewable versus guaranteed renewable policies

Health insurance is available to individuals and groups from insurance companies and service plans, the most notable of which are the Blue Cross (hospitalization) and Blue Shield (surgical and medical) plans. There also are service plans of various types sponsored by employers, labor unions, groups of physicians or private citizens, or community organizations. One type of service plan that is worthy of consideration is the so-called "panel" or prepaid group-practice plan. Such a plan, available primarily in large metropolitan areas, encourages preventive care, and therefore covers diagnosis and observation. A major limitation, in the eyes of many people, is that a participant does not have free choice of doctors. He must choose from a panel or group of physicians and specialists.

The price of health insurance plans varies widely, depending on the benefits offered, as well as on the age, sex and occupation of the applicant. As a general rule, the cheaper the policy, the more limited the contract, and the more exceptions, conditions and reductions it contains. To make his wisest choice, the prospective buyer must comparison shop, talking to representatives of several insurance companies and service organizations.

A policy's type of renewability is a price factor. The most costly is the *noncancellable guaranteed renewable policy*—referred to as "non-can"—which the insured person may continue in force by timely payment of premiums set forth in the contract until at least age 50, or for at least five years if issued after age 44. While the policy is in force, the company has no right to change any of its provisions.

The second type, *guaranteed renewable,* differs to the extent that the insurer may seek rate changes by class, that is, for all outstanding policies of the same type. This is less expensive than the "non-can" policy, but more costly than the optionally renewable contract. That policy is offered on a short-term basis and is renewable at the option of the company, up to specified age limits or for the insured person's lifetime. Though more costly, the "non-can" policy is worth considering, particularly if it may be carried until age 65, when Federal Medicare takes over. With such a contract, a person will not find late in life that he no longer has insurance and cannot buy any.

The consumer should consider buying only from a reputable representative of a recognized company, one that is licensed to operate in his state. Litigation can be costly, if not prohibitive, against an out-of-state company, such as those that promote sales by mail. A person could expect little help from his state's insurance department, which has no control over such companies.

He must fully comprehend the coverage afforded by the policy or plan he owns or contemplates buying, and relate that coverage to medical costs in his area and to his particular needs. Some governing factors are the hazardousness of his work and his family's size and general health. Answers should be sought for all questions raised by a reading of the policy. What are the definitions of "confining" and "nonconfining" illnesses, and what are the payments in each case? What does the company mean by the term "total and permanent disability?" Some companies will pay only when the insured person cannot perform his regular work, others will pay only when he can do no work of any kind. There are still other questions: How much time must elapse before a new policy will honor claims for certain illnesses or surgery? What physical conditions or illnesses does the contract exclude? What are the provisions of the cancellation and renewability clauses? Can rates be increased? Are existing health problems excluded?

As a rule, health insurance does not pay all medical-care bills. Some items are not always included, and others are not insurable. A family must take this into account, when deciding on the size of the "emergency fund" in its financial program.

Long-term Illnesses and Disabilities

A young family—parents and three children—were getting by with little economic strain, though the father had been ill and unable to work for a number of weeks. They were, that is, until the day the money stopped. Then, to meet basic living expenses and to make insurance, automobile and other periodic payments on time, they had to dip into savings and other assets earmarked for a down payment on a home, for college for the children. Before long, cracks began to appear in the foundation of the family's entire financial program.

It did not seem possible to the wife that this was happening to her family. They had made provision for most emergency situations, she thought. Through her husband's place of employment, they carried group hospitalization and surgical insurance, along with major-medical coverage to pay a large proportion of the bills above those covered by basic health insurance in the event of catastrophic illness or injury. Their life insurance was adequate. And the husband had accumulated 12 weeks of full-pay sick leave. It had seemed such a long shot that illness would put her family into such dire straits.

But was it really such a long shot? According to 1963 figures of the *National Underwriter,* an insurance publication, the chance of disabling illness lasting more than three months is about three times greater than the chance of premature death among men in the 30-to-50 age group. One man in every three of those disabled, it was found, will be disabled for three months or longer before age 65, and the average disability period for these men will exceed five years.

True, there are certain additional benefits available to the disabled worker. If it is an employment-related disability, he will receive workmen's compensation benefits. Otherwise, he may receive disability income under a state insurance program, such as that in New York which provides up to $55 a week. If the disability is total and is expected to continue for at least 12 months, he and his dependents may be eligible for Social Security's disability benefits (see Chapter 6).

None of these is generally sufficient to sustain a family, but collectively they provide a base on which to build a protective program against loss of income. Recognition of these needs has increased the importance of individual and group disability-income insurance, especially in this age in which many families have committed themselves so extensively to pay-as-you-go credit buying.

A 1965 survey by the National Industrial Conference Board of more than 1,000 manufacturing, banking, insurance, trade and utility companies showed that the possible loss of earning capacity through long-term or lifetime disability—"one of the last chinks in the wall of employe 'social security' "—is being closed. More than 25 per cent of the companies surveyed provide such coverage. Of 103 company plans studied in detail, most were less than two years old, almost all covered salaried employes and three-quarters of them asked employes to share the cost. The emerging coverage pattern was of disability income of 50 to 60 per cent of pay up to $1,000 a month until age 65.

A person interested in obtaining disability (or loss-of-income) insurance should survey his needs. That would include learning from his employer what his current benefits are. Then he could determine his minimum supplemental disability income need, and how long after the start of a disability it should begin. The longer this initial elimination period—7, 14, 30 or 90 days—the lower the premium. An aid in selecting a policy is a pamphlet, "Guide to Your Disability Income Insurance," published by the Health Insurance Institute, 27 Park Avenue, New York, N.Y. 10017.

The first step in evaluating a policy is to determine the conditions of disability under which an insurer will pay benefits. Total disability is commonly required, but the definitions vary. For example: Inability to perform any duty of his (the insured's) occupation, business or employment; inability to engage in any gainful occupation for which he is fitted by education, training or experience; or inability to engage in any occupation or employment for wage or profit.

The institute points out that some policies, especially those with lifetime benefits for sickness, also contain a clause that requires the insured to be confined indoors to qualify for benefits.

Disability payments commonly range from a year to a lifetime for accident and a year to age 65 for sickness, but may vary in duration between accident and sickness within a contract. The amount may be as much as $800 a month for long-term duration, such as five years or more, and up to $1,500 a month for short terms, such as two years or less. While these amounts may in some instances be higher, they normally are limited to 40 to 60 per cent of the insured's gross earnings. While most policies cover both occupational and nonoccupational disability, some cover only claims that are unrelated to employment. Some policies waive premium payments, usually after a specified disability period, such as 90 days. Buyers must be cautioned that some policies do not contain this feature.

Disability income insurance, like life insurance, has been called "essential primary coverage," but a man can only do his best within the limits of his income. Doing with less or none of this protection might be wiser than being "insurance poor." Each man must make his decision, not allowing concern with tomorrow's possible dangers to negate completely today's pleasures.

Insurance for Housewives

A housewife who reads the Personal Finance column in *The New York Times* called to ask about the availability of disability income insurance for persons like herself. "A housewife's work must be done," she stressed, "whether she is there or not. This may mean hiring someone, or having her husband stay home at a sacrifice in his pay, or intruding on friends and relatives. Any of these can be costly and inconvenient."

A number of insurers agree to the need, and some offer limited plans and claim to be studying the matter further. One industry source said that housewife coverage is not popular in the business because of difficulty in administering it. The general industry objection is that, if a housewife does not have income from a job or business, she does not have an insurable interest. However, the relatively few policies available to housewives generally offer a maximum of only $100 monthly for a year. A woman who has a noncancellable policy while working may continue it as a housewife, but at a reduced benefit. The benefit usually is limited to $200 or $300 for working women. A substitute often offered is a hospital indemnity policy, which may pay from $25 to $200 a week while the housewife is hospitalized.

For Persons 65 or Older—Medicare: The Hospital Insurance Plan, The Medical Insurance Plan; Supplementing Their Benefits

The Federal Medicare program, provided under the Social Security Act, actually offers two related health insurance plans for persons who are 65 or older. The first, the Hospital Insurance Plan, pays much of the cost of hospital and related care. The second, the voluntary Medical Insurance Plan, helps pay for physicians' and surgeons' services and other medical and health services not covered by the hospital plan.

Basically, the *Hospital Insurance Plan* provides benefits in four areas:

- Services while hospitalized;
- Extended-care services, such as are provided in a nursing home, after having been in a hospital;
- Health services at home, after having been in a hospital;
- Outpatient hospital diagnostic services.

With one exception, all benefits under the hospital plan, as well as under the medical plan, became available July 1, 1966. The exception is nursing-home benefits, which became available January 1, 1967.

Benefits during hospitalization would help pay the cost of services provided by participating hospitals for up to 90 days in any one "spell of illness." A spell of illness is defined as a period beginning with the first day a person receives hospital or extended-care services. It would end when the person has been out of the hospital or nursing home for 60 days. Thus, if a person returned to a hospital within 60 days of his discharge from a hospital or home, he would be deemed to be in the same "spell of illness." The 90-day-benefit restriction would apply. In the first 60 days of hospitalization, a person would pay for the initial $40 in costs. With few exceptions, the plan would pay for all services normally provided by the hospital to its bed patients. From the 61st day through the 90th, the person would pay $10 a day toward these costs.

Payments will be made for psychiatric services in general and psychiatric hospitals. However, there is a lifetime limit of 190 days in benefits for inpatient psychiatric hospital care. The intent of the law, it has been said, is to cover only active care intended to cure or improve the patient's condition, not to cover custodial care. If he is in a psychiatric or tuberculosis hospital when he becomes entitled to benefits, the days he already has been hospitalized would count toward the 90-day limit on such benefits during a spell of illness.

As to "post-hospital extended care" in a nursing home or comparable institution, the hospital plan will pay for up to 100 days of care during each spell of illness. However, the patient must pay the first $5 in costs for each day in excess of 20.

In the area of home health services after hospitalization, the plan will pay for up to 100 home visits by nurses, therapists or other home health aides. Payment for such services will be available for a year after discharge from a hospital (after at least a three-day stay) or nursing home, and before the beginning of a new spell of illness. To receive the benefits of home health service, a person must be in the care of a physician and under a plan calling for such services. The plan must have been established within 14 days of discharge from the hospital or home.

In the fourth benefit area—outpatient hospital diagnostic services—the plan will pay 80 per cent of the cost above $20 for each diagnostic study. The complete study must be furnished by the same hospital within a 20-day period. The plan excludes services not provided in a hospital, or not supervised by a hospital or its medical staff.

The plan contains another deductible factor. It will pay the cost of the administration of blood, but not the cost of the first three pints. This, it was said, is to encourage the replacement of blood by donors, giving recognition to the problem of replacing large quantities.

To be eligible for hospital insurance benefits, a person must have attained the age of 65. He is automatically covered by this basic protection if he is collecting monthly Social Security benefits. However, if he is not collecting benefits only because he is working and earning too much to collect, he and his wife, if she is 65, still are protected under the basic hospital insurance plan but they must enroll at a Social Security Administration office. In addition, a person who will turn 65 by 1968 will be eligible for the hospital insurance, even though he never had been covered by the Social Security program.

The voluntary *Medical Insurance Plan* supplements the basic hospital plan. It provides benefits in the following major areas:

- Physicians' services;
- Certain psychiatric care;
- Other medical and health services;
- Home health services.

Enrollment at a Social Security Administration office during prescribed enrollment periods is open to United States residents 65 or older, who are citizens or lawfully admitted aliens living in this country for at least five years.

While the hospital plan will be supported primarily by a stipulated portion of the Social Security taxes paid by workers, employers and self-employed persons (see Chapter 6), the medical plan will be financed equally by participants and the Federal Government. Thus, each person enrolling in the supplementary medical plan will pay $3 a month, which the Government will match with contributions from general revenues. Every two years, beginning in 1967, the rates will be reviewed and increased, if necessary. Premium payments will be deducted from monthly checks of persons receiving Social Security, railroad retirement or Federal civil service retirement payments. Other insured persons pay their monthly premiums directly.

Benefit provisions of the medical plan are comparable to those of a major-medical policy in that the insured person pays the first $50 of covered costs in a calendar year and 20 per cent of the amount above that deductible sum. Payments for psychiatric care are limited to $250 or one-half the charges, whichever is less, in a year. For physicians' services, the medical plan will help pay the cost of surgery (including certain dental surgery), consultation, home, office and institutional calls. It excludes services covered by the basic hospital plan, immunizations and routine physical, eye or hearing examinations. Other exclusions are cosmetic surgery, unless for repair of accident injury, and routine dental care. Within the limitation already mentioned, the plan's psychiatric-care benefits include outpatient care for mental, psychoneurotic and personality disorders.

As to medical and other expenses, the medical plan's benefit schedule includes the following: diagnostic tests; X-ray, radium and radioactive-isotope therapy; surgical dressings, splints and casts; rental of durable medical equipment; ambulance service when necessary because normal transportation would endanger the patient's health, but only to the extent provided in the plan's provisions; prosthetic devices (other than dental) to replace internal organs; braces and artificial limbs and eyes.

While some of these services also are provided under the basic hospital plan, they are not payable under that plan unless the insured person is a bed patient. If that is the case, the hospital plan covers the services, the medical plan will exclude them.

The home health services section of the medical plan provides for up to 100 visits by nurses, therapists or other home health aides, as does the same section in the basic hospital plan. However, previous hospitalization is not required, as it is in the hospital plan. It is notable that the supplemental medical plan can be used to extend the duration of the home health services provided under the hospital plan. An eligible person may enroll in the optional medical plan any time within three months before or after his 65th birthday. If he fails to enroll during that initial enrollment period, he may do so during a general enrollment period, which will run from October 1 to December 31 in each odd-numbered year, starting in 1967. However, his monthly premium will be increased by 10 per cent for each full 12 months between the end of his initial enrollment period and the end of the general enrollment period in which he signs up. A person must enroll within three years after the first period in which he could have enrolled, or forfeit his opportunity to be covered. If a person enrolls in the plan and later drops out, he may re-enroll in a general enrollment period beginning no later than three years from the date his previous enrollment was terminated. He is allowed only one re-enrollment.

The surcharge and time limits on late enrollment and the restrictions on re-enrollment were designed to prevent persons from participating in, and supporting, the medical plan only when they have need for it. That practice would generate an abnormally large volume of claims in excess of premium income.

Aside from the specific exclusions of items or services under the various provisions of the Social Security Act, there are some general exclusions that apply to both the basic hospital plan and the supplemental medical plan. In general, payment will not be made for services and items that are: furnished outside the United States; covered under workmen's compensation; not subject to payment by the insured individual; unreasonable or unnecessary; required as a result of war; for custodial care; for personal-comfort items.

The scope of the Medicare program is so broad, that our discussion could not cover all its aspects and ramifications. However, complete details, as they pertain to an individual's particular situation, may be obtained from any Social Security Administration office. This may be done well in advance of eligibility, or during a person's initial enrollment period, whether or not he decides to retire and apply for Social Security's cash retirement benefits.

Supplementing Medicare: As comprehensive as Medicare's combination of hospital and medical insurance plans is, it will not provide total protection. On average, it will finance "some 40 per cent" of an aged person's medical costs, according to Wilbur J. Cohen, Under Secretary of Health, Education and Welfare.

In review, among the items not covered by either plan are routine physical checkups and dental care, drugs for use outside an institution, eyeglasses, hearing aids, private-duty nurses and protracted nursing-home stays. In addition, both plans call for payment by the insured person of an initial amount (the deductible) or of a percentage of certain costs, or both. Many of these gaps can be filled with supplemental plans being offered by insurance companies and health service organizations. It is likely that an employed person who becomes eligible for Medicare will find that his employe-group-insurance benefits have been reduced to serve as Medicare supplements. The reduction usually would apply only to him or his wife, if she also is 65, but not to other dependents entitled to full benefits under his group plan. The supplemental coverage usually can be carried into retirement, and some employers have agreed to continue paying for it.

Other older persons who do not have any form of supplemental coverage would be wise to buy it on their own. Their children might consider buying it for them, especially if they contribute to the parents' support, or would be responsible for large medical bills. The extra protection that is bought may take the form of a family benefit payment while the insured person is hospitalized or may be directly related to medical expenses not covered by Medicare. The plans being offered vary widely and several should be compared for price and coverage before a decision is made.

Workmen's Compensation

All states have workmen's compensation laws, which require that most employers provide benefits to workers who sustain occupational injuries or illnesses. But the laws vary widely, ranging from comprehensive ones, such as New York's, to some that are sorely inadequate. The appropriate state agency, perhaps its labor department, could give a person the details of his state's workmen's compensation law. An employer also may provide that information, as well as tell what additional protection he provides for the employe. In New York, workmen's compensation pays for all necessary medical care. It also provides the disabled worker with weekly cash benefits equal to half his average earnings, but not less than $20 or more than $60. There is no cash benefit in the first week unless the disability exceeds two weeks.

Off-the-Job Disability

Many companies provide benefits, such as "sick pay" and health insurance, for employes who suffer illnesses or disabilities that are not related to work. However, only four states, California, New Jersey, New York and Rhode Island, require that most employes be provided with benefits for off-the-job disabilities. Under New York's law, only a cash benefit need be paid for off-the-job disability. After the first week of absence, up to $55 is paid weekly for as many as 26 weeks. Employers may have their workers help pay the cost at the rate of half of 1 per cent of income, but no more than 30 cents a week.

Dental Insurance

"Well, I guess dad never will get the periodontal work he needs."

This was the observation of a dental hygienist, as her boss told a young father that two of his children required orthodontic treatment.

A couple of months earlier, the father had been advised by the dentist that he should see a periodontist for preventive gum and root work, lest he eventually lose good teeth because of the deterioration of their foundations. Straightening children's teeth generally is expensive, as is periodontal work. Deciding that he could not afford both, the conscientious father proved the hygienist right. He tended to his children's needs and "postponed" his own.

A backdrop to this story is the United States Public Health Service's recent finding that, in any given year, six of every 10 persons in the nation do not receive dental care. Of the rest, only a small proportion receives adequate attention within a year. And most of those probably are children. Indications are that the situation may change in time, thanks to dental insurance, a relatively new form of coverage that promises to improve the nation's dental health—and, therefore, total health—by reducing the economic pain of treatment.

In a sense, dental insurance is more a prepayment plan than insurance. For, while fire or automobile insurance provides protection against a hazard that may not occur, dental insurance is protection against the high cost of care that almost everyone may need. Thus the premiums may more closely approximate the "average" cost of dental care, giving some assurance to the insured person and his family that their dental costs will be reasonably stable. This is underscored by the fact that, upon entering a dental insurance plan, most persons, or their dependents, already need care, or will within the year.

The bulk of dental insurance is available only on a group basis, primarily through employers and unions, but also through fraternal, social, community and other organizations. The organizations may pay all or part of the premium for the protection, which usually extends to the participant's family. Insurance companies, dental societies, labor, consumer and nonprofit insurance corporations largely comprise the formal insuring organizations providing the group protection. A few companies sell policies to individuals, but, as far as could be determined, none is sold, for example, in New York State.

While coverage provisions vary from contract to contract, many policies include a deductible provision, under which the insured person pays the first part, perhaps $25 or $50, of the dental-care bill for the year. Beyond that, the insurer pays a part of the cost, usually 75 or 80 per cent. However, even within a particular policy, these payment provisions may vary with the type of treatment or service. For example, some contracts provide for payment of only half the cost of dentures while allowing larger percentage payments, up to 100 per cent, for other services. Still other contracts reimburse the insured, according to a schedule, for each service rendered. For example, he may receive $4 to $7 for an extraction, $24 to $40 for bridgework and so on. Then there are plans that provide stipulated services, rendered at specified centers or by participating dentists, and there is no exchange of claim money between the insured and the insurer.

According to a Public Health Service estimate, more than 1.8 million people had group dental protection under 460 plans in 1965. The plans were in operation in 30 states, including New York, and in the District of Columbia and Puerto Rico. About 600,000 of the people carrying dental-care protection subscribe to group-practice plans or clinics, which represent the earliest form of dental insurance. Subscribers to these plans must go to the clinics or to the offices of participating dentists for their dental care. The role of the insurance industry, however, soon may eclipse that of the clinics. About 40 insurance companies offer dental protection on a group basis, and the industry hopes its actuarial studies will allow it to broaden sales to individual consumers. Dental service corporations, that is, nonprofit organizations chartered in the states in which they operate, sell dental insurance in about the same way that Blue Shield sells medical insurance. As physicians control Blue Shield operations, dentists control the dental service corporations. A major difference between the insurance companies' plans and those of service corporations is that insurers pay policyholders who pay the dentists, while service corporations generally pay the dentists directly. Among the states in which service corporations are operating are California, Colorado, Connecticut, Michigan, New York, Ohio, Oregon and Washington.

While it may be some years before individual policies become available, it is expected that group coverage will continue to grow in popularity as labor unions continue to stress improvement in "fringe benefits" in their contract negotiations with managements. Enlightened consumers might accelerate the trend by urging that their unions, professional associations or other organizations weigh the many advantages of dental insurance.

8

PROTECTING AGAINST PROPERTY LOSS AND LAW SUITS

Most people cannot assume the economic risk of loss of their personal property to fire, theft or other potential perils. Neither could they easily pay a large cash settlement or court judgment arising from injuries or damages they accidentally cause other people or their property. Their means of protection against these economic hazards, of course, is insurance. Many persons each pay a relatively small sum regularly to an insurance company, which then has sufficient funds to pay the financial losses of the comparatively few unfortunate individuals and families whose property is damaged or who are sued. This sharing of economic losses, or spreading of risk, is the essence of insurance.

The price an insurance company charges for protection is based on the amount it expects to pay in claims, as well as on its operating costs and, if it is stockholder owned, reasonable profits. A mutual company, one that technically is owned by its policyholders, operates on a nonprofit basis, but sometimes, whether because of management problems or other reasons, its rates are not always lower than those of a stockholder-owned company. Therefore, as in most consumer situations, comparison shopping for the most suitable "product" at the best price is essential.

A person may obtain his protection by buying a number of separate policies covering the risks to which he feels he is most vulnerable, or he may buy a "package" policy that combines several types of insurance at reduced over-all cost.

Among the separate policies available are those protecting against fire and related perils, personal liability, burglary and theft. There also are "floater" policies that insure personal property—most frequently, furs and jewelry—against almost all perils wherever the owner takes it.

The most common of "package" policies is the homeowner's policy, which, in its most comprehensive form, could combine all of the protection listed above. There is a comparable package policy for persons who rent their living quarters. There also is a money-saving package policy for the automobile owner who wants the full range of coverage it affords.

We first will discuss the major separate personal insurance policies, and then turn to homeowner's and tenant's policies and automobile insurance, closing with a few suggestions as to how insurance costs might be reduced.

The Most Basic Insurance: Fire

Fire insurance, the most basic of property coverages, grew out of the great London fire of 1666, which wrought $13 million in damages. However staggering that sum may have been in those straitened economic times, however great the impact of such a disaster, the conflagration was like a lone torch in the night, when compared with "the great United States fire of 1965." With a blaze flaring up every 24 seconds, fire claimed $1.4 billion in property that year. It took a human life every 45 minutes.

Though everyone is generally aware of the hazard, many individuals think of it as something that "happens to the other fellow." This rationalization is justified to the extent that it helps to ease the tension of day-to-day living, but having the right kind of insurance protection goes a lot further in that direction. While most people have some form of fire insurance on their home and its contents, many of them are not knowledgeable about what they paid for, what the policy covers, what it doesn't, how to get the most out of it.

Illustrations of this would be revealed by a reading of a fire insurance contract. The basic contract consists of a "standard form" used by insurers in most states and a dwelling-and-contents form, the application of which depends on whether the policy specifies coverage of the home, its contents or both. The basic policy will indemnify for "all direct loss by fire, lightning and by removal from premises endangered by perils insured against," with certain exceptions, such as loss from explosion, war and nuclear perils. Damage from water used to fight a fire is covered, as is the cost of removing debris, but there is no coverage for such property as accounts, bills, currency, deeds, securities. Protection against other perils may be added by endorsement at extra cost.

Much of the surprise of most people centers on the basic, unadorned policy's "coverage extensions," which include the following:

1. Up to 10 per cent of the amount of insurance on a home's contents covers personal property of the insured and his family while it is off the premises. Under an $8,000-contents fire policy, for example, there is up to $800 of protection on property outside the home, whether it be clothing carried on a vacation trip within continental North America, or property left at a cleaning or repair shop.

2. A tenant may apply up to 10 per cent of his contents fire insurance to cover improvements, alterations or additions he provided in his rented residence. Thus, if a tenant has a $5,000 contents fire policy, and the paint job he just paid $400 for was destroyed by perils covered by the basic policy, he would collect the $400, because it was within the 10 per cent limit of $500.

3. A homeowner may apply, as additional insurance, up to 10 per cent of the amount of fire insurance on his house to the rental cost of temporary shelter, if he is forced to vacate his house because of damages inflicted by perils covered in the policy. However, only one-twelfth of that 10 per cent may be received in any one month, and it may not exceed the "rental value" of his house. A man with a $24,000 fire policy on his house, therefore, may apply for a total of $2,400 in temporary shelter cost, but no more than $200 a month, provided the rental value of his house is at least that amount.

4. A homeowner also may apply as additional insurance up to 10 per cent of the fire insurance on his house to cover other noncommercial buildings on his premises, such as a private garage or a gazebo.

Extended Coverage Endorsement: Storm, flood, explosions, riots, vandalism

The *extended coverage endorsement* is the most popular additional to basic fire policies. It protects against exterior windstorm damage and interior damage from rain, snow, dust or hail, provided that they entered the house through an opening caused by the wind. This coverage usually carries a $50-deductible clause, under which the insured pays for the first $50 of a damage claim.

In general, this endorsement also indemnifies for damage from: explosion, except those caused by steam boilers or steam engines; riots; aircraft or objects falling from them; vehicles not owned by the insured; smoke from sudden, unusual and faulty operation of a heating or cooking unit connected to a chimney by a smoke pipe. Fireplaces are excluded.

A fire policy may be broadened further with purchase of other endorsements or additions, their type depending on the particular state's regulations. One available in a number of states, New York not among them, is the "additional extended coverage" endorsement. This protects against water damage from plumbing and heating systems, from the overflow of such domestic appliances as dish and clothes washers and, if the house has been heated and occupied 72 hours before the loss (or the insured used "due diligence" to maintain heat), from freezing of plumbing or an appliance. It also generally protects against damage from the following: Heating-system explosion; vandalism and malicious mischief, provided the house has not been vacant for more than 30 days before the loss; vehicles, including those owned by the insured. The damage-exclusion under basic extended coverage applies; glass breakage, provided the building has not been vacant in the preceding 30 days; ice, snow, sleet, hail and freezing; fall of trees, including intentional felling, topping or trimming; partial or total collapse of the building, except when caused by subsidence. Protection against flood damage generally is unobtainable.

It is not wise to overinsure, because only the actual cash or replacement value of the property will be paid in the event of total loss, regardless of the amount of coverage bought. It is even more unwise to underinsure, because the policy may not be adequate to pay the full cost of major repair or replacement when property loss or damage occurs.

In New York, the only state in which fire policies include the "co-insurance clause," claims for partial damage or loss to the insured property will be paid in full if the amount of insurance protection equals at least 80 per cent of the property's total replacement value. Payment otherwise would be proportionately less. For example, if coverage is only 60 per cent of value (three-quarters of 80 per cent), claims payment could be at the rate of 75 per cent of the loss.

With real estate values and replacement costs on the rise, insurance amounts should be reviewed when policies are up for renewal. It is helpful to have a house or other valuable property appraised periodically by experts. Fire insurance rates vary widely with location and type of house. A policy may be bought for one year or, at a 10 per cent saving, for three years. The prime advantage to the longer term is freedom from rate increases in that period. Equally aware of this rate advantage to policyholders, some insurers do not heavily promote the three-year policy and most long since have stopped selling the five-year contract.

When There Is a Loss: Inventory, "proof of loss"

There is a general procedure that should be followed when a person has suffered a loss of property covered by his policy, be it a fire, burglary and theft, or other contract. He immediately should notify the insurance company, either directly or through his insurance agent or broker, and should safeguard remaining property from further loss. He then should prepare an *inventory* of lost or damaged property, and, within 60 days of the loss, submit a certified *"proof of loss"* form to the company.

Normally, no one need be paid for helping an insured person settle a claim, unless he chooses to engage his own adjuster or other specialist. He should either deal with the company's claims adjuster himself, or have his agent do so. If dissatisfied with the final offer, he may seek arbitration, involving two appraisers (one chosen by him and the other by the company) and an umpire (chosen by the appraisers). The policyholder and the company each pays for its own appraiser, and they divide other costs. The majority decision of the appraisers and umpire is binding on both parties.

Lawsuits and Comprehensive Personal Liability

While entertaining guests recently, a young executive placed a cocktail shaker on a window seat. A gust of wind twirled the curtains around the glass container and sent it plummeting six stories to the street, where it struck and seriously injured a man who sued. The jury award: $7,500.

An avid golfer went out on the links one day last summer, confident that it was his day to break 80. The first four holes went beautifully; he was only one over par. He enthusiastically teed off on No. 5, and the ball flew straight as an arrow over a rise toward the unseen pin. It never got there; it struck a man, fracturing his skull. The man sued. The jury award: $15,000.

The party host had to clean out his savings account, sell the securities in his still meager investment portfolio and take a loan to meet the judgment against him. He will be a long time in making up that loss. But the golfer was luckier—or wiser. The judgment against him was paid by his insurance company, which also provided his defense.

The coverage involved is known as "comprehensive personal liability" insurance, or simply C.P.L., which most people tend to associate with home ownership. Owning a home may increase a person's liability exposure, but not owning one does not eliminate it. Anyone is responsible for injuries or damages caused by his unintentional acts, or those of his children and other members of his household. In essence, the C.P.L. policy protects the insured and his family from much, if not all, of the economic loss that could result from those acts, whether the accidents occur at home or away.

While a basic policy provides $10,000 of liability protection for each occurrence and $250 in medical payments to injured persons, most people are generally advised to buy at least twice those amounts of protection. If the policy buyer is reasonably affluent, he should buy even higher limits, especially in view of the increasing number of large jury awards. The most basic coverage costs about $17 a year in New York, but $25,000 in protection against lawsuits, with $500 in medical payments, would cost only $6 more, or $23 a year, according to the Insurance Information Institute.

A C.P.L. will pay damages up to that maximum limit. It also

provides the insured person's legal defense, whether he is proved legally liable or not. But damages are not paid until it is determined that he is liable—at fault, or to blame. The medical-payments section of the policy will pay an injured party's medical expenses after a minor accident, regardless of who is at fault. It is designed for the small claim, the minor injury. It does not cover medical expenses of the policyholder or members of his household.

An optional section indemnifies for minor damage to the property of others, regardless of who is at fault. For example, if the policyholder's child accidentally throws a ball through a neighbor's window, the policy will pay the repair bill. If the child is under 12, the policy even will pay for damage he causes intentionally.

Instances of protection are countless. The following illustrations suggest the range:

—The homeowner who is sued by the mailman who falls on an icy sidewalk or a broken step, or who is bitten by a dog.

—The parent who is sued because his son seriously injured a playmate while playing Tarzan.

—The hostess who is sued by her guest, because of injuries sustained in a fall down the cellar-stairs, which were behind a door she had thought was a closet.

—The fisherman, particularly the caster, who is sued when his hook snags another outdoorsman.

—The hunter who ends up in court, because he had thought his target was a deer, rather than another hunter.

Boating enthusiasts should find the personal liability policy's protection especially comforting, for it covers the operation of small craft, whether rented or owned. The coverage is limited to inboard motorboats of less than 50 horsepower, outboard motorboats of no more than 24 horsepower and sailboats no more than 26 feet long. Additional coverage can be bought for larger craft. Such coverage is especially important, when one considers the surge in popularity of pleasure boating and its companion, water-skiing. Injuries and property damage can be extensive in an accident on the water, perhaps involving the boatman's passengers, as well as swimmers, water-skiers and persons in other boats. Consider the potential cost of an accident in which a speedboat rams and sinks a $25,000 cruiser, injuring several of its passengers.

Among the major exclusions in the policy are accidents arising out of "business pursuits." This sounds simple enough, until it is studied more closely. For example, an electrician who does some wiring work as a favor to a friend may have a problem in proving it was not a "business pursuit." And he might have to do that, if he was sued by someone injured in an accident attributable to his wiring job.

Among other exclusions are claims of the insured's employes, if state law requires that they be covered by workmen's compensation, which the employer must provide. This raises a sticky question concerning occasional employes. For example, experts say it is possible for an insurance company to question its legal need to defend a policyholder in a suit filed by a baby sitter, if it is established that the sitter had been employed from time to time by the insured. The point is that if a person is employed with some frequency, though not on a regular basis, that person should have workmen's compensation coverage, thereby freeing the company that issued the personal-liability policy. However, protection would extend to a suit filed by a person employed for only the single day in which the accident occurred.

There are other areas of protection that may not occur to the average policy owner. For example, the policy will pay for damages inflicted on a neighbor's property by a fire that started with a spark from the insured person's barbecue grill.

Operation of automobiles and most other vehicles is not covered. The policy, however, will indemnify for damage to a borrowed lawn mower or nonbusiness equipment, if it contains the "minor-damage" option.

There is one other thing owning a C.P.L. policy can do: It can help give a golfer the peace of mind that just might allow him to break 80.

Stop, Thief!: Limited and broad form personal theft insurance

A theft insurance policy would provide financial protection against burglary, robbery and larceny. Coverage of loss by "mysterious disappearance" and of damage caused by thieves to the insured's home and other property also may be desired. A "broad form personal theft policy," rather than a "limited" form, would provide this additional protection. The policy may cover loss "from the premises or a depository" of all personal property but jewelry and furs, or may include those items at additional cost. It also could afford protection, at the policy buyer's option, against loss away from his premises. He should discuss the coverage thoroughly with his insurance man, and should read the contract, for there are many insuring agreements, conditions and exclusions worthy of note. Premium rates vary widely, depending on many factors, not the least of which are the police protection and the crime rate in the insurance applicant's area. It is difficult, if not impossible, to buy a personal theft policy in some city sections that are major crime targets.

"All-Risks" Protection: Personal property

Policies known as "inland marine floaters" protect property, wherever it may be taken, against all risks, with major exclusions, such as wear and tear, pet damage, earthquake, war and riot. In general, there are inland marine lines to cover most transportable belongings. Personal policies are most widely written on furs and jewelry, but they also may be bought to insure cameras, costly sports equipment, stamp and coin collections, musical instruments, works of art and most other belongings and personal effects.

The broadest personal inland marine policy, the personal property floater, protects all of the personal property of the policyholder and members of his household. The completed policy form includes a categorical list of unscheduled items, ranging from silverware and clothing to furniture and lawn tools, with estimates of their values. Then there is a list of scheduled items, such as furs, jewelry, artworks and cameras, each of which is described and given a certified valuation, which may be an appraisal or sales receipt.

The total premium on a personal property floater is made up of the charges for its various component parts, each of which carries a different rate. Thus, the premium is calculated for furs at their particular rate, for jewelry at its rate and so on, after which the sums are totaled to arrive at the policy's full price. As is the case for theft insurance, the rates for personal property coverage vary widely, and for many of the same reasons. For example, the annual rate for each $100 of jewelry insured may range from $1 in Indianapolis to $2.40 in New York City; the annual rate for each $100 of furs insured may range from 30 cents in Indianapolis to $1.05 in New York City, or, if it's mink, to $1.35 in Chicago, where thieves have a special preference for those skins.

The Homeowner's Policy: Standard, broad, and comprehensive forms

By buying a homeowner's policy, a person enjoys the convenience and simplicity of having full protection in one contract, while saving up to 20 per cent or more on his insurance bill. The companies have been able to reduce the cost, in large measure, by eliminating what has been called "antiselection." In other words, certain types of protection would be bought, as part of the "package," by many more people than those who feel they are especially vulnerable to the specific risks covered. Thus, the risk is spread more broadly over more "safe" people, reducing the individual cost.

A homeowner's policy covers the house, or "dwelling," and other noncommercial structures on the policyholder's land, including a garage, tool shed or guest house. In addition, it covers personal property, including household contents and other personal belongings used, owned, worn or carried by the policyholder or his family. The protection applies whether the loss occurs at home or away. This coverage may be broadened, at extra cost, to apply to personal property of guests, while at the insured person's home or temporary residence. Items of unusual worth, such as antiques, furs, jewelry and paintings, should be insured under a separate policy, or added at extra cost to the homeowner's policy, because they may not be covered for their full value under the limits set for personal property not specifically listed in the homeowner's contract.

Another feature of the homeowner's policy is the provision of additional living expense, should the policyholder and his family find it necessary to move from their home because of excessive damage caused by an insured peril. Within policy limits, he would receive the difference between living expenses incurred while his house is being repaired and what they would have been had his property not been damaged. The specific perils insured against would depend on whether the homeowner bought a standard, broad or comprehensive form, each of which being progressively more expensive because it provides more protection. In most states, the forms are designated as 1, 2 and 5, and in a few states, including New York, as A, B and C. Form 3 is a blend of 2 and 5, and form 4 is for tenants.

All of the forms include the same protection limits for comprehensive personal liability coverage: $25,000 for personal liability, $500 for medical payments and $250 for minor physical damage to the property of others. These limits may be increased at the policy buyer's option. However, the differences among the three forms is in the number of perils against which the property is insured. The *standard form,* in general, protects against the standard fire and extended coverage perils, as well as against vandalism and malicious mischief, theft and breakage of glass constituting a part of the building.

The *broad form* protects against those, and the following:

- Falling objects;
- Weight of ice, snow and sleet;
- Collapse of buildings or any of their parts;
- Sudden and accidental tearing asunder, cracking, burning or bulging of a steam or hot water heating system, or of appliances for heating water for consumption;
- Accidental discharge, leakage or overflow of water or steam from a plumbing, heating or air conditioning system;
- Freezing of plumbing, heating and air conditioning systems and domestic appliances;
- Sudden and accidental injury to electrical appliances, devices, fixtures and wiring (television and radio tubes not included).

The amount of insurance bought on the house determines the amount of coverage for subordinate buildings, personal property and additional living expenses. For example, suppose the replacement value of a house is $20,000, and the owner decides to insure it for 80 per cent of that value, or $16,000, so as to receive full replacement cost for all partial losses or damages. On that basis, if he bought a homeowner's standard form, his subordinate structures would be insured for $1,600, or 10 per cent, of the amount on the dwelling; his personal property would be insured for $6,400, or 40 per cent, and he would be allowed additional living expenses of up to $1,600, or 10 per cent. If he had bought the homeowner's broad form, he would have been allowed up to 20 per cent, or $3,200, for additional living expenses.

The homeowner's *comprehensive form* protects against all risks, with major exclusions, such as earthquake, landslide, flood, surface water, waves, tidal water or tidal wave, the backing up of sewers, seepage, war and nuclear radiation. In essence, the comprehensive form lists the perils it does not cover, while the other two forms list the perils they do cover.

DEDUCTIBLES. Homeowners' policies are commonly being written with an automatic $50 deductible that applies to all property losses, including those caused by fire and lightning. However, it is of the "disappearing" type, reducing in size as the total claim increases. Thus, a policyholder might pay the first $50 (the deductible) of a claim of less than $200, the first $33.50 of a $200 claim and nothing on a loss of $500 or more. The insurance companies' objective reportedly was to eliminate, or at least reduce, the volume of administratively costly small claims. The comprehensive homeowner's form generally contains a "disappearing" deductible of $100 on all insured perils but fire and lightning. These deductibles may vary from area to area, depending on each state's laws.

Package Policies for Tenants

For the family that lives in an apartment or rented house, there is the residence contents broad form, or tenant's form, designated as Form No. 4 in most states. It is comparable to the homeowner's broad form, but with the building protection naturally eliminated.

Household Inventory

It would be easier to determine adequacy of insurance and prove future property losses if the policyholder took a household inventory and periodically reviewed it, getting revised appraisals of especially valuable items. Many insurance companies have forms available for this purpose. Inventory photographs may be taken and filed with the written forms in a fireproof box at home or, preferably, outside the home, perhaps in a safe-deposit box, lest they burn with the house.

Automobile Insurance: Liability, medical payments, uninsured motorists, fire and theft

Among the most prevalent of insurance bills paid by Americans are for highly complex policies on the 70 million passenger cars they own. The persistence of these payments, which can be monumental in accident-cluttered metropolitan areas, should be stimulant enough for families and individuals to seek ways of reducing them. They should attempt to remain abreast of changes in rates, policy provisions and underwriting practices. This will provide greater assurance that they are getting the most for their dollar.

There is little dispute among most people about the necessity for auto insurance, but there is a broad range of opinion as to what amount of insurance is adequate. While the level of adequacy will vary with each individual's circumstances, it should be borne in mind that jury awards to accident victims have been substantial, many exceeding $100,000, and that the car itself represents a sizable investment that should be protected. Those thoughts coincide with decision-making in the two primary auto insurance categories: liability insurance, which protects the motorist against law suits, and physical damage insurance, which protects him against damage to his own car.

LIABILITY INSURANCE. The chief policy components that protect the motorist against lawsuits are bodily injury and property damage liability insurance. If there is an accident, and claims or suits are brought against the policyholder, his insurance company provides protection in the form of legal defense. If it is agreed by the parties involved, or judged by a court, that he is legally liable, the company will pay the damages up to the limits of his policy.

Amounts of bodily injury and property damage coverage often are referred to as, for example, 10/20/5. The figures represent thousands of dollars. The first, $10,000, is the most the insurance company will pay for the injury of any one person in an accident. The second, $20,000, is the most it will pay for all of the injuries resulting from one accident. The third figure, $5,000, is the maximum it will pay for property damage in one accident. While it is important to know the minimum limits of coverage that would satisfy his state's financial responsibility law, the motorist probably would want more than that basic protection. It is 10/20/5 in 33 states and the District of Columbia; less than that in most other states, and more in a few.

Financial responsibility laws were designed to reduce the number of drivers who cannot pay for the injuries or damages they cause. A motorist involved in an accident, whether he was at fault or not, may be required to show proof that he can pay up to the minimum amounts prescribed in the state's law. If he cannot show a policy, he may be required to put up cash or a bond. Inability to do that could result in suspension or revocation of his driver's license and car registration. It should be noted that these laws do not require that a motorist carry insurance, though that is his most sensible means of staying within the law. Compulsory auto insurance laws are in effect only in Massachusetts, New York and North Carolina.

As has been noted, rising claim settlements make an increase above basic coverage an important consideration. If a man had only 10/20/5 coverage and was judged legally liable for injuring a person to the extent of $25,000, his company would be obliged to pay only $10,000. He would have to pay the other $15,000. The cost of additional insurance is relatively small. For example, in one major city, it costs an additional 28 per cent of the basic 10/20 bodily injury premium to increase limits to $100,000/$300,000, and an additional 8 per cent of the basic $5,000 property-damage premium to increase the limit to $25,000.

The liability coverage applies when the car is driven by the policyholder, members of his family or others who drive it with his permission. In addition, the policyholder and members of his family are covered while driving someone else's car, provided they have the owner's permission.

MEDICAL PAYMENTS INSURANCE. This optional auto policy coverage pertains to medical expenses resulting from injuries suffered by the policy owner and members of his immediate family while riding in his car or someone else's, or when struck by a vehicle while walking. It also applies to guests occupying the insured person's car. The insurance company will pay all "reasonable" medical expenses incurred, up to the policy limit, within one year from the date of the accident, including those for necessary medical, surgical, X-ray and dental services, prosthetic devices, ambulance, hospital care, professional nursing and—if it comes to that—funeral costs. Payments are made regardless of who is at fault in the accident.

The maximum amount that will be paid to any one person injured in an accident is limited to the amount stated in the policy. The coverage is available in amounts ranging from $500 to $5,000. Merely as a comparative price guide, in an area where $500 of coverage costs $10 a year, $1,000 of coverage would cost $12, $2,000 would cost $14 and $5,000 would cost $17.

UNINSURED MOTORISTS. An automobile policy may include, sometimes automatically, protection against injury caused by a hit-and-run driver or by a motorist who carries no liability insurance. This protection applies to the policyholder and members of his immediate family, whether occupying the family car or someone else's, or walking. It also applies to guests occupying the family car. The insurer will pay damages up to the limits specified in the policy—usually 10/20—if it is established that an uninsured motorist is legally liable for the injury and the insured person was unable to collect from him.

FIRE AND THEFT. A motorist may protect his car with basic fire and theft insurance, or may broaden that protection with comprehensive physical damage insurance. Among the perils insured against by that coverage are fire, theft, glass breakage, flood, falling objects, missiles, explosion, earthquake, windstorm, hail, water, vandalism or malicious mischief, riot or civil commotion, or collision with a bird or animal. The coverage applies only to the insured person's car. It does not cover wear and tear or mechanical difficulties, nor damages resulting from a collision with another car or object, or caused by upset. Price relates to the degree of exposure to the insured perils in the policy buyer's area. For example, some areas are more vulnerable than others to theft, or to damaging storms. Many policies are issued with a $50 deductible on all claims but fire and theft, particularly in urban areas.

COLLISION INSURANCE. If a person's car is in a collision or turns over, his collision insurance would cover the damage regardless of who was responsible. The protection does not extend to personal injuries suffered in auto accidents, nor to damage to other people's property. The insurance usually is written on a $50 or $100 deductible basis, meaning that the policyholder pays the first $50 or $100 in repairs and the company pays the rest. The larger the deductible, the smaller the premium. As the car gets older, the annual cost of collision insurance decreases. However, at a certain point, the car continues to lose value, but the premium does not continue its decline. An advantage of collision insurance is that a person may have his car repaired immediately, even in cases where the damage was caused by another driver. Without the coverage, he might have to wait for payments until negotiations have been completed, or until a court has decided the case.

INSURANCE COSTS. Auto insurance costs depend on many factors. They vary from individual to individual, area to area, and, in some instances, even from company to company. A mutual company or a company that sells directly to the public through salaried or exclusive agents may charge less than stockholder-owned companies that sell through independent agents and brokers, but this is not always the case. Company selection is based on product, service and convenience, as well as price.

Basically, each state is divided into "rating territories": part or all of a large city, a suburb, a rural area. For each territory, insurance companies compile statistics on claims relating to cars garaged in that area, regardless of where those cars may have been involved in accidents. An Indiana car responsible for an accident in Maine would affect Indiana rates, not Maine's. Among the individual factors considered are the insurance applicant's age, sex, marital status, driving record and the use to which the car will be put, such as pleasure, business or driving to work. Further, the owner of more than one car may get a discount, perhaps 25 per cent, on each additional car, and persons with approved driver-education credit would qualify for premium discounts.

The highest rates are paid by unmarried young males who own or are the principal operators of automobiles, because they, as a group, have the highest accident rate and most costly accidents. In some states, such as New York, all single male drivers under age 25 are bracketed in one group for rate-making purposes. In most other states, however, a distinction is made among youthful drivers under a rating system that was put into effect in 1965. Under that system, which applies to all auto insurance coverages, the cost continues to be highest for young unmarried males, but it is scaled downward year by year from age 17 through 29. Unmarried girls also pay more than the base rate, with their costs scaled downward from age 17 through 20. A premium credit is allowed, if the young driver of a family car is a resident student at a school more than 100 miles from home. Women drivers aged 30 through 64 are in a low-premium class, if they are the only operators of their cars.

A driver may win a premium discount of from 10 to 20 per cent if he has a "clear driving record." That would mean that he has not been involved in an accident where he was at fault, nor has been convicted of a serious traffic-law violation for the past three years.

A person also may cut his costs by obtaining a "package" policy that contains liability, medical payments, collision, comprehensive and other automobile insurance coverages. Assuming he wants all that protection, he could get it in this one policy at a saving of from 10 to 20 per cent.

CAR POOLS AND ACCIDENTS. Members of a cooperative, nonprofit car pool should ask the question: Who will pay the bills should one of us be injured in an accident? In certain states, including Connecticut, New Jersey and New York, the injured riders could sue the auto owner, and his liability insurance would pay if it is established that he was at fault. In other states, among them Illinois, so-called guest statutes preclude such suits, unless it can be proved the driver was "grossly and wantonly negligent." These laws, generally inspired by the insurance industry, are supposed to reduce the chance that a rider might take advantage of his host. Further, it is said, there are many interfamily suits in states not having "guest" laws.

But, in states where it is permitted, some persons may be hesitant to sue their friends, and, even if they did, litigation might be protracted. In guest-statute states, the driver might feel personally responsible for medical bills. Of course, if the driver of another car caused the accident, the car-pool riders would be free to sue him. But here, too, it might be a long time before they saw any money. Part-time chauffeurs can reduce their worries by adding the previously discussed medical-payments coverage to their auto policies, thereby providing injured riders with cash for medical bills, no matter who was at fault in the accident.

Noncommercial motorists who conduct car pools for profit may run the risk of voiding their policies, which specifically exclude "any automobile while used as a public or livery conveyance."

A final note: After pool riders collect medical expenses, they still may decide to file negligence suits against the driver.

CANCELLATION OF POLICIES. If a policy is canceled by the company, it is terminated on five or ten days notice on a pro-rata basis, that is, all of the premium for the unexpired period is returned. If the insured person cancels, it usually is on a short-rate basis, and he receives less than the premium for the unexpired period, in accordance with a short-rate table on the policy. For example, if a company cancels a one-year policy after six months, the policyholder would receive a refund of half the total premium. However, if he canceled, he would get back only 40 per cent of the one-year premium.

9

A USEFUL PLACE FOR SAVINGS

Wherever a person saves, he should be familiar with the policies, regulations and services of the institutions he uses. Beyond that, he should know why he is saving, and not swerve from his goal. Every sound personal financial plan includes a program for systematic saving, that is, saving for a purpose. While those funds initially may be represented by a relatively small savings account and nominal cash values in life insurance policies, ultimately they may be made up of cash, securities, a house and other real estate, larger amounts in life insurance policies, pension plans or annuities and other assets.

However, whatever the proportions of a family's total "savings," there generally always is a need for keeping part of it in readily accessible form. This may be in interest-bearing accounts at banks and other financial institutions or perhaps in Federal savings bonds. Those accessible savings would be made up of the family's emergency fund of perhaps six months' or more income, funds to meet near-term family goals and that part of the investment reserve held aside to take advantage of special investment opportunities that might arise.

This raises the question as to how one selects a savings institution that offers the happy combination of maximum return on savings, safety, convenience to the depositor and a range of services that fulfill his needs. Finding the perfect repository would be difficult, if not impossible, so the compromise may be to use two or more.

This chapter will consider the major ones, which are commercial banks, savings banks, savings and loan associations and credit unions. It also will delve into the advantages and disadvantages of Government savings bonds, the methods of determining exactly how much interest actually is paid on your savings, the possible pitfalls of check-writing in this electronic age, and the systematic savings and Christmas and vacation club plans being offered by many banks.

Commercial Banks: Services, special and regular checking accounts, analysis plans, savings accounts, loans and notes, investment service, collection and payment services

Because of the wide range of services it offers, a good commercial bank can be one of the most useful and convenient of financial institutions, when properly used. Most people know of the basic services: checking and savings accounts, safe-deposit box rental and personal installment loans. In addition, however, a full-service commercial bank may offer a variety of other less-costly personal loans, home mortgage loans, investment custodial and management services and trust administration. It also would transfer a customer's funds to out-of-state or foreign banks, issue letters of credit and travelers checks, automatically pay some of his bills for him and collect regular payments due him.

As the name indicates, a commercial bank serves the financial needs of commerce, business and industry, but the individual customer has become increasingly important to bankers over the years. There are no figures to show how much of total commercial banking funds are attributable to nonbusiness customers, but that banks are interested in their money is evidenced by the aggressive consumer advertising campaigns.

A brief survey of the services of commercial banks provides an individual with another measurement in selecting the institution that best suits his needs. Does it provide all of the services he requires at the lowest cost or, in the case of savings accounts and investment management, at the highest return? In addition, the prospective customer must consider the institution's financial stability and reputation, its convenience and the competence and attitudes of its personnel. A bank might offer all of the services a man would need, but would not be the best choice if it was inefficient or inconveniently situated, or if the employes with whom he came in contact were discourteous or unable to give him adequate guidance in banking and investment areas.

Many people divide their banking business among two or more institutions of different types. For example, the bulk of a person's cash savings might be in the institution paying the highest interest rate, be it a commercial or savings bank, a savings and loan association or a credit union. The small remainder might be kept in a "convenience" savings account at the commercial bank where he has his checking account.

It generally is recommended that a person place with one bank as much of his business as is economically feasible, so as to build a good relationship with that organization. This would be useful in the future in terms of bank references, special assistance and advice.

CHECKING ACCOUNTS. The most widely used banking services are checking accounts, which, when properly handled, provide safety, convenience, accurate records and proof of payments made. The primary types are the special and regular accounts. The special generally is best for the person who writes relatively few checks and prefers not to maintain a minimum balance of any size. He would pay 10 or 15 cents for each check he writes and a monthly maintenance charge, which typically is 50 cents. A monthly charge for a regular checking account usually is based on the amount of money kept in it, the number of checks written and, sometimes, the number of deposits made. A certain number of transactions are allowed "free," when the balance rises to a certain level, perhaps $300 or $500. The cost of free transactions is covered by the income the customer's money in the account earns for the bank.

A type usually restricted to business or large personal accounts is the analysis plan. While the customer is charged for each transaction, he also is credited with an "earnings allowance." The credit, which in effect is interest on the money left in the account, is deducted from the charges, and the customer pays the difference, if any. The credit would not be called interest, because the law no longer allows commercial banks to pay interest on "demand deposits," which checking account balances are.

Some banks have variations on the basic checking account plans. The consumer must determine how extensively he would use a checking account and find the bank that would best provide it at least cost to him. His cost would include the interest lost on money he might have to keep in the account as a "minimum balance." He may not want a checking account at all, if his need is for only a few checks a month. Such a person might make withdrawals from his savings account in bank-check form, or might buy bank money orders, registered checks or cashier's checks.

SAVINGS ACCOUNTS. As to savings accounts, a person should consider not only conventional passbook savings accounts, but also savings bonds, savings certificates and other time-deposit plans that offer relatively high interest rates. In periods of money scarcity, commercial banks are willing to pay those rates to customers who agree to leave their money on deposit for a given period of time. However, if the money is withdrawn before that period ends, the interest rate is reduced.

The Federal Deposit Insurance Corporation insures depositors for up to $15,000 against bank failure in more than 90 per cent of the nation's commercial banks. All Federally chartered commercial banks must be members of the Government insuring agency, and state-chartered commercial banks may join. If a bank should fail, the insuring agency either pays the depositor directly for his loss or opens an account in the same amount for him at a nearby bank.

The $15,000 insurance limit applies to a single depositor in a particular bank, regardless of the number of savings and checking accounts he may have. However, it does not prevent him from spreading his funds among several banks, or among several accounts in family names at the same bank, though some institutions impose restrictions. Joint accounts, such as those naming husband and wife or parent and child, also would be separately insured to the $15,000 maximum, provided that the accounts were jointly held "with the right of survivorship" (on death of one depositor the remaining co-owner would get the whole sum). Accounts in the same name in two or more branches of the same bank would be added together, with the excess above the $15,000 limit uninsured.

While few banks fail, it is wise, where there is a choice, to select the bank that carries deposit insurance.

INSTALLMENT, PASSBOOK, COLLATERAL LOANS AND NOTES. The cost of a personal installment loan at a commercial bank can range up to a 6 per cent add-on or discount rate, meaning that the cost is added to or subtracted from the loan amount. (See Chapter 3 for a discussion of these and other loans.) The true interest rate is about twice that discount or add-on rate, because, in making monthly repayments, the borrower has use, on average, of only about half the loan from the time he receives it until it is fully repaid.

There are cheaper ways to borrow money from commercial banks. Among them are passbook loans with the savings account as security; collateral loans with stocks or bonds as security; and, if the applicant qualifies, 90-day or longer notes. The cost of all of these generally is predicated on a simple annual interest rate, which is less than the true annual interest rate on the installment loans. Repayment usually is made in a lump sum at the end of the loan period.

If a man does not have the collateral, a savings account or the credit standing to qualify for a note, he would have to consider a personal installment loan. Banks usually charge less for those than do small-loan or finance companies, but sometimes more than credit unions.

Passbook loans also are offered by savings banks and savings and loan associations, both of which are more active than commercial banks in the home mortgage market. Therefore, the savings and loans and the savings banks should not be overlooked when shopping for a mortgage.

INVESTMENT SERVICE. A person could have his commercial bank hold his securities in custody, collecting dividends and interest and crediting them to his account. The bank also would maintain records of payments and receipts, buy and sell securities on his orders and advise him of stock splits, the issuance of rights and other developments pertaining to his securities. Rates vary and would have to be comparison shopped. The investor could go still further by having his bank's trust department manage his securities, advising him as to what he should buy or sell. The securities or other property managed could be in trusts set up while he is alive, or established by his will for the benefit of his heirs.

EXECUTORS OF ESTATES. A bank also could be designated as executor, or co-executor with a relative, friend or lawyer, of an estate. The prime advantages ascribed to a good bank (or trust company) as executor are its financial knowledge and the reasonable assurance that it would outlive an individual executor. Fees may be prearranged or set by law or the probate court so they would not necessarily be greater than those paid to an individual.

COLLECTION AND PAYMENT SERVICES. Among other services that a person might find useful are payment collection and bill payment. If a person has a loan outstanding—perhaps a mortgage loan he issued to the buyer of his house—he could have his bank make collections, deposit them in his account or forward them to him or to another bank, and handle all paper work. Fees can range up to $1 or more per payment. On the other hand, a bank also would pay certain of the customer's bills, such as insurance premiums or mortgage payments, withdrawing the money from his account. There may not be a fee for handling the mortgage payments if the same bank holds the mortgage.

A person moving to a distant and unfamiliar area would find it helpful to have his bank open an account for him there, sending a letter of reference to the new bank. This would give him immediate access to cash and status as a good credit risk.

There are many other services a commercial bank can perform for the individual, so it would be wise for the prospective customer to have a talk with one of its officers.

More About Checks: Certified checks, stop-payment orders, endorsements, electronic check processing

Checks are negotiable legal instruments that permit safe and convenient transfer of funds and provide accurate payment records for tax and legal purposes. Maximum effectiveness in their use can be achieved by a person acquainted with the procedures available to him, such as certification of a check by a bank to assure payment, stop orders to prevent payment when warranted and special endorsement forms. Awareness of the reasons why a bank might not honor a check also would be helpful in avoiding these pitfalls.

A *certified check* may be required in cases in which a person is unwilling to accept an ordinary check or in which the finality of a transaction, such as transfer of real estate, makes payment in cash or its equivalent necessary. To have a check certified, it must be brought to the bank on which it is being drawn. The bank will establish that there is a sufficient amount in the account to cover the check, set that amount aside and stamp the word "certified" across the face of the check, thus guaranteeing its payment. A check may be presented for certification by the bank's customer (the maker of the check), or by the recipient of the check (the payee). A bank sometimes imposes a small fee for certification.

To avoid difficulty in having a check canceled in the event that a transaction is not completed, it is recommended that a person make a certified check payable to himself. If the transaction is completed, he would endorse the check over to the person to whom he is making payment. If the deal falls through, he merely deposits the check in his own account.

A bank may be asked to *stop payment* on a check, if a person has reason not to want payment made. Among the reasons may be that the check was lost or that the person or organization scheduled to receive payment did not fulfill the agreement. To obtain a stop order, a person must go to the bank, where he completes and signs a stop-payment form, providing the check's date, number and amount and the name of the person or organization to whom it is payable. Most stop-payment forms contain a clause relieving the bank of liability if one of its employes inadvertently pays on a check that had been stopped.

Aside from a stop order, there are a number of reasons why a bank may refuse to honor a check that was drawn by one of its customers. For example, there may be insufficient funds in the depositor's account. If he does not make the check good within a specified period after notification of the deficiency, he may be subject to prosecution. Among other reasons are that the check was altered, that it was postdated and presented for payment prematurely or that the words and figures on the check do not agree as to amount.

If an error is made in writing a check, a new one should be written. A person using a regular checking account and certain special checking accounts may tear up the old check. However, a special-checking account user who pays for his checks in advance may mark the old check "void," and exchange it at the bank for a new blank check without charge. If a person must issue a postdated check, he should caution the recipient not to attempt to cash it before the specified date. As to a discrepancy between the figures and the written amount on the check, one can try to avoid it by rereading each check he writes. Some banks will pay on the written amount, because the law recognizes that over the figures.

In addition, a bank would not honor a check if it believes the signature is not genuine, if the bank learns that the person who wrote it died, or if the person presenting the check for payment is unknown and cannot properly identify himself.

Before a person can cash or deposit a check he must endorse it, signing it on the back. A check passing among several persons would carry several endorsements, starting with the one by the person to whom it had been made payable by the writer. If that first person's name is incorrectly spelled or incomplete as it appears on the check, he should write his endorsement in that way and follow with his correct signature.

There are several *endorsement* forms, the most widely used being the "blank endorsement," which simply is the person's signature. However, that form is safe to use only after arrival at the bank where it is to be cashed or deposited, for it makes the check payable to whoever has it in his possession. Losing a check carrying a blank endorsement, therefore, is almost equivalent to losing cash. (For the same reason, a person normally should not make a check payable to "cash" or "bearer.") To protect himself, a person may use the "restrictive endorsement" or the "special endorsement." The restrictive form would include the phrase "for deposit only" above the person's signature, and the special form would carry the words, "pay to the order of (the recipient's name)." For added protection, a person may use the combination, "pay to the order of the XYZ Bank for deposit only."

The "qualified endorsement" is rarely used, and one should think twice about accepting a check carrying it. That endorsement carries the phrase "without recourse," and frees the endorser of responsibility if the check bounces and its maker will not make it good. On the other hand, a person should attempt to use a qualified endorsement himself, if there is insistence on an endorsement when he is passing to another party a check that is payable to the bearer.

Checks should be cashed or deposited as soon after receipt as possible. While a check legally is valid for the full term of the statute of limitations (generally six years), a bank may not honor it after a reasonable period of time has passed, usually six months, without the consent of the person who wrote it. Aside from this complication, the recipient may lose out if the check is not payable for a reason not attributable to its maker. For example, the maker may have had sufficient cash in his account to cover the check, but the bank in which he kept his account subsequently failed. He would not be liable for the loss suffered by the recipient who could have gotten his money if he had made timely presentation of the check for payment.

ELECTRONIC CHECK PROCESSING. It once was common practice for a person to take a blank check, or one from someone else's checkbook, and write a draft, adding his own account number and bank's name. However, in our automated age, there is possible risk and inconvenience in these practices. The use of a blank-check form could cause delays in processing and payment. The use of a check from another person's book could result in its being debited against the other person's account, though his account number had been crossed out.

To cope with the billions of checks that are written each year, banks use highly sophisticated electronic equipment which even reads numbers that are crossed out. All check-processing systems include steps handled by human beings, who, in effect, check up on the machines. But people, not always precision made, err occasionally. In essence, check processing involves the sending of checks received for payment by banks to a clearing house, which, in turn, sorts and sends them to the banks on which they were drawn.

Machines read check numbers that are crossed out, because the numbers are printed with magnetic ink—regular printer's ink with iron-oxide filings in it. The system is known as Magnetic Ink Character Recognition (M.I.C.R.). When checks in process are put through electronic sorting or reading equipment, the iron-oxide filings in the ink give off wave lengths. The numerical configurations are such (take a look at a check) that each number gives off a different wave length, thus making it possible for the machine to "read." Crossing out a number with a conventional pen or pencil does not eliminate or disturb the iron-oxide filings; neither does a paste-on label. To obliterate an unwanted number, one must use a magnetic-ink pen. Banks may use one on a "made-over" check they spot, so that it will not be misrouted; but magnetic-ink pens are not usually handy to most people. Therefore, according to a banker, they should tear or cut the bank and account numbers out of the checks they use that are not their own.

The blank checks often are delayed in processing because they do not bear the transit-routing (bank) numbers in either magnetic or conventional form and must be handled manually.

Savings Banks: Deposit insurance, services, life insurance

The first mutual savings banks were established in the United States—one in Boston and another in Philadelphia—in 1816 to encourage thrift among families and individuals of moderate income by providing them with a safe place for savings. This remains the objective of the more than 500 savings banks in the 18 states in which such institutions may be established.

As "mutual" corporations, the banks are technically owned by their depositors, and not by stockholders. Thus, all earnings, after operating expenses are met, go to benefit the depositors, either as savings dividends (interest) paid to them directly, or in the form of additions to reserves for protection against loss. The earnings primarily are from placement of savings deposits in sound investments, primarily first mortgages on homes, United States bonds and other high-grade securities.

Most mutual savings banks carry some form of deposit insurance. More than two-thirds are members of the Federal Deposit Insurance Corporation, and their depositors are protected in the same way depositors in member commercial banks are protected. Within 10 days of a bank's failure, depositors would receive their savings, up to $15,000, in cash or as a new account in a solvent bank. The limit could be increased with accounts in other family members' names or with joint accounts that carry the survivorship right. There also are insurance plans in Connecticut, Massachusetts and New Hampshire, and, depending on the state, most or all banks are covered.

In addition to a variety of nonbusiness savings accounts and competitively rated home mortgage and improvement loans, mutual savings banks offer other services, including passbook loans, banking by mail, rental of safe-deposit boxes, sale of money orders and travelers checks and, with the cooperation of employers, systematic saving by payroll deduction. In some states, they, like other institutions, also may provide student loans. In New York, the loans are backed by the state, which also pays part of the interest cost.

For those who find it convenient or useful, withdrawals may be taken in bank-check form, payable to the customer or to the individual or organization to whom he is making payment.

Savings banks in Connecticut, Massachusetts and New York also sell life insurance. It is relatively low priced, because it is sold directly to customers, at the bank or by mail, but not through salesmen whose commissions would add to the price.

Savings and Loan Associations: Interest rates, deposit insurance, services

A savings and loan association, either state or Federally chartered, accepts savings with which it makes loans secured by mortgages for the construction, purchase and repair of homes. There are nearly 6,300 of these specialized financial institutions in the nation, of which nearly 2,000 are Federally licensed and the rest state licensed. Though there may be periodic exceptions, the associations generally pay a higher *interest rate* on savings than do mutual savings banks and commercial banks. This is because the associations have most of their assets, up to 85 per cent, on loan in high-yield mortgages. Like the savings banks, the majority of the associations are "mutuals," being owned by their shareholder-depositors.

A depositor in an association technically is buying savings shares on which he receives dividends (interest), and legally is a shareholder. The commercial bank's checking or savings account depositor, by contrast, is a creditor of the bank, which owes him the money he has left with it.

Passage of the Federal Home Loan Bank Act in 1932 created a system of regional reserve banks. The system's member associations have greater financial flexibility, because they may borrow from the 12 reserve banks, using as security the mortgages they hold. Federally chartered associations must be depositor owned and must belong to the system, as well as to the Federal Savings and Loan Insurance Corporation, which insures savings accounts up to a maximum of $15,000 each. State-chartered associations may subscribe to these Federal agencies, and in some states they must to meet their charter requirements. As a result, state and Federally chartered members of the Home Loan Bank system account for more than 95 per cent of all association assets, and more than two-thirds of the nation's savings and loan associations carry *deposit insurance.*

Insurance is provided for up to $10,000 in each account, and, as is the case in commercial and savings banks, an individual or family may have insured accounts in several associations, or several accounts under family members' names in one association, though some institutions impose restrictions.

Aside from home mortgages and improvement loans, associations provide a variety of other *services.* Among them are passbook loans, banking by mail and the mailing of dividend checks to owners of certain types of savings certificates or savings accounts.

Savings and loan associations also are known as savings associations, building and loan associations, in New England as cooperative banks and in Louisiana as homestead associations.

Credit Unions: Savings plans, life insurance, loans

A credit union, a state or Federally chartered nonprofit corporation, is a group of people who agree to save their money together and to make loans to each other from the savings pool at low interest. It is organized by persons with a common bond, such as employes of a company, members of a fraternal order, church or labor union, or residents of a closely knit community. The members elect officers and committeemen and set policies at annual meetings.

More than 15 million people belong to the nation's nearly 22,000 credit unions, which have a total of more than $10-billion in assets. Credit unions can offer attractive interest rates on savings and loans, because they are tax-sheltered, nonprofit corporations with limited overhead. Sponsor groups often absorb certain expenses. The effectiveness to an individual of a credit union lies in the creative blending of its basic features, which are:

1. *Savings plans:* Regular savings, often by payroll deduction, are encouraged. In most credit unions, the allowable maximum savings (called "shares") in an account is $5,000.

2. *Life insurance:* Most credit unions provide life insurance without extra charge. Each savings dollar, usually to a maximum of $2,000, is matched with a dollar of insurance on the life of the individual account owner or the first-named owner of a joint account, provided that he or she is between the ages of six months and 55

years. Under six months, or between 55 and 60 years old, the insurance is 75 cents for each dollar on deposit, and between the ages of 60 and 65 it is 50 cents.

3. *Loans:* These are made "for provident or productive purposes," including home-improvement and education. While the maximum allowable interest charge is 1 per cent a month on the unpaid balance, some credit unions charge three-fourths of 1 per cent. Others charge less, but they generally do not provide loan-protection insurance, which automatically pays the debt, up to $10,000, if the borrower dies. A monthly interest rate of 1 per cent on the unpaid balance comes to an annual true interest rate of 12 per cent, and is equivalent to a 6 per cent advance-discount loan for one year from a bank. The three-fourths of 1 per cent rate equals an annual true interest rate of 9 per cent, and compares with a 4½ per cent discount loan.

A great benefit of an effective credit union is the financial counseling it can provide for its members. While most families and individuals may require financial guidance and information from time to time, there are dramatic cases of debt-ridden and desperate families who have been nursed back to financial health by their credit unions. In addition to budgetary and general financial counseling, their programs included consolidation loans with weekly repayments that they could handle, and elimination of most or all high-interest debts with the loan proceeds. The credit union, where possible, dealt with the creditors, minimizing the penalties of loan prepayment.

While credit unions do not provide deposit insurance, there are devices that protect savers against loss resulting from an institution's failure. Among those devices are external (governmental) and internal supervision, a bonding program, a mandatory reserve requirement and member participation.

Interest-Payment Policies: Compounded interest, dividends, interest periods, bonus plans

The bank or other savings institution that offers the highest annual interest (or dividend) rate is not necessarily the one that pays the largest dollar amount in interest on savings. The primary telling factors behind the stated annual rate are how often accounts are compounded (paying interest on interest), how account balances are calculated for interest-payment purposes, and whether a service charge is imposed for "extra" withdrawals.

Because the rate of return is such an important factor in selecting a place for one's money, close inquiry should be made of institution officials as to what their interest-payment policies are. The institution whose policy incorporates a combination of factors that make its actual interest rate the best one available would be the consumer's choice, provided that it also measured up in terms of safety, convenience, competence, courtesy and service. By knowing his savings institution's interest-payment rules, a depositor could achieve a higher return on his savings, because he would be able to coordinate his deposits and withdrawals with that policy.

Here is how *compounding* works. If the interest rate is 4 per cent compounded quarterly, 1 per cent interest would be paid every three months. Thus, interest would earn interest. A $1,000 balance would grow to $1,010 at the end of the first three months. The extra $10 also would earn interest in the next quarter, so that the account would increase by $10.10. That would bring the total balance to $1,020.10, all of which would earn interest in the third quarter, thus growing by $10.20. By the end of the year, the original $1,000 balance would have earned a total of about $40.60. By contrast, an account offering a straight 4 per cent a year would have paid $40 on the $1,000 balance.

The greater the frequency of compounding, the more interest an account will earn during the year. But the increase in return is not as great as one might be led to believe. At 4 per cent compounded semiannually, the actual yield is 4.04 per cent. It grows to 4.06 per cent when the account is compounded quarterly, to 4.07 per cent when compounded monthly and 4.08 per cent when compounded daily. For short periods of time and for small accounts, the advantages derived from compounding perhaps would be nominal. But, on larger accounts held for long periods, compound interest pays a sharply higher return than does simple interest. In illustration, $5,000 invested at 4½ per cent compounded quarterly would grow to $7,821.85 in 10 years, compared with $7,250 at 4½ per cent simple interest.

Accounts generally are credited with earned interest or *dividends* at the end of each period. For example, interest usually is credited at the end of December in a simple-interest account, at the end of June and December in a semiannually compounded account, and at the end of March, June, September and December in a quarterly compounded account. However, there are exceptions. Some banks may operate on a fiscal rather than a calendar year, crediting interest at the end of other than the usual months. Other banks may credit interest on the first day of the month following the end of each period, such as on April 1, July 1, October 1 and January 1.

Since a depositor will lose interest payments at many banks if he makes a withdrawal before the *interest-payment date,* it is important that he know what his bank's payment policy is. And that touches on the most influential factor determining how much the actual return on savings accounts is. How are account balances calculated for interest-payment purposes? A corollary question: When does money in an account start earning interest?

As to premature withdrawal of funds, some institutions allow several "days of grace" at the end of each interest period. If money is withdrawn within the specified number of days, usually three, before the interest-payment date, it still will earn interest until the end of the period. However, if that is not part of an institution's policy, and a customer must withdraw his money prematurely, he should consider a passbook loan. The interest he would pay on the loan for the few days until his account's interest-payment date generally is considerably less than the interest he would receive on the savings for the whole earnings period, be it three, six or twelve months.

As to when money in an account starts earning interest, the most favorable plan computes interest on the actual amount in the account from the day it is deposited until the day it is withdrawn. Thus, provided there is still some money in the account on the interest-payment day, all money that was in the account during the interest period would have earned interest for the time it was on deposit. This is the policy of only a relatively few banks; in New York City, for example, it's limited to only about five commercial banks. The device is especially useful to a person who must have a large amount of cash on hand for a special expenditure, such as for a house, but does not know exactly when the expenditure will be made. If, for example, he deposits a large sum in early January and withdraws it in mid-March, he could receive interest on the entire sum for that two and one-half months simply by leaving a few dollars on deposit until the interest-payment date. In a more typical acccount, he would have forfeited that interest.

Most banks and other savings institutions allow a certain number of grace days at the beginning of each interest period, so that money deposited on or before the last grace day would earn interest from the first of that month. One must question whether the grace days are calendar or business days: for example, 10 business days of grace would actually be about two calendar weeks. Depending on the institution, money deposited after the grace period may earn interest from day of deposit, or may not earn interest until the first of the next month or until the beginning of the next interest period, which could be several months off, thus allowing the money to lie fallow. Other institutions, particularly some savings banks, allow a few grace days at the beginning of each month. There is value, of course, in knowing the number of grace days allowed at the beginning of each interest period or month and at the end, before the interest-crediting day, but, as has been observed, it is even more important to know what happens to the money deposited at other times. Will it earn interest?

As has been noted, the most favorable interest-payment policy is the computation of interest on the money in the account from day of deposit to day of withdrawal. The next best is payment of interest from day of deposit on all money remaining in the account until the end of the interest period. However, there are other plans that could be economically painful to the regular saver. For example, there are some institutions that pay interest only on the lowest balance for the period. Thus, if the least a person had in his account during the interest period was $250, the most was $1,500, and his balance on interest-crediting day was $1,200, he would receive interest only on the $250.

The method used to calculate the interest-earning balance is especially important to the person who has made a number of deposits and withdrawals, thereby causing the actual balance to fluctuate widely. Aside from the "low-balance" method already mentioned, the two primary ones are the "last-in, first-out" (LIFO) and "first-in, first-out" (FIFO) methods. The LIFO method is the more advantageous one, because it assumes that the last amount of money deposited is the first withdrawn. Thus, interest is lost for a minimum span of time, that is, from the last deposit date to the day of withdrawal.

However, the FIFO method assumes that the first money on deposit during an interest period is the first money withdrawn. This means that money withdrawn toward the end of an interest period could lose interest for the entire period. For example, money withdrawn toward the end of the interest period would lose up to 1 per cent or more in interest in a 4½ per cent account that is compounded quarterly, and up to more than 2 per cent if it is compounded semiannually.

Then there are institutions that offer *bonus plans,* under which they promise to pay an additional dividend or interest over and above the regular savings account rate to depositors who keep money on deposit for long periods, typically a year. Most plans pay the extra interest retroactively at the end of four consecutive quarters. Thus, if, say, $1,000 is deposited on January 1 and left through the year, it will be credited with the regular passbook interest during the year, and will be credited on the following January 1 with the extra interest, applicable to the whole sum for the whole year. Thereafter, the bonus is paid, on a pro-rata basis, at the end of each regular interest period. Some institutions begin the bonus payment after four consecutive quarters, but do not make it retroactive, thereby reducing the "reward."

United States Savings Bonds

One of the most popular and reliable of savings media is the United States savings bond. There are Series E bonds, which are bought at a 25 per cent discount ("Get $4 back for each $3 you invest") and gradually grow in value to the full face amount in seven years. Then there are the "current-income" Series H bonds, for which buyers pay the full amount shown on their face, and receive interest payments by check twice a year.

The Series E bonds are the most widely bought, because they are available in denominations as small as $25. The Government has increased the yield from time to time by reducing the amount of time it takes for them to mature. Initially—during and after World War II—a bond grew from 75 per cent of face value to full face value over a span of 10 years, thereby providing an average annual yield of 2.9 per cent if held to maturity. Now the E bonds mature in seven years, providing an average annual yield of 4.15 per cent compounded semiannually if held to maturity. Bonds may be held for an additional 10 years after maturity, earning interest at the 4.15 per cent rate.

Though interest rates on savings accounts at many banks and savings and loan associations have risen above the 4.15 per cent level, these rates are not guaranteed for as long a period as are those of savings bonds. Further, savings account interest must be claimed as taxable income in the year in which it is credited to the account. E bond interest is not taxable until the bond is cashed in, and that may be in lower tax-bracket retirement years.

Series E bonds should be bought for long-term savings, because they do not increase in value in the first six months, and have a low rate of growth in the early years thereafter. They grow at a greater than 4.15 per cent rate in the later years, thereby producing the average yield of 4.15 per cent compounded semiannually, when held to maturity. The graduated scale was designed to encourage investors to retain the bonds to maturity.

Many individuals have found value in the "enforced savings" method of buying E bonds by payroll deduction, an accommodation provided by employers. This, like most other payroll-savings plans, has proved to be a painless and popular savings device.

Series H bonds may be bought in denominations of $500, $1,000, $5,000 and $10,000, and that is what the investor pays when he buys the bonds, and what he gets back when they mature, or when he cashes them in. In the meantime, he receives interest checks twice a year, which he must claim as taxable income in each of the years in which he receives them. As with E bonds, the H bond interest is on a graduated scale to encourage investors to hold them to maturity. However, if held to maturity, the bonds provide an average annual return of 4.15 per cent compounded semiannually.

An important feature of all Federal savings bonds is that they are readily redeemable at most banks and other authorized financial institutions or at a United States Treasury office. E bonds are redeemable any time after the first two months of ownership, and the full purchase price, plus interest, will be paid. There is no commission charge on purchase, and no penalty on premature sale (aside from the reduced early-years' interest rate). Similarly, H bonds may be redeemed at the full purchase price (the face value) after six months of purchase and on one-month's written notice.

Both the E and H bonds may be bought in the name of one person, in the names of two as co-owners or in the name of one person, with a beneficiary. Co-ownership could be useful, for either owner could cash it by endorsement without the consent of the other. If one of the owners dies, the other becomes sole owner without having to establish proof of death or transferring the bond to his name. To eliminate or change the beneficiary on a bond, one would have to cash it in and buy a new one.

Savings bonds are registered with the Treasury, and would be replaced if they were lost. In such a case, a person may write to the Bureau of the Public Debt, Division of Loans and Currency, 536 South Clark Street, Chicago, Illinois. While bonds are recorded in that agency by name as well as number, it takes longer to track down the records, if it only has the owner's name. It would be expeditious, therefore, to provide the bureau with the lost bond's serial number and the date of its purchase. Such data could be recorded by the owner, and kept separately from his bonds, so that it would be available in the event of loss.

Programed Savings: Payroll deduction, bank incentive plans, Christmas and vacation clubs

Some people have the discipline and money management ability to conduct their own cash savings programs, methodically putting aside a predetermined amount for each payday or budgetary period. Others save on an irregular basis, but are so financially sophisticated that they can end the year with the amount of additional savings that satisfies their needs.

However, there is a great army of individuals and families that find it impossible to follow either course. For them, the solution may be a systematic and perhaps "enforced" program for cash savings. For many of them, the most valuable of plans are the *payroll-deduction programs*. Each payday, a certain amount is deducted from an employe's check by a cooperative employer. Depending on the plan, the employer will buy Series E savings bonds in the employe's behalf, or forward the money for deposit in a credit union, bank or other designated financial institution. Other persons, who either are self-employed or do not have a suitable payroll-deduction plan available, may authorize their bank to withdraw a certain amount each month from their checking accounts for deposit in a savings account or for purchase of Government savings bonds.

Some banks and savings and loan associations offer a *bonus incen-*

tive to consistent savers in the form of additional interest or an extra dividend. Savings banks that also sell life insurance offer a savings package that combines regular savings with purchase of Series E savings bonds and life insurance. Programs may be arranged for as little as $3 a week, and they may extend for five, 10 or 20 years.

Among the sharply modified systematic savings plans available are the *Christmas* and *vacation clubs* offered by many banks. Under these plans, a person would make a weekly deposit of a fixed amount, which could range from 50 cents to $10, and in 50 weeks he would receive a check for the amount deposited. Most banks do not pay interest or dividends on these accounts, and those that do pay only a nominal rate. Such plans are useful to those persons who have difficulty in budgeting and cannot save for these special expenditures by any other means.

10

TAILORING WALL STREET TO THE INVESTOR

It is something of a milestone when a family decides, on reviewing its financial program, that it is ready to consider investments in securities. For it indicates that, in addition to having met other goals over the years, the family has acquired adequate life insurance, possibly bought a home and accumulated relatively substantial savings. Those savings, less an emergency fund and amounts needed for more immediate family plans, would be earmarked for investment. This does not mean that a family must immediately seek to commit all of it at once, whether it is less than $1,000 or considerably more. It does mean that the savings are available for use as timely and suitable investment opportunities arise. And they will, if the potential investor makes an intelligent and systematic search for them.

Meanwhile, it is worth noting again that other parts of a family's financial program enhance its total economic status, thus aiding in the attainment of long-term goals. Permanent policies in the life insurance program are building cash values, a form of disciplined savings. As a mortgage is repaid over the years, the family increases its equity in the house, which also may appreciate in market value. In addition, the family may be paying toward an annuity, or the breadwinner may be contributing with his employer to a pension plan.

Aware of these other areas, a family may sensibly formulate its securities investment plan. In so doing, it would take into account the span of time and amount of cash it has to work with in achieving its goal, perhaps the children's education or the parents' retirement security. The cash may be from current income, as well as savings. The amount of time and capital available determine whether emphasis should be on the investment's growth, its income, or the preservation of its purchasing power. Because achievement of one of these primary investment objectives is generally at the sacrifice, at least in part, of the other two, careful planning is crucial.

Flexibility in Investment Policies: Growth or income?

A young couple of moderate income would be most interested in seeing their few investment dollars multiplied over the broad span of years until their children are ready for college or they themselves are ready for retirement. For the sake of that growth, or capital appreciation, they would forgo immediate income, which would be small on their limited, perhaps periodic, investments. However, on retirement, this same couple would shift their primary objective to income, just as much as their nest egg could safely provide.

However, anyone, whatever his age, might wish to stress immediate income, if his investment were sizable. If he were young, his goal might be a combination of income and growth. But, if he were more concerned with preserving his capital to protect his retirement program for use in a relatively few years, or to protect the interests of his heirs, he would stress capital stability, forgoing part of the income potential.

There are persons of modest means who have relatively few years in which to accomplish their goals. They may be a middle-aged couple planning retirement, or the parents of a 12-year-old looking forward to college. These persons cannot absorb the large inherent risk of highly speculative growth stocks, but some capital appreciation is essential to at least moderate success. The compromise may be investments that combine moderate growth potential with stability.

Thus it becomes apparent that there can be much flexibility in investment planning. Securities, that is, stocks and bonds, are the most popular of investment media, but a family or individual may consider real estate, or, if they feel qualified, their own business. As to securities and real estate, the investor has the choice of two procedures in selecting investments, and he may use either or a blend of both. He may adopt a do-it-yourself role, utilizing available professional advice but depending mainly on his own research efforts and judgment. Or, he may rely entirely on the professional guidance available from an investment counselor (if the investor's capital is large enough) or through an investment company (the most popular of these investment pools is the mutual fund) or a real estate syndicate or trust. But, even this second course is not as easy as it may sound, because the investor must do a conscientious investigative job if he is to end up with the best available adviser or investment vehicle.

Whatever the route selected, the rewards can be high, especially if the investor is willing to do some work for the rewards, which is a form of working for himself.

The Investor's Internship: Study, practice investment clubs

Almost every craftsman and professional must serve an apprenticeship of a sort. Why not the investor? His on-the-job training could be extremely costly, so he should gain his experience without risking capital. This can be done by making "paper" investments, actually recording the securities he would have bought and sold over a period of time, and ultimately seeing what he would have gained or lost. Admittedly, he might hate himself for having missed some golden opportunities, but what if it had been the other way around?

A person may begin the practice long before he is actually ready to invest. Having by this time read extensively on investment and having acquired the habit of regularly reading a newspaper's financial pages and at least one financial publication, he would come to view his "dry-run" investing as a game, a game that could pay off handsomely when he is ready for the real thing. For this total effort would develop in him an investment savvy that cannot be bought. Ultimately, he will be able to evaluate a particular stock or bond, to relate business and general economic developments to the market.

He may supplement his training with an investment course offered by the adult education division of his local high school or college, or perhaps by a stock brokerage house. Later, combining nominal investment with education, he may join an investment club, thus learning from others and by experience. These clubs, which usually have about a dozen members, hold regular meetings at which an appointed committee reports on its study of a particular industry or securities group. Specific investments, which must have majority approval, are regularly made from a fund fed by each member's monthly contribution, as well as earnings from previous investments. Further information about investment clubs may be obtained from the National Association of Investment Clubs, 1300 Washington Boulevard Building, Detroit, Michigan.

In time, when the investor decides that he has sufficient investment capital and experience, he will be ready to invest on his own. It is hoped that his training would have hardened him to the emotional impulses to which many investors yield. Ideally, there should be no emotionalism and no "hunches" in making investment decisions. Decisions should be based on objective analysis. The urge by many investors to follow the crowd generally results in their buying a stock at too high a price, or selling too low.

Common Stocks: Risk and potential

Common stocks are the greatest risk and have the greatest profit potential. They are the most popular of securities investments, primarily because they extend the promise of capital gains, that is, investment growth; though many unknowledgeable investors who were eager to "get rich quick" have been sorely disappointed. With proper selection, they allow investors to share in the nation's economic growth, and usually are considered to be a hedge against inflation, historically rising as the value of the dollar declines.

Common stock, which is divided into equal units called shares, represents ownership in a corporation—a legal entity that can live indefinitely, surviving owner after owner, management official after management official. The corporation may issue common stock and preferred stock, or several classes of both; but if only one type is issued, it is almost sure to be common. Its owners have the right to profits of the corporation only after the company has met its obligations to creditors and preferred stockholders, who usually receive income at a stated rate. The common stock's lure is that profits in excess of those "priority" claims could rise steadily in an expanding, well-managed company, thereby increasing the return on investment. It also could provide capital gains, if buyer interest has been sufficiently stimulated to cause the stock's market price to rise.

This discussion naturally centers on "publicly owned" corporations, all or a significant part of whose stock is widely held by the investing public and traded in the securities markets. The converse is the "closely held corporation," whose shares are primarily, or exclusively, held by family members, management officials or some other limited group of associates, friends or investors. There not being any real market for such stock, it must be sold privately at a negotiated price, or, as is required in some cases, it must be sold back to the company or its other stockholders.

A corporation receives the proceeds from the sale of newly issued stock, less underwriting costs, and uses the money to begin or expand operations. Thereafter, the stock is traded from investor to investor, with no additional benefit to the company. In the case of a "secondary offering," stockholders of a closely held corporation or large stockholders of a public company decide to sell all or part of their holdings to the public, with the proceeds going to the selling stockholders.

When two or more classes of common stock are issued, the difference generally is in voting power, with only one class having majority or exclusive voting control—the right to elect directors, who, in turn, run the company and appoint officers. With this device, managements have raised capital by publicly selling stock with little or no voting power, thus retaining control by holding as much of the voting stock as they can.

The voting stock often represents only a small percentage of the total stock the company has outstanding. It is New York Stock Exchange policy to deny listing to nonvoting common stock. To the average investor, his miniscule right to share in corporate management generally is of small concern to him, provided that the stock otherwise measures up as a sound investment. Some concerns, perhaps primarily for public relations reasons, urge stockholders to attend annual meetings, and occasionally a small investor raises an issue that distresses or embarrasses management, and could have greater ramifications if it gets press attention.

Standards of Value: Book value, market value, earnings-and-dividend value

The worth of a common share may be given as its book value, market value or earnings-and-dividend value. A company's book value, in effect, is its value at corporate dissolution, for it is the net of its assets after all creditors and preferred stockholders have been paid off. This assumes, of course, that historic book value is identical with value of the corporate assets on liquidation. The book value per share is arrived at by dividing the number of outstanding shares into that net.

Book value generally is of nominal significance to the average investor, whose interest is in going concerns, not dead ones. However, it may be worthy of consideration in the case of a stock that is selling for substantially less than book value, because of a generally depressed market or for some other reason that does not detract from its intrinsic value as a sound investment. Perhaps it was caused by an easily explained temporary decline in earnings. If that is the case, the stock may qualify as a bargain.

Market value is the price set in the securities market; it is the share price that the last buyer of the stock was willing to pay, and the seller was willing to accept. The price itself, large or small, sheds little light on the quality of the stock, but its price pattern in recent days, weeks, months or years may. Did it steadily rise or decline, or did it fluctuate wildly? Too many people, accustomed to shopping for merchandise, arbitrarily decide whether or not they can "afford" a stock by its per-share price. They automatically shy away from "high-priced" shares, concentrating instead on "cheaper" issues.

This is unwise. The investment determinant is not the price per share, but the potential percentage of return and capital gain on the amount invested. If $1,000 investments are made in two stocks, one selling at $10 and the other at $500, and both pay a 5 per cent dividend, the return in each case would be $50 a year. If the "cheap" stock advanced $1 in market price, and the "expensive" stock advanced $50, the gain in each instance would be $100 on the $1,000 investment.

There may in fact be an advantage to the high-priced stock in that a decline of 10 per cent, or 50 points, generally would be far less rapid than a decline of 10 per cent, or one point, in the $10 stock. This would give the investor more time in which to protect his investment by selling to minimize his loss, if he decides to sell in the belief that the setback is not a temporary one.

On the other hand, the investor should be aware that the public affinity for moderately priced stocks could, under the right circumstances, be another favorable influence on market value. Many corporations, also aware of this lure, have split their stocks, creating two or more smaller shares where there was one large share. There are countless cases of share prices rising after stock splits.

In essence, most corporations that split their stocks do so in the hope of achieving greater marketability and wider distribution of their shares. The practicality of this device is evident, since the share price of some companies' stocks, had they not been split many times, would be astronomical. That price, which in some instances might be in the tens of thousands of dollars, would make it impossible for most investors to buy even one share. Further, some companies split their stock to qualify for listing on one of the exchanges, which usually set minimum requirements for number of shares outstanding and number of shareholders.

These factors, all other things being equal, may tend to enhance a stock's market value. They would be reinforced by the more subtle psychological factor: the public's affinity for moderately priced stocks.

The price-enhancing factors represent the prime advantage to a shareholder in a company that splits its stock or distributes large stock dividends. He has no immediate benefit, aside from possession of another impressive stock certificate, for the size of his interest in the company remains unchanged. If a man has a share worth $100 in a company that splits its stock five for one, he ends up with five shares worth $20 each for the $100 total he started with, and a second certificate covering the four additional shares. He is ahead if the relative dividend rate is increased, and if investor interest is stimulated by the new low price, and the bigger yield.

The third, and perhaps most important, measurement of a stock's worth is *per-share earnings and cash dividends.* The per-share earnings are arrived at by dividing the number of outstanding common shares into the company's net income, after having allowed for taxes and any preferred dividends. A company's earnings and cash dividend payment pattern is an indication of its quality as an investment. Adjusting for past stock splits and stock dividends, have share earnings consistently advanced, or are they in decline? How much has been passed on to the shareholders as cash dividends, and how much plowed back into the business? If a good deal has been plowed back with little or no resulting growth, or if all earnings are paid in dividends, the company may be standing still, if not losing ground.

Share earnings are related to market values under the "price-earnings ratio" concept; that is, over the long term, shares tend to sell at a multiple of earnings. Thus, if in the general market, or perhaps within a particular industry list, the multiple is 20, then a company's shares should be selling at about 20 times the current year's estimated earnings. The multiple for certain very promising growth stocks might be considerably higher than for the general market. If a stock is selling for a smaller earnings multiple than comparable stocks, and there are no sound reasons why, then it might be worthy of investment consideration.

Rights and Warrants

The investor who receives stock rights and does not exercise or sell them is throwing money away. The same can be said, in many instances, about warrants.

Rights certificates are issued by a company that chooses, or is required by law or charter, to give its stockholders the first opportunity to buy new securities that it issues to raise money. Each certificate allows the shareholder to buy the new securities, usually common stock, in proportion to the number of shares he already owns. Because the additional stock is usually offered to stockholders below the current market price per share, rights generally have a market value of their own and are actively traded.

The rights certificates usually expire after a relatively short time. They get their name because they represent the pre-emptive right often granted by state law or charter to a company's investors, usually its common-stock holders. That right is to buy a proportionate part of new stock issued so that they may maintain their proportionate ownership in the company. For example, if an investor has a 1 per cent interest in the company, he has the right to buy 1 per cent of the new stock.

Thus, if a shareholder does not exercise his rights, he ends up with a reduced interest in the company. This can mean an actual loss, unless he makes it up by selling the rights. The lower-than-market price of the new shares may not be a bargain, because the new stock issue enlarges the number of shares outstanding, thereby reducing the value per share. This may be reflected in the market price of the stock, unless the old price is sustained or advanced for other reasons. In that case, the investor who did not act on his rights also deprived himself of a potential profit.

Warrants also are options to buy securities, usually common stock, at a stipulated price, but they usually are valid for years or perpetually. A warrant sometimes is offered with other securities, such as bonds, as an inducement to buy. The market value of warrants can fluctuate more widely than the price of the stock to which they apply, depending on the warrant's expiration date and the degree of potential seen in the stock.

A warrant allowing purchase of a stock at $21 a share would be quite valuable, if investors believed the stock had a potential far in excess of that price. When the market price of the stock exceeded $21 a share, an immediate profit could be realized by exercising the option. But, if there was little likelihood that the stock would even approach the warrant price in the foreseeable future, the warrant certificate would lose attraction.

Bonds and Preferred Shares—Investments for Safety

There probably would be a broader demand for bonds and preferred shares if the investing public had a greater understanding of their nature and purpose. When properly chosen, these senior securities can provide greater immediate income and safety of investment than most common stocks, which generally put the promise of capital gain ahead of income and safety. Preferreds and bonds, therefore, may best serve the investor who, by inclination or circumstance, should not speculate with part or all of his capital. He may be retired and dependent on his investment income, or he may be a family man with too little time to risk speculation of his child's college tuition.

Bonds and preferred stock are called senior securities because they rank ahead of, or are senior to, other securities of the issuer. The prime difference between the two classes of senior securities is that a bondholder is a creditor of a corporation or government, and a preferred-stock holder is an owner of a company. Bonds, furthermore, are senior to preferred shares.

Thus, a preferred stock's interest in a corporation ranks after debts, but ahead of common stock. Preferred also has a claim on the corporation's earnings and assets—and sometimes its control—ahead of common stock. A company may issue preferred stock in series, such as preferred A, B and C or Class A, B and C, or first preferred, second preferred and so on. Dividends must be paid on the first in a series, such as Class A, before they can be paid on the second, and so on.

Because a preferred stock's dividend is usually at a set rate, it is often called a fixed-income security, as are bonds. Preferred dividends may be cumulative or noncumulative. Cumulative dividends not paid by a company are carried over from year to year and must ultimately be paid in full before dividends can be declared on common stock. A company has no obligation to make up dividends missed because of insufficient income if the preferred stock is noncumulative.

It should be emphasized that common-stock holders bear the greatest risk, but they usually have the greatest control. Further, they are entitled to the largest profits, if earned, since dividends are contingent on earnings. Variations in a company's earnings can cause the market value of its common stock to fluctuate widely.

A bond is an interest-bearing certificate of debt, usually for $1,000. It binds the borrower to pay interest regularly and repay the principal sum on a stated future date. A bond's term usually is five years or longer; if less, it usually is a note. Callable bonds may be redeemed by the issuer at a fixed "call" price before the maturity date.

If bonds are secured with a mortgage on corporate assets, they are called *mortgage bonds*. Others are *debentures,* which are unsecured and merely a promise to pay. *Government bonds* generally are, by definition, debentures, but they can represent the highest class of investment because their payment rests on the taxing power and general credit of a government.

The most highly rated of government bonds are those of the United States. These range from savings bonds—such as the Series E mentioned earlier, which are not traded, but may be redeemed at predetermined prices—to other Treasury Department issues that are marketable.

Other government bonds, such as those of state and local governments or their "authorities," are attractive because their interest generally is exempt from income taxes of the Federal Government and some states. These *"municipals,"* as they are called, may be backed by the full credit of the government, by specific tax income, or by revenues of toll roads, electric utilities or other special facilities built with the borrowed funds. Care must be taken in selection. A few toll-road bond issues, for example, have declined in credit standing and, consequently, in price.

Some companies enhance their bonds by making them convertible, allowing the holder to convert his bond into the company's common stock. This would lure an investor who is convinced of a concern's growth potential. Other companies may issue bonds with warrants, which would entitle the owner to buy common stock at specified prices. The purchases generally are made with cash, rather than through surrender of the bonds. Thus, if a company's common-stock price advances substantially, the bondholder may exercise his warrants at a profit, or sell them if they are detachable.

Because bonds can vary widely in quality, it is wise to check the ratings set by several independent statistical services, such as Moody's, Standard & Poor's, and Fitch. Standard & Poor's and Fitch rate bonds from AAA down to D. Moody's uses Aaa down to C. Bonds that merit one of the four top ratings are considered of investment grade. The speculative element, as far as the credit of the issuer is concerned, is almost nonexistent at the top rating and predominant at the seventh or beyond. A bond's rating could be provided by your stockbroker.

Generally speaking, the greater the speculative element, the greater the return on investment, based on the interest rate stipulated in the bond as originally issued, on the discount below "par," or a combination of these factors.

Bonds are quoted on the market as a percentage of face value. Thus, par, or 100 (per cent), represents the full face value of a bond, which usually is $1,000. If the market price falls below par, the investment yield—a percentage return on the investment to maturity—increases. If the market price rises above par, and the bond sells at a premium, the investment yield decreases. For example, a 15-year bond that paid 3 per cent interest on its $1,000 face value would actually yield 4 per cent to the buyer who had bought it for 88.80 (per cent), or $888. But it would return only 2.5 per cent a year to the man who had bought it at the premium price of 106.22 (per cent), or $1,062.20. In either case, if the investor held his bond to maturity, he would receive the $1,000 face amount.

High-grade bond prices are influenced almost exclusively by money market conditions. If the market tightens, and interest rates rise, high-grade bonds decline in price, increasing yield. If money becomes "cheap," and interest rates decline, the prime bonds rise in price because of the demand generated by investors seeking safe, relatively high-yield securities.

Second-grade bond issues are influenced in price not only by the money market, but also by the changing credit standing of the issuer and by general business conditions. This is true because the security of these obligations never is beyond reproach.

To compare various bond rates, if the best Treasury bond rate is 4.23 per cent, the average high-quality corporate bond might pay 4.5 per cent and tax-exempt bonds might return 3.26 per cent. Thus, the investor is rewarded for the slightly greater risk of corporates over Governments, but he must grant a concession, if he wants the tax advantage of the "municipal" bonds.

Banks and savings and loan associations at times offer higher interest rates than do senior securities, but bond advocates maintain that those institutions cannot guarantee their rates beyond the current year. A bond's rate is fixed until it is redeemed.

A Personal Investment Plan

Once a person has some investment capital, backed by the knowledge and experience he acquired during his investment internship, he is ready for the real thing. He may choose to invest all or part of his funds directly in securities, as opposed to an indirect investment vehicle such as a mutual fund. In that case, his ultimate aim, as his investment portfolio grows over the years, is diversification. That means reducing the risk by spreading investments over several promising industries and, perhaps, over several types of securities.

Most investors, particularly young people with long-term goals, concentrate on common stocks. Some common stocks, of course, are more speculative than others, and the investor would assume only the degree of risk commensurate with his total program and funds. On the other hand, a combination of high-quality common stocks, preferred shares and bonds may be ideal for persons dependent on investment income, or for those wishing maximum safety for funds earmarked for fast-approaching family or personal plans. The sophisticated investor might shift emphasis from stocks to bonds, when convinced that the stock market is on the verge of general decline. The procedure would be reversed in a rising stock market.

A person's investment training and his habit of reading general and financial newspapers and magazines will equip him to select industries that have the greatest growth potential, from the investor's view. Over the years many promising industries have run out of promise, as technological advances, social and economic changes and other factors made their products and services obsolete. Thus, carriage making was eclipsed by the automobile industry, railroads by airlines. Among today's front runners are the office equipment, electronics and aerospace industries.

Having selected an industry, the investor then must find its best companies. No matter how glorious an industry's total picture, there are unsuccessful companies—poor investments—in it. The investor would evaluate all material on the industry and its components that he can glean from his financial reading, his broker, the companies themselves and, perhaps, from an investment service. His choice of specific investments will come out of comparative studies of several companies' capitalization, earnings, rate of growth, announced plans, backlog of orders, research and development programs and other measurements, relating all of them to stock-price trends.

The task is less formidable than it sounds. Reports containing this factual information are readily available from a broker. His firm may have prepared them, or obtained them from an independent investment service, such as the Standard & Poor's Corporation, Moody's Investors Service or the Value Line Investment Survey.

In the course of his evaluation, the investor must not lose sight of general business conditions, Federal spending and tax policies, interest rates and other relevant economic factors that are subject to change.

Annual Reports: Value, how to read them

A prime source of information about a company is its annual report to stockholders. Yet, it often is cast aside by investors, usually because it appears too formidable, or because it was pedantically or confusingly prepared. The situation is changing, however, for the trend is toward more comprehensive and attractive reports. Corporate motivation extends beyond the simple desire to meet moral and legal obligations to stockholders by providing them with vital company information. Reports often are promotional pieces used to generate business, attract individual and institutional investors, or to stimulate merger talks with other companies.

Annual reports are more accurate and straightforward than they ever have been, but, taken collectively, they are far from perfect. Controversy continues to rage over the lack of conformity in accounting procedure and presentation, with the implication, in some instances, that accurate figures can be manipulated to present inaccurate corporate pictures. This is kept at a relative minimum because reports must pass muster with independent auditors, income-tax examiners, the Federal Securities and Exchange Commission and the stock exchange on which the company's shares may be listed. Aware of the difficulty that many stockholders have with annual reports, many brokerage houses, stock exchanges and industrial companies distribute explanatory literature.

Upon receiving a report, a stockholder first should turn to the "highlights" page near the front of the pamphlet. That immediately will show how much money was earned on what volume of business. A comparison with preceding years will indicate the company's performance record. A comparison with the performance of other companies or the particular industry as a whole will pinpoint the position of the investor's company. For example, if in the last year the industry showed a 10 per cent gain in sales, a company would be doing extraordinarily well with a sales increase of 20 per cent. However, only a 5 per cent rise should raise questions in the investor's mind.

The next stop in the annual report is management's statement to stockholders. The shareholder should look for and evaluate the officers' reports of trends and new developments, their explanations as to why the dividends are small or nonexistent, or why sales declined.

Turning to the report's "cash-flow" page, the stockholder would learn whether the company is putting its spare cash to work. The cash-flow page may have other titles, such as "source and application of funds." The source ordinarily would include with net income such items as depreciation and amortization, deferred income taxes, proceeds of additional borrowings or from the sale of securities, and possibly the value of capital (common) stock exchanged for business and assets. Under "application of funds" may be listed the cost of plant and equipment purchases, research and development, debt reduction, dividend payment and treasury-share purchases. This section may indicate, for example, why dividends are not being paid, though the company is doing extraordinarily well. It may be that large sums are being sunk into research and development or new productive facilities, which create products and services that foster company growth. If this be the case, the stockholder may conclude that the growth and potential income warrant the sacrifice of current cash dividends.

Among other major elements of an annual report are the balance sheet and the income statement. The balance sheet—the product of double-entry bookkeeping—represents a company's financial picture on a given day, the last day of the period being reported. On the left side are listed all assets, and on the right all liabilities and stockholders' equity, or the amount for which the company is accountable to them. Both sides must be in balance, thus the name.

A 1964 booklet of Merrill Lynch, Pierce, Fenner & Smith on "How to Read a Financial Report," puts it another way: "Assume that the corporation would go out of business as of the date of the balance sheet. Assume also [what is probably never so] that the assets when sold bring dollar for dollar the amounts in the balance sheet." Then the amount remaining for the stockholders would be total assets less liabilities.

As to footnotes in annual reports, Merrill Lynch says: "Most people do not like to read footnotes, because they may be complicated and they are almost always printed in small, hard-to-read type. Nevertheless, it is well worth the effort, for a careful reading of the footnotes in conjunction with the statements gives greater meaning to the financial story of a corporation." This raises the question: Why can't footnotes be put into simpler language and larger type?

A company's net worth, its assets less its liabilities, also gives some indication as to how much book equity remains for its stockholders. Its relative size in the industry would be indicated by its total assets, the number of people it employs and its total sales or revenues.

The income statement, also referred to as the "operating statement" or "profit and loss statement," shows which income during the period increased the surplus (stockholders' earned equity in the company) and which expenses reduced it. The final figure is the amount of net profit added to surplus, or the amount of net loss subtracted from it.

Choosing a Broker

Once a man decides to invest in stocks, he faces the next difficult question: How do I choose a broker? Many sage advisers advance the cliché that one should choose his broker as carefully as he chooses his doctor. Of course, both the physician and the broker must be men of integrity, knowledge, dependability and other qualities, but that is where the parallel ends. Every business or professional man with whom one deals obviously should have such qualities, from the automobile mechanic to the accountant.

When a physician diagnoses a medical condition and prescribes treatment, his patient usually does not declare that he is wrong and proceed to prescribe his own treatment. Instead, if he becomes uncertain of the doctor's judgment, or if he simply wants confirmation, he consults another physician. The point is that the advice almost always must stem from the physician, whose patients rarely can lay valid claim to extensive knowledge in his highly technical areas of training and experience. This is not always true in the investment field. Medicine may not be an exact science, but investment is not even an art. Rather, it is a analytical business, one in which the customer can and should have sufficient knowledge to make his own decisions, based on the information and advice obtained from—and through—his broker, and from other sources.

Of course, there is the affluent investor, one with perhaps $100,000 or more of investment capital, who might engage an investment counselor, who would manage his portfolio, possibly making all buy-sell decisions without consulting him. But, even here, the client's investment knowledge would serve as a check on his counselor's effectiveness.

Other investors, large or small, who choose to deposit all or part of their investment money with a mutual fund, turn over investment decisions to the manager of that investment pool. Here again, the investor's knowledge guides him in the selection of a fund whose management's performance seems best for his needs, and in the continuous evaluation of that performance.

The problem is different for the individual seeking to build and maintain his own securities portfolio. This is reflected in an observation made by Keith Funston, president of the New York Stock Exchange. "There is no substitute," he asserted, "for studying the merits of a particular issue and then deciding, with the help of a reputable broker, whether the stock meets one's personal needs."

This observation highlights two major points that have been stressed in previous investment discussions in this chapter: First, to study competently the merits of a stock, one must have acquired a sound basic investment knowledge. Second, to be able to determine whether a particular stock meets one's personal needs, the investor already must have clearly established his investment objectives. If his goal is growth, the attributes of a highly attractive income-producing stock without such a characteristic should not appeal to him. If he cannot afford to absorb the inherently greater risk of a highly speculative stock, he must not allow himself to be baited into buying one, no matter how appealing it is made to appear.

A guiding rule for the small investor is that he should be an investor and not a trader whose many transactions demand much time, investment knowledge and acumen, and risk capital. This does not mean that the small investor should make a purchase and then forget it; no stock merits such faithful inattention. Rather, he should invest for the long term, and subject his securities to regular review.

The question remains as to how a person should choose a broker. Unfortunately, there are no hard and fast rules, because one is dealing with an intangible business of ideas and analysis that is only as good as its people. Only extreme cases of incompetence or malfeasance become public knowledge. Further, most brokers, like doctors, but unlike many manufacturers, would be violating their code of ethics to say anything negative about a competitor. Nonetheless, there are some general guidelines.

The New York Stock Exchange urges that investors seek a firm that belongs to the exchange, and this is good advice up to a point. Member firms must abide by the exchange's rules and regulations, which, in some areas, are more stringent than those of the Securities and Exchange Commission. But logic and the law of averages tell us that not every one of the 667 member houses could qualify as the ideal broker for every investor.

Many nonmember firms also are highly reputable. In considering one, however, it would be wise to ascertain whether it is a member of the National Association of Securities Dealers. Membership in that quasi-official self-regulatory body requires, in essence, filing of statements of financial condition and conformity with regulations on trading procedure and commission rates.

A brokerage house might be recommended by a highly respected friend or business associate; a person who got his first taste of direct investment through an investment club might decide that the broker serving the club's needs can serve his own equally as well.

However the investor comes by his list of prospective brokerage houses, he should visit them personally, becoming acquainted with the company and the particular registered representative (also known as an account man or customer's man) with whom he would be dealing. To some investors, it is important that they like and get on well with their brokers. To others, the only concern is with a man's competence.

Questions must be asked about the adequacy of the brokerage house's research department, its ability to provide reports on companies from independent financial reporting organizations.

What other services are provided? They may include the safekeeping of customers' securities in the brokerage house's vault, and the forwarding of dividends on that stock to the customer, sometimes spreading quarterly dividend checks over monthly intervals. Are there charges for these services?

Knowledge and "comparison shopping" are the tools with which the investor can evaluate and select his broker. Once he has a broker to whom he will confide his needs, objectives and pertinent financial information, his experience will tell him whether his decision was sound.

One Wall Street man recommended that the average investor make investment a two-step operation. "After having waited so many years within which to accumulate sufficient savings to make his long-term investment," he said, "the small investor should take sufficient time to appraise his needs and select a proper vehicle.

"That should not be a 10-minute deal with the first broker he talks to. He first should check with at least two brokers, supplementing their information with data from other sources, and then make his own investment decision, based on an evaluation of all material."

Oscar Lasdon, a New York financial consultant and associate editor of *The Bankers Magazine,* suggested: "It would be desirable if the broker himself had some research training or experience, if your problems are more sophisticated." On the other hand, the former New York Stock Exchange member noted: "If you don't need the advice, you might just as conveniently go to your local bank which would execute your orders for you, usually through a member firm."

Big customers get better service from brokers than do smaller investors who buy only a few shares at a time. But that does not mean that the small investor is left in the cold; he can demand service. Brokers want him, as evidenced by their extensive advertising, because he represents an overwhelming majority of the nation's 20 million investors. The big ones are relatively scarce.

To the investor who wants to rely completely on his broker and therefore is looking for a wizard with all the attributes, including a perfect batting average, one must put the question: Why should such a marvel be a broker?

Investment Expenses: Sales commissions

Sales commissions are the primary extra expense for any securities purchase or sale, and those set by the New York Stock Exchange are among the lowest for the transfer of any property, averaging about 1 per cent. Commissions on the purchase or sale of 100 shares (a round lot) would depend on the value of the investment, as follows:

Less than $100—commission is negotiated
$100 to $399.99—2 per cent plus $3
$400 to $2,399.99—1 per cent plus $7
$2,400 to $4,999.99—one-half of 1 per cent plus $19
$5,000 or more—one-tenth of 1 per cent plus $39.

On transactions of $100 or more, the minimum commission may not be less than $6, and need not exceed $1.50 a share or $75 per round-lot or odd-lot (less-than-100-share) transaction.

When buying or selling odd lots, the regular commissions generally prevail. In addition, the odd-lot broker gets a price differential of

12½ cents a share for stock selling at less than $40 a share and 25 cents a share for stock selling at $40 or more. The investor pays this much more per share when he buys, and receives this much less when he sells.

Mutual Funds: Value of diversification, choice of fund, voluntary accumulation and contractual plans, withdrawal plans, reinvestment privileges, operating costs

Mutual funds could be the answer for the man seeking professional management and immediate diversification for all or part of his long-term investment capital, however much or little it may be.

When a person buys shares in a mutual fund, his money becomes part of an investment pool, which is managed by financial experts. He achieves immediate diversification in that, in effect, he owns a proportionate part, no matter how small, of each stock or bond in the pool, be there 10 holdings or 500.

A mutual fund also is known as an open-end investment company, because it continuously issues new fund shares to new investors. It "buys back" fund shares of investors wishing to redeem them. Redemption is usually at net asset value per share, which is arrived at daily by dividing the number of fund shares outstanding into the market value of the securities in the investment pool (total net assets).

On buying fund shares, the investor generally will pay not only the net asset value per share, but also a commission charge. That charge generally is an 8.5 per cent deduction from the total purchase price, putting the true rate at about 9.2 per cent of the actual amount invested.

Mutual funds are best as long-term investments, because their performances with few exceptions are not dynamic except in the long view. First, the investor must recoup the commission charges before he can start counting gains. Second, the very investment diversification that reduces the risk of major loss also dampens the potential for gain, for in a general market rise or decline, not all the stocks in the fund will rise or decline accordingly. The argument in favor of mutual funds is that most investors have neither the time nor the ability to get better investment results on their own.

Once a person decides to invest in a fund, he may be stymied by the deceptively simple question: Which one? Equally simple-sounding is the answer: The one that best meets your investment requirements and holds the greatest promise of helping you to achieve your financial goals.

But there are more than 250 mutual funds. While these investment pools usually state their investment objectives—growth, income, safety or a combination of these—their actual results may vary widely from fund to fund, even within the same category.

Thus, the task of choosing a fund may appear difficult, but it is hardly insurmountable. A few inquiries and a little research will achieve an answer, provided the investigator does not expect to find the absolutely perfect, foolproof fund. That would require clairvoyance, for the future performance of most securities investments cannot be assured, however superior their past performances may have been. An investor should not let himself be cajoled or coerced into a decision by an agressive high-pressure salesman of the type that has made the industry the object of not unfounded criticism and of Federal study.

Whatever the investor's goals, there are funds to match them. While mutual funds issue financial statements at least twice a year and offer sales literature, it would be far simpler for the investor to compile a list of eligible funds with the aid of a reputable securities broker or mutual fund dealer, or by consulting reference works available in most libraries and brokers' offices.

Among those works is *Investment Companies,* a statistically dependable book published annually by Arthur Wiesenberger & Co., a New York Stock Exchange member firm. Another is *Investment Trusts and Funds from the Investor's Point of View,* published annually by the American Institute for Economic Research in Great Barrington, Massachusetts. These and other reference materials also will be useful in completing the next two steps: eliminating funds that do not meet personal requirements and standards, and rating the remainder by their past performances.

A primary personal requirement may be for a fund that offers accumulation plans if it is decided to buy shares on a systematic basis, perhaps monthly or quarterly, rather than in a single large purchase. Most funds offer *voluntary accumulation plans* that allow the purchaser to set his own pace. There often is a $25 or $50 minimum for each investment, and sometimes an annual minimum of $300 or $500. The minimum initial investment sometimes is set at $300 to $500 as well.

Some investors favor the *contractual plan,* under which they agree to invest a fixed sum (as little as $20) regularly, usually monthly, over a number of years, usually 10. It is an enforced savings plan in that a major part of the total 10-year sales charge or "load" is deducted in the first year. Thus, only about half the first year's payments are actually invested, the rest going to the "front-end load." This type of program must be avoided by a person unsure of his ability to complete it, because the penalty—loss of the prepaid sales charges—can be high.

In the 1963 report of a special study for the Securities and Exchange Commission of the nation's securities markets, it was charged that the front-end load was excessive and that high-pressure selling caused many unqualified persons to buy contractual plans.

Otherwise, sales charges should not necessarily be a prime determinant. While most funds include an 8½-cent sales charge in every dollar an investor pays, there are some 40 so-called "no-load" funds sold directly to the public by their manager-distributors with little or no sales charge. If a person can select a no-load fund that suits his needs and also is a good performer, he'd be wise to buy it. But he'd be far less wise if he passed up an even better performing, more promising fund just because it had a sales charge.

Among other factors to be measured in qualifying a fund are the following:

Life insurance: Low-cost protection combined with systematic investment provides a practical means of assuring the achievement of a financial goal for the benefit of one's family in the event of death.

Withdrawal plans: An investor may want a fund that provides regular withdrawal options that he may exercise for some special purpose or in retirement.

Reinvestment privileges: The relative ease and cost of reinvesting dividends and capital-gain distributions may be important to an investor unconcerned with current income.

Operating cost: The fund's annual overhead and expenses, as a percentage of its total net assets (the investors' pooled funds) should be compared with that of other funds.

As a final step, the investor should compare the performance record of the funds remaining on his list, after having eliminated those that did not meet one or more of the requirements he considers important.

To decide which fund's management was most expert in accomplishing its stated objectives, the investor must compare all the remaining funds' records—as far back as possible—of share-value fluctuations, dividend payments and capital-gain distributions (profits realized by the fund from sales of securities in its portfolio). If growth was a fund's objective, the investor must determine whether it surpassed others in the growth group in share-value advances and in total capital-gain distributions. If current income was the objective, the investor must ask whether the fund provided a consistently high percentage of dividend income each year in relation to its share value at the time. Did it bolster income with capital gains obtained from premature sales of securities, thereby depressing share values? If stability was the stated goal, the investor should learn whether the fund's share price held up, on a comparative basis, when the market declined in 1957, 1962 and 1966.

Little by little, the investor's list will be reduced to just a few qualifying funds. A final decision may be made, based on more current information available from the broker or mutual fund representative. Some experts recommend that an investor with sufficient capital spread it among several of the best-performing funds—the survivors of his grueling test.

Closed-end Investment Companies

Sometimes confused with mutual funds is the closed-end investment company. It, too, operates an investment pool, but differs from a mutual fund in that it neither continuously offers additional new shares nor buys back shares that owners wish to redeem. Instead, the organizers of a closed-end investment company make an initial offering of stock to the public, as does any other business or industrial corporation. The money received from that initial sale, and sometimes occasional subsequent sales, makes up the investment pool, the funds used to compile a portfolio of securities of other corporations.

After the initial sale, the shares in a closed-end are traded on the open market, as are the securities of business and industrial companies. Some closed-end funds are listed on exchanges. The Lehman

Corporation and the Tri-Continental Corporation, for example, are listed on the New York Stock Exchange.

The market value of a closed-end fund's stock may be above or below the value of the underlying securities in its pool. An undervalued stock can look attractive in terms of income from the more valuable securities it represents, provided its discount price is not attributable to poor management or some other detracting reason.

Investment Timing: Dollar-cost averaging, market fluctuation, review of investments

Deciding when to buy or sell securities always is a problem to most investors, including professionals. For most typical investors, evaluation of a stock's fundamental values and the market's general condition is adequate. Then there are the professional and highly sophisticated nonprofessional investors who indulge in charting and other technical market analysis procedures that are beyond the ken of some fairly skilled investors, let alone the average family man with a few dollars to spare.

But there is one somewhat mechanical procedure that most people can put to use, particularly those who can invest only small sums periodically. That is *dollar-cost averaging,* which usually is much discussed whenever the market is rising sharply or declining rapidly. With the stock market climbing, many investors have been hearing much about dollar-cost averaging, just as they did when the market plummeted in 1962. Some investors may have the impression that it is a magic formula that takes the worry out of investment. It is not. Rather, it is a stock-purchase plan that takes some of the worry out of investment timing. Its success or failure rests with the investor's choice of a security, be it a particular corporation's stock or shares in a mutual fund.

By definition, dollar-cost averaging is a systematic method of building a securities portfolio by investing fixed amounts in particular stocks at regular intervals, perhaps monthly, quarterly or even annually. The result is that the average cost per share generally will be lower than the average of the market prices during the investment period, because more shares have been bought with the fixed sum when the market price per share was down.

To illustrate, a person may decide to invest $120, plus commissions, quarterly in a common stock that, after investigation, he is convinced has long-term growth potential. If the share prices on five consecutive purchase dates were $6, $2, $4, $8 and $10, his $120 would have bought 20, 60, 30, 15 and then 12 shares, or a total of 137 shares in the five quarters. The average market price for the period was $6, but his average cost (the $600 total investment divided by the 137 shares held) was only $4.38. With the last market price $10 a share, his total investment would be worth $1,370, for a capital gain of $770, or $5.62 a share.

There are several major points that should be noted from this illustration. One is that the investor must have the emotional stability and the confidence in his investment choice to make his purchases on schedule, even in a market slump. It is in periods of price decline that he brings his average per-share price down most sharply, because he gets so many more shares for his money. However, the investor's concern with dollar-cost averaging must not be so great that he forgets to review his investments periodically. If a stock soars to fantastic price levels, he must study the wisdom of further purchase. Conversely, if the price of his chosen stock had been steadily deteriorating, he must determine whether the long-term outlook for the issue remains promising, or whether further investment would be "throwing good money after bad." This underscores a truism: Dollar-cost averaging is as good as the latest market price. Whatever an investor's average share cost, his prime concern should be with what his total investment will be worth when he needs the cash.

If, in the illustration, the sequence of market prices in the five quarters had been $10, $8, $6, $4 and $2, the average market price in the period would have remained at $6, and the average per-share cost would have been the same $4.38. But the market value of the 137 shares acquired would have been only $274, at $2 a share, for a capital loss of $326 (based on the $600 total investment in the five quarters), or $2.38 a share. It appears clear that, in such a situation of consistent price erosion, the investor should have re-examined his choice of security. If, upon review, he remained convinced that the stock's market price would recover in a reasonable period of time, he would decide to continue buying under his dollar-cost averaging program. If not, he could sell, putting the salvaged cash into a stock with greater potential. As a second alternative, he might stop buying but hold the shares he had thus far accumulated, in the perhaps justified hope that the market price would improve in time.

There are stocks that have extremely promising long-term potential growth, but their market prices may fluctuate widely. This, too, can cause a problem, for the price may be down at the very time that the investor planned to sell and use the cash for a special purpose. It is for this reason that the person with established financial-planning goals must be cautious. While such a long-term systematic investor may find a useful tool in dollar-cost averaging, he must carefully survey his marketing position well before the day that his personal plans mature.

When a child is ready for college, a parent must raise the cash, whatever the market value of the securities earmarked for that purpose. When a couple are physically and emotionally ready for retirement, they don't want to discover suddenly that, because of investment negligence, they are not economically ready.

Periodic reviews of investments would minimize such problems. If, within a few years of a personal goal, be it education, home ownership or retirement, the inherent risk of certain stocks appears too great, the investor could preserve his profits by selling. Depending on general market conditions and the amount of time he has left to achieve his goal, he may decide to invest in especially conservative "blue chip" stocks, high-yield preferred shares, corporate or Federal bonds or tax-exempt state and local government bonds. If time is short, or no other investments appear attractive, he may put the money into a high-interest savings account.

Buying Stocks on the Installment Plan

The advantages of dollar-cost averaging are stressed by New York Stock Exchange member firms, primarily Merrill Lynch, Pierce, Fenner & Smith, who promote the Monthly Investment Plan. Under the plan, a person may accumulate shares in a listed stock by investing as little as $40 quarterly or as much as $1,000 monthly. The commission charges range from 6 per cent for payments under $100 to 1.5 per cent on $1,000, plus the price differential on odd-lot (less-than-100-share) purchases, which most of them are. Several exchange-member firms allow a lump-sum investor in a given stock to become an M.I.P. member, so that he may elect automatic reinvestment of his dividends. Some employers allow employes to invest by payroll deduction in M.I.P. plans.

Buying Stocks on Credit

Borrowing part of the purchase price of securities is known as buying "on margin." Use of credit allows larger purchases, thereby increasing the profit potential. But it also increases the risk of loss. Thus, the margin device should be restricted to the sophisticated investor, that is, the trader or speculator with the knowledge, money and temperament to assume large risks. A margin investor must maintain a minimum ownership interest, or margin, in his stocks. When that equity falls below the minimum, he gets a "margin call," to which he must respond with additional cash. If he cannot, his broker sells enough of his securities to raise it.

Since 1934, the Federal Reserve Board has been empowered to set the margin rate, the percentage of the stock purchase price the investor must pay in cash. Depending on the Board's concern with credit expansion, the trend of securities prices and the volume of margin buying, the rate has ranged from 40 to 100 per cent. Rate increases do not affect money invested at the lower rate, which may be retained on reinvestment of that money, provided certain procedures are followed. The margin rate was cut from 70 to 50 per cent on July 10, 1962, in an effort to augment the market's recovery after the May debacle. It recovered so well that the board restored the 70 percent rate on November 6, 1963.

Once the stock is bought the exchange's and brokers' rules pertaining to maintenance of a broker's account take over. The Federal Board, in general, restricts its regulation to initial, or point-of-purchase, margin requirements, because its chief objective is to limit the volume of credit used for speculation. While some brokers have more stringent rules, the exchange requires that a broker issue a margin call to a customer when the amount of money the customer has left in his margin stocks is less than 25 per cent of the stocks' current value.

The Investors' Protectors: S.E.C., Federal Reserve Board, New York Stock Exchange, National Association of Securities Dealers

Securities dealings are closely regulated by the Federal Government and, to a lesser extent, by various state governments. Federal control is primarily through the Securities and Exchange Commission, which regulates the public sale of securities and the operation of the exchanges and over-the-counter markets. The Federal Reserve Board regulates the use of credit by brokers and, as has been noted, by investors. In addition, there is sometimes stringent self-regulation within the industry. The exchanges, particularly the New York Stock Exchange, the world's largest, set down principles and procedures that must be adhered to by members and member firms. The National Association of Securities Dealers, a quasi-official organization of over-the-counter, or nonexchange, securities dealers and brokers, also sets guidelines for its members. These organizations hold the threat of suspension or expulsion, which can destroy a man's business.

11

TAXATION, A REDUCIBLE FACT OF LIFE

Those inevitable tax bills can be reduced, at least to the minimum required by law. That may not sound like too great a accomplishment, but each year more than a million of the nearly 70 million individuals who file Federal income tax returns overpay on the basis of information included in their returns. In addition, there are millions of others who overpay simply because they do not take advantage of all the tax saving opportunities available to them under the law.

The only sure way to avoid costly mistakes or oversights is to acquire some knowledge about taxes. Even taxpayers who have their returns prepared by professionals should take time to familiarize themselves with tax procedures. This will enable them to keep proper records, present their cases intelligently to their advisers and evaluate the advice they receive. The do-it-yourself taxpayer—and most people are—can get answers to his questions from local Internal Revenue Service and state tax offices. Of course, Government personnel do not actually complete returns for individuals, but they can be quite helpful.

Becoming familiar with tax rules does not mean that a person is expected to become an accountant or tax lawyer overnight. That is neither possible nor necessary. If such expertise is required for his particular tax situation, he had better turn to a professional. However, the average taxpayer can glean enough tax knowledge from available materials to complete his return competently. It is especially important that he carefully review the rules each year, lest he miss recent regulatory changes.

While the instruction book that comes with the tax return will answer most questions, other more comprehensive Government publications are available. Among them are: "Your Federal Income Tax" and "Tax Guide for Small Business," which may be bought for 50 cents each at local tax offices. In addition, a wealth of tax material is distributed free by many companies, or sold by private publishers.

Filing a Tax Return

Every person under age 65 must file a Federal income tax return, if he had a gross income of $600 or more in the taxable year. Persons who are 65 or older on January 1 of the year after the tax year must file a return only if gross income was $1,200 or more, because they are allowed two $600 exemptions, rather than one, because of age. A person who earned less than those minimums, but who had taxes withheld from income, must file a return to obtain a refund. As part of the Treasury's massive computer program, each taxpayer has a tax identification number, which is the same as his Social Security number, if he has one. If not, it is the tax identification number assigned to him by the Internal Revenue Service. A taxpayer who needs an account number may apply for one on Form SS-5 or Form 3227.

Tax Withholding and Estimates

Most persons' taxes are paid during the year by being withheld from income. However, if a person earns income not subject to withholding, or if withholding is not sufficient to cover most of his tax liability, he may be required to file a Declaration of Estimated Tax Form 1040 ES.

In general, an estimate must be filed by an individual earning more than $5,000, or by a head of household, a widow(er), or a married couple earning more than $10,000 a year, or by anyone expecting to have more than $200 of additional income that will not be subject to withholding. In any case, an estimate is not required, if the estimated tax—in essence, the amount in excess of what is expected to be withheld from earnings—is less than $40. A 6 per cent penalty may be imposed on taxpayers who underestimate their taxes, or who fail to file a required estimate form. The rationale behind the penalty is that the delinquent estimated-income taxpayer has use of tax funds he had not paid until the April 15 date, while the average wage earner had his income tax deducted regularly from his salary.

The taxpayer who files an actual estimate of income may be penalized for underestimating, unless he amends his estimate quarterly to keep it accurate. However, the taxpayer who files a "protective estimate" based on the preceding year's income or tax would escape any risk of penalty, even if he greatly understated his actual tax liability for the current year.

The estimated tax, less the amount expected to be withheld, may be paid in equal installments on April 15, June 15, September 15 and January 15.

Taxable Income

Unless specifically exempt, all income is taxable. Examples of exempt income are qualified scholarship and fellowship grants up to certain limits, most payments and benefits to veterans and their families, unemployment and workmen's compensation, Social Security and Railroad Retirement Act benefits, gifts, inheritances and bequests, interest on state and local government bonds and most insurance proceeds.

Among the income reports that arrive shortly after the end of the tax year and that should be checked are the W-2 forms from employers and the information returns (Form 1099) from organizations that have paid $10 or more in interest or dividends, or $600 or more in royalties, pensions, annuities or other income not covered by withholding. Among these organizations may be banks, credit unions, stockholder-owned companies and life insurance companies paying interest on a policyholder's accumulated dividends. Accuracy is essential; necessary corrections should be formally requested, because copies of these forms, which carry the taxpayer's identification number, automatically go to the Government.

All taxable income should be included in the return, if received or credited to an account within the tax year, and the recipient operates on a cash basis, as do most taxpayers. For example, bank interest not entered in a passbook, but credited to the account, must be included. However, cash dividends on stocks, declared in the tax year but received in the next year, would be included in that next year's income.

Income, in addition to wages, interest and dividends, also would include profits (or losses) from the sale of securities or other property and rental fees received on real estate. In addition, there may be income from taxable pensions and annuities, trusts, estates or from a supplemental business, such as that of a free-lance writer, artist, handyman or hobbyist-turned-commercial.

Social Security Overpayment

If a person worked for two or more employers during the tax year, he well may have overpaid his Federal Social Security taxes, which are listed on the W-2 form under the heading, "F.I.C.A. Employe Tax Withheld." Any excess over the maximum required payment during the tax year can be claimed as a credit against income taxes. If one employer withheld more than the maximum, he must pay the difference to the worker himself.

Basic Tax Forms

A person may use the "short" card form 1040A, if his income was less than $10,000, and if all but $200 of it was reported on his W-2 form, and if he prefers to take a standard deduction rather than to itemize all deductions. All other persons must use the "long" Form 1040.

A person who has income other than salary and wages must use one of the following supplemental forms:

- Schedule B for such income as from dividends, interest, rents, royalties, taxable pensions and annuities, partnerships, trusts and estates;
- Schedule C for income from a personally owned business;
- Schedule D for income from the sale or exchange of property;
- Schedule F for income from farming;
- Schedule G for income averaging.

Separate or Joint Returns

For tax purposes, a couple is married for the whole year even if they were wed on the last day, and a couple is not married for the whole year even if they were divorced on the last day. If either spouse dies before the close of the year, the surviving spouse is considered, for tax purposes, to have been married for the entire year. If the survivor did not remarry within the tax year, a joint return usually may be filed for the survivor and the deceased.

A married couple may file a joint return, even though one spouse had no income. The joint return involves the split-income tax computation method, which usually results in a smaller tax bill than if husband and wife file separate returns. Under the split-income method, the couple pays twice the tax computed on half their net taxable income, thus usually putting them into a lower tax bracket. However, because it sometimes is advantageous for a couple to file separate returns, this alternate to joint filing should not be ignored. For example, suppose a husband and wife have about equal incomes, but one had unusually large medical bills in the tax year. They need not file jointly to have their combined income treated as though it were earned half-and-half. Therefore, the large medical deduction of one spouse is more useful in offsetting her income. In dollars, the medical deduction reducing 3 per cent of the joint income is twice the 3 per cent of half the income reported separately. In filing separately, both partners either must itemize deductions or take one of the standard deductions.

Head of Household Benefits

If a person is single, divorced, widowed or legally separated and maintains certain dependents in his household, he may qualify for "head of household" benefits. By using the Head of Household tax-rate table, he will enjoy about half the tax benefit obtained by a couple filing a joint return. To be eligible, a taxpayer must meet the following requirements:

—He must be unmarried on the last day of the tax year.

—He must furnish more than half the cost of maintaining a household for at least one relative.

—If the relatives are his parents, they need not live in his home to qualify, but he must be able to claim them as dependents, and must maintain their household.

—If the relative is his child or grandchild, the child must live in the taxpayer's household. It is not necessary that the child qualify as a dependent unless he is married. The child must live with the taxpayer for the entire year, except for temporary absences.

—Any other person will qualify the taxpayer as head of household provided the person lives with him during the entire year and qualifies as a dependent.

Exemptions

A single person may claim a personal exemption of $600 and an additional exemption of $600 if he was 65 by January 1 of the year following the tax year. He may claim still another $600 exemption if he is blind. A married taxpayer may claim a personal exemption of $600 for himself, his spouse and any dependents. The additional exemptions for age or blindness may be claimed for himself and his spouse, if applicable, but not for a dependent.

In general, apart from the taxpayer's own primary exemption, his status at the end of the year controls whether additional exemptions may be claimed. For example, if he marries on December 31, he is entitled to a $600 exemption for his spouse. (Husband and wife filing jointly each is regarded as a taxpayer and therefore is entitled to the personal exemption.) A full $600 exemption may be claimed for a child born on December 31. An exemption also may be taken for a dependent who dies during the tax year.

A parent may claim a dependency exemption for a child regardless of the amount of income the child may have, if the child is less than 19 years old at the end of the tax year or is a full-time student and, in either case, received more than half his support from his parent. Moreover, the child also is entitled to a $600 personal exemption on his own return.

Generally, a dependency exemption may be claimed only if the taxpayer contributes more than half the support of the dependent. An exception, however, is the case in which two or more persons jointly contribute more than half the support of an individual. Assuming none of the contributors pays more than half, one of them may claim an exemption, if he furnishes more than 10 per cent of the support. The other contributors cannot claim a dependency exemption and each must file Form 2120 with his return, stating that he will not do so.

A taxpayer may claim a dependency exemption for a person living in his household for the entire year, even if he is not related to the taxpayer. However, the individual may not have adjusted gross income of $600 or more for the year, and the taxpayer must have furnished more than half his support.

A qualified relative may be listed as a dependent, even though the relative does not live with the taxpayer or is not a member of his household. The relative, however, must be his child (adopted or natural), grandchild, great-grandchild, stepchild, brother, sister, half-brother, half-sister, stepbrother, stepsister, stepfather, stepmother, uncle, aunt, niece, nephew, parent-in-law, child-in-law, brother-in-law or sister-in-law.

A taxpayer who is divorced or legally separated at the end of the year may not claim an exemption for his spouse, even though he may contribute all of her support. However, divorce does not terminate relationships established by marriage. Thus, a taxpayer may claim a dependency exemption for his mother-in-law, even after a divorce, if he claimed the exemption before and no other changes have occurred.

Sick Pay: Taxable and nontaxable

Contrary to widespread belief, an employe who receives as sick pay more than 75 per cent of his regular weekly salary while absent from work cannot exclude any of that sick pay during the first 30 days' absence, whether hospitalized or not. An employe who receives as sick pay 75 per cent or less of his regular salary while absent from work can exclude his sick pay or $75 a week, whichever is less. That exclusion is allowed from the first day of absence, if the taxpayer is hospitalized for at least one day during his total absence. If not hospitalized, his exclusion would begin with the eighth calendar day of his absence. After the first 30 days of sick leave, an employe may exclude up to $100 a week of his regular salary. Sick pay received in excess of the $75 or $100 ceilings is fully taxable.

Dividend Income: Taxable dividends, return-of-capital distributions, capital-gains dividends, tax-free distributions

Ordinary dividends, sometimes called "taxable dividends," are the most common type of corporate distribution. Others are return-of-capital distributions, capital-gains dividends and tax-free distributions.

The ordinary or *taxable dividend* is paid out of corporate profits and included in the taxpayer's return as ordinary income. Unless otherwise indicated by the paying corporation, cash dividends received on stock generally can be assumed to be ordinary. When paid by qualifying corporations, the initial $100 in dividends received during the tax year by an individual may be excluded from his gross income. Whether filing joint or separate returns, husband and wife are each entitled to the $100 exclusion, provided both received dividend income.

One spouse may not use any of the other's unused portion of the $100 exclusion. When a couple hold stock as joint tenants with equal rights of survivorship, half of the dividends received on each stock, together with other dividends, may be excluded by each spouse up to $100. Thus, if a husband received $120 in 1965 on stocks held in his name, and his wife received $80 on stocks in her name, he could take the full $100 exclusion, but his wife could take only $80. The wife may not use the $20 her husband was unable to exclude. However, if all their stock had been jointly held, all of the $200 in dividends could have been excluded from taxable income, because each could have claimed half the total, or $100.

The $100 exclusion applies only to dividends paid by qualifying corporations, which are taxable domestic companies. Among those that do not qualify are foreign companies, exempt farmers' cooperatives, real estate investment trusts, and corporations doing business in United States possessions, if 80 percent or more of their income is derived from those possessions and 50 per cent or more from the active conduct of business there.

Dividends paid on insurance policies, including veterans, or G.I., insurance policies, are not taxable, because they are not dividends. Actually, they are a partial return of premiums that were paid.

Return-of-capital distributions are not paid out of corporate profits, and are not listed on the investor's tax return as income. They are a return of his investment, and, as such, reduce the cost of his stock. Thus, upon the sale of the security, his capital gain is increased or his capital loss reduced in comparison to what it would have been had the distribution not been made. If the investor's total cost is recovered through these return-of-capital distributions, all such distributions in excess of that cost are taxed at the capital-gain rate.

Capital-gains dividends are paid or allocated to stockholders' accounts by regulated investment companies (closed-end investment companies and mutual funds) and by real estate investment trusts. The total distributions paid or allocated by a regulated closed-end investment company or mutual fund during the year might include ordinary dividends, return of capital distributions and capital-gain dividends. For tax purposes, the organization normally will designate how the total should be apportioned. All investment-company distributions must be reported, whether taken in cash or left with the fund for reinvestment.

Tax-free distributions usually are in the form of additional stock or rights to buy stock in the corporation, and generally are not reported on the investor's tax return. They must be reported, if the investor had the option to take cash or other property in lieu of the stock or rights, or if such stock or rights were issued to discharge preferred-stock dividends for the tax year or the preceding year.

The Federal income tax on dividends of some corporations also is eliminated or substantially reduced as a result of accelerated depreciation and amortization deductions, depletion reserves or loss carry-overs. The paying corporation usually advises the stockholder as to tax treatment. Some companies can treat depreciation and accelerated amortization charges differently for tax purposes than for regular corporate accounting purposes. Thus, dividends can be paid on earnings that do not exist for tax purposes.

Companies engaged in oil drilling, metal and coal mining, natural gas and other extractive industries may pay part of their dividends out of the depletion reserves, in which event, the dividend payments are tax-free to the investor to that extent.

A corporation may have net operating losses that are carried over from previous years. These act to reduce current-year earnings. In addition, a company may sell assets that, when sold, have a market value much below original cost. These losses can offset realized capital gains as well as current income. As a consequence, dividends are distributed free of Federal income tax and are considered as a return of capital.

Dividends on stocks that are sold would be claimed as income by the buyer, if they were declared and paid after the sale, or if he became the holder of record in time to receive them. The seller would claim them as income, if they were declared before he sold, but received by him after the sale.

Capital Gains and Losses

Any net loss in excess of gains, as in securities transactions, may be applied against other income up to $1,000. Any remaining loss may be carried into as many subsequent tax years as necessary to exhaust it. The losses carried over will be treated as long term or short term, depending upon their origin. Long-term capital gains or losses are those realized on property held for more than six months, while short-term gains or losses are on property held for six months or less.

The distinction is important, because the tax rate on short-term gains is the same as for regular income, while the tax rate on long-term gains is half the taxpayer's highest tax rate, but no more than 25 per cent.

Basically, here is how the offset works in the initial and carry-over years. A taxpayer having long-term or short-term capital losses, or both, first would offset them against the kinds of gains to which they apply: long against long, short against short. If an excess of either type of loss remains, he would offset it against any other gain he might have, short or long. If an excess of loss still remains, he may offset up to $1,000 of it against regular income. Any excess beyond that would be carried into subsequent years. A taxpayer who has both short-term and long-term losses in a taxable year, but no realized capital gains, first must apply the short-term losses against regular income.

Income Averaging: Regular and averagable income

Income averaging benefits the person whose income fluctuates widely from year to year by allowing him to average his income retroactively, at least in part, over up to five years. This can be done without recomputing prior years' taxes.

Most income qualifies for averaging, if it exceeds $3,000, with the exception of capital gains, wagering gains, income from gifts and bequests, and premature distributions from employment pension plans.

The procedure is complex, and the instructions should be read carefully before it is attempted. Here, in general, is how it works. To be eligible, a taxpayer and his wife, if he is married, must have been United States citizens or residents in the computation year (the tax year) and not nonresident aliens in the base period (the four prior years). They also must have furnished at least half their own support during the base period. In addition, the taxpayer's tax-year income must be at least $3,000 greater than a sum equal to one and one-third times his average annual income—his "average base period income" —in the four preceding years. The tax-year income in excess of that adjusted average is called his "averagable income."

To compute his tax, the taxpayer would break his income into two parts: "regular" or nonaveragable income, and "averagable income." He determines the tax on his regular income and then adds to that tax amount five times the amount of tax computed on one-fifth of his averagable income. This device provides him with a lower tax rate.

To illustrate, suppose a person, after properly adjusting his base-period incomes to conform with averaging procedure, determines that adjusted taxable income for each of the four base years was $4,000, $5,000, $7,000 and $8,000. In the tax year, it was $18,000. His average annual taxable income for the base period is $6,000 (the four-year total divided by four). Under the rules, he increases that by one-third, putting his "average base period income" at $8,000. Subtracting that from his tax-year income of $18,000 puts his "averagable income" at $10,000. In determining his total tax liability for the year, we will follow the procedure in Schedule G, the tax form provided for income averaging. First, he calculates the tax on $10,000 (his average base period income, plus one-fifth of his averagable income); it comes to $2,190. Next, he calculates the tax on $8,000 (his average base period income), and that comes to $1,630. He subtracts that from the tax due on $10,000, and arrives at a $560 difference. Multiplying the difference by four, he gets a total of $2,240. Adding that sum to the $2,190 tax due on the $10,000 gives him a total tax liability for the year of $4,430. He thus would save $740; for his tax liability would have been $5,170 had he calculated in the regular way the tax due on $18,000 of taxable income.

One must be cautioned that the computation in the illustration would have been much more complex, had the hypothetical taxpayer been required to make the various other income-averaging adjustments described in the I.R.S. instruction book.

Deduction Methods: Standard deductions, medical deductions, charitable contributions, unrelated student in home, deductible taxes, casualty and theft losses, interest deductions, child-care deductions, education expenses, moving expenses, occupational expenses, alimony, nondeductible items

The taxpayer may use the 10 per cent standard deduction or the minimum standard deduction. If the total of his charitable contributions, medical expenses, mortgage interest, real estate taxes and other deductible expenditures exceeds the limits of those two procedures, he may itemize his actual deductions.

Under the *standard deduction,* the taxpayer may exclude from taxation 10 per cent of his total income, but no more than $1,000, or $500 if he is married and filing a separate return. Under the minimum standard deduction, the taxpayer may exclude a basic $200 and an additional $100 for each exemption, including his own, with the same maximum limits as above. Thus, a single person would be allowed a $300 deduction; a childless married couple, $400; and a couple with three children, $700.

Whatever deduction procedure is followed, the taxpayer continues to deduct $600 from gross income for each exemption—for himself and his dependents.

MEDICAL DEDUCTIONS. Within certain restrictions, a taxpayer may deduct from taxable income the cost of medical care for himself, his wife and his dependents, if he itemizes all deductions. Costs to be considered for deduction must be net amounts, excluding expenses that were reimbursed by insurance or otherwise.

Medical expenses of a dependent are deductible, even if, for tax purposes, he does not otherwise qualify as a dependent, because his gross income was more than $600 in the tax year. However, the taxpayer must have furnished more than half his support. Such a dependent may be, for example, a child over 18 who is not a full-time student, or one who married late in the tax year and is filing a joint return with his or her spouse.

The taxpayer must reduce his medicine and drug expenses by 1 per cent of his adjusted gross income, and then add the difference to other qualified medical and dental expenses. The total then must be reduced by 3 per cent of his adjusted gross income. Beginning with the 1967 tax year (on returns due April 15, 1968), these rules also apply to taxpayers over age 65, who were exempt from them in previous years. There also were certain limitations for all taxpayers on total medical deductions, but these, too, have been lifted, effective in the 1967 tax year. Also, beginning in the 1967 tax year, a taxpayer may deduct half the cost of his medical insurance, up to a maximum of $150, without the 3 per cent rule applying. The other half and the excess, if any, over the $150 limit may be added to other medical deductions, as was the case for all medical insurance premiums before 1967. Under the new rule, however, the taxpayer will not be able to deduct any part of the insurance premium attributable to coverage for disability income payments or indemnity payments for loss of life or limb.

In general, after subtraction of required percentages of income, a taxpayer may deduct all bills from hospitals, physicians, dentists, optometrists, chiropractors, chiropodists, podiatrists, osteopaths, psychiatrists, psychologists and Christian Science practitioners. He also may deduct the cost of transportation for obtaining deduction-qualifying medical or dental care. Only travel costs are deductible, not meals or lodging. If the taxpayer uses his car, he may deduct 5 cents a mile, or the actual cost of gasoline and oil, as well as tolls and parking fees. Auto depreciation and insurance are not deductible.

The same transportation deductions are allowed for a health or convalescence trip, provided that the person taking the trip is actually going for medical reasons, that he has a specific ailment or condition requiring it, that it is not a permanent change of residence and that the destination is medically recognized as a help in curing or easing the person's particular problem.

Transportation costs incurred for trips taken to improve general health have been disallowed by I.R.S., even when taken on medical advice. If it is necessary for a person, such as a relative, companion or nurse, to accompany the ill person, the taxpayer may deduct those additional transportation costs.

Among other allowable medical deductions are:

—Special schooling required for a physically or mentally handicapped child.

—Nursing services. No deduction may be taken for domestic help, even if hired on the physician's recommendation, because the tax-payer's wife is medically unable to do the work herself.

—Confinement in a nursing home, home for the aged or similar institution, if the patient is there because his physical condition requires the medical services provided. The deduction may be challenged, if the Internal Revenue Service believes the person was institutionalized, not for medical, but for personal or family reasons. At best, only the medical portion of the deduction may be honored.

—At least a portion of the cost of installing a home improvement, such as a wheel-chair ramp, elevator or air conditioning, if the installation was medically necessary. Full cost is deductible if the item is detachable. If it is part of the house, however, the deductible portion is the excess of the cost over any resulting increase in the home's value. For example, if installation of a $1,200 air-conditioning system increases a home's value by $800, the taxpayer may deduct the $400 difference.

—The cost of prosthetic devices and other special aids to the ill or disabled, among them, eyeglasses, hearing aids, artificial teeth and limbs, braces, crutches, wheelchairs, special mattresses and boards, and oxygen equipment. The cost and upkeep of a seeing-eye dog are deductible, as are the expenses of a special vehicle that enables a disabled person to get about, provided it is not used only to commute to work.

The Internal Revenue Service will not allow medical deduction of transportation costs between work and home, even if a person's ailment requires a special mode of transportation.

All medicine and drugs bought during the tax year may be deducted, whether obtained with a prescription or not. This, it appears, would include household remedies usually bought and used without the advice of a physician, such as aspirin, cold remedies and laxatives. However, vitamins, according to a specific I.R.S. ruling, are deductible only if prescribed or recommended by a doctor, but not if taken for general health purposes. This is presumed by experts to apply also to sleeping tablets and tranquilizers.

No deduction for special food or beverages is allowed if they substitute for those normally consumed. However, deductions are allowed, if a doctor prescribes foods or beverages that are not part of normal nutritional needs and are taken in addition to the regular diet.

A physician's statement to that effect must accompany the return. In one example, the I.R.S. said the cost of whiskey was deductible if the doctor prescribed that two ounces be taken daily for relief of angina pain resulting from a coronary artery disease. In another example, in which a patient was put on an ulcer diet, the I.R.S. said the cost of food and beverages was not deductible, because the special diet simply replaced the normal diet.

Among other items that are not medically deductible are funeral expenses, maternity clothes, the cost of diaper service and any expenditures for the improvement of general health, such as for dance lessons, vacations, health club dues, steam baths and reducing treatments.

It often is difficult for a taxpayer to determine his allowable medical deductions, because the I.R.S. tends more toward broad description than specific instruction in this area. A person with a complex problem should engage a tax specialist or visit his local Internal Revenue Service office.

CHARITABLE CONTRIBUTIONS. Within limits, Federal income tax law allows a person itemizing all deductions to deduct from his taxable income all charitable contributions made in the tax year to qualified organizations. In general, an organization is qualified, for the contributor's tax purposes, if it was established and operates exclusively for charitable, religious, educational or scientific purposes. Net earnings of the organization may not benefit any private shareholder or individual. An organization will be able to advise whether contributions it receives may be deducted by the donor from his taxable income. Local Internal Revenue Service personnel also will tell you whether an organization qualifies.

Among the examples given by the I.R.S. of the types of organizations that qualify are: nonprofit schools and hospitals, the Salvation Army, churches, United Funds, Community Chests, the Young Men's Christian Association and other "Y's," Red Cross, Police Boys Clubs, Boys Clubs of America, Boy Scouts, Girl Scouts, and Government agencies, such as Civil Defense. Also qualified are nonprofit organizations engaged in research or education for the alleviation and cure of disease, such as cancer and heart disease.

Contributions to or for the use of a nonprofit cemetery company, whose funds are irrevocably dedicated to the perpetual care of the cemetery as a whole, are deductible. However, one may not deduct a contribution for the care of a particular plot or mausoleum crypt, or the purchase price of that plot or crypt.

Among other major nondeductible contributions or payments are:

—Gifts to relatives.

—Amounts paid for raffle tickets, to play Bingo or other games of chance. This is considered wagering, and any losses incurred by wagering are deductible elsewhere in the tax form only to the extent of wagering gains.

—Contributions to chambers of commerce, labor unions (though dues are a deductible occupational expense), civic leagues, social clubs and certain international organizations.

—Gifts to political parties and candidates.

—Amounts given to charitable organizations, if the donor is permitted to specify that his contribution is to benefit an individual of his choice.

—The cash value of blood donated to the Red Cross or to other blood banks.

—Payments to a hospital for care of particular patients or for services rendered to such patients by the hospital, even though the hospital may be operated exclusively by the local or state government, or by a charitable organization.

The value of time or service a person contributes to a qualified organization is not deductible. However, unreimbursed out-of-pocket expenses incurred in rendering the service are deductible as contributions. They may include the cost of transportation from the taxpayer's home to the place where he served, and reasonable amounts for meals and lodging while away from home in rendering the donated services to a qualified organization.

However, the taxpayer may not deduct expenses incurred to attend a church convention solely as a member of his church, rather than as a duly chosen representative. Unreimbursed expenses directly connected with and solely attributable to gratuitous service he may perform for his church during the convention are deductible.

If he uses his car in donating his services to a qualified organization, he may deduct 5 cents a mile, or the actual cost of gasoline and oil, as well as parking fees and tolls, as a contribution. Depreciation, insurance costs and repairs are not deductible.

As for tickets to charity benefits, only the difference between their price and the value of the entertainment may be deducted. For example, if a person paid $10 to see a benefit showing of a movie, and the regular price for the movie, including tax, was $2.50, he could deduct a charitable contribution of $7.50.

Gifts of property to a qualified organization may be deducted as contributions to the extent of their fair market value. If the value is more or less than its original price (or other cost basis), the donor, for tax purposes, would have neither a gain nor a loss because it was not a taxable exchange of property. That could be a double advantage to the taxpayer. For example, suppose he could afford to give $2,000 to his church and had a stock that was worth that much, though he had bought it for $400. By giving the stock instead of cash, he avoids the capital-gains tax he would have had to pay on his $1,600 gain, if he had sold the stock, and can claim all of the $2,000 as a charitable contribution. Of course, this is assuming he had decided either that the stock's potential had diminished, or that he wanted his church to enjoy the stock's further growth.

In claiming deductions for contributions of property, a taxpayer must attach a statement to his return containing a description of the property, the date of the gift and the method of valuation. Property appraisals are a good protection. There are additional requirements that may apply, and the taxpayer should refer to his instruction book or talk to the I.R.S., unless he has an accountant or tax lawyer completing his return.

In general, deductions for contributions may not exceed 20 per cent of adjusted gross income. However, an additional 10 per cent is allowed for contributions to churches, tax-exempt educational organizations with a regular faculty and student body, tax-exempt hospitals and, under certain circumstances, organizations directly engaged in continuous medical research in conjunction with a tax-exempt hospital, and certain college endowment associations.

Also includible in the additional 10 per cent are donations to:

—Most domestic government bodies, if the money is given for public purposes.

—An exempt charitable, religious, educational, scientific or literary organization, or one established to prevent cruelty to children or animals, if it normally receives a substantial part of its support from a governmental unit or from contributions from the general public.

Gifts to private foundations are not included in the additional 10 per cent.

Qualified contributions made within the tax year that are in excess of 30 per cent may be carried over into the succeeding five years. Deductions, including the carry-over amounts, would be limited to the 30 per cent in those years.

It is imperative that the taxpayer be able to substantiate all claims for charitable deductions, particularly those paid in cash. If he cannot do so, should his return be audited by the I.R.S., he may be limited to cash deductions of $78, provided the auditor thinks his oral statements are credible. The $78 guideline, used extensively in the Service's North Atlantic Region, including New York, is neither an automatic allowance nor a rigid rule.

UNRELATED STUDENT IN HOME. A taxpayer may deduct, as a charitable contribution, the amount he pays to maintain in his home a full-time student in the 12th or lower grade. The student, who must not be a dependent or relative, may be foreign or American. He must be in the taxpayer's home under a written agreement between the taxpayer and an organization that qualifies as one to which contributions are deductible for Federal income tax purposes. No deduction is allowed, if the taxpayer is otherwise compensated or reimbursed. His allowable deduction may not exceed $50 for each "full month" in which the student is in his home. A full month, for this purpose, is any month in which the student resides with the taxpayer for 15 or more days.

DEDUCTIBLE TAXES. Most state and local taxes, but no Federal taxes, may be deducted from Federally taxable personal income, provided the deductions are itemized on the "long" Form 1040. Among the allowable state and local taxes are those on real estate, gasoline, personal property, general sales and income, but they must have been imposed directly on the taxpayer. Among those not deductible are taxes on cigarettes, tobacco and alcoholic beverages. Neither are fees for automobile driver's licenses or for license plates, unless the car is used for business, and unless the tax is based on the car's value and is therefore qualified as a personal property tax. Like other Federal taxes, excise taxes on telephone service, gasoline and cars are not deductible. Neither are the Social Security taxes paid for domestics, or the water taxes (actually assessments) paid by homeowners.

CASUALTY AND THEFT LOSSES. A taxpayer may deduct only amounts in excess of $100 on each personal loss from casualty or theft. The amount of loss, less insurance or other compensation, generally reflects market value or cost less depreciation. To qualify, a casualty loss generally must be caused by a sudden, unexpected or unusual event, such as a fire, storm, tornado, hurricane, flood, sonic boom of a jet aircraft, or an auto accident that was not the result of the taxpayer's willful act or willful negligence. However, there are exceptions. An admissible deduction, for example, may be damage from termites or from drought.

INTEREST DEDUCTIONS. Interest actually paid by a taxpayer during the tax year is deductible, provided it was paid on debts for which he was legally liable. Interest paid on debts related to his trade or business or to his rental property or investments may be deducted on the appropriate form—Schedule C or Part II of Form 1040's Schedule B—whether or not he itemizes all other deductions. All other interest he pays may be deducted only if he itemizes all deductions.

Interest paid on a home mortgage usually is shown in his monthly-payment record, but, if not, the taxpayer may ask the lender for the exact interest figure, that is, total payments less amortization. If the lender imposes a penalty for prepaying the mortgage, that penalty may be deducted as interest. A tenant-stockholder in an apartment cooperative may deduct his share of interest paid on any indebtedness of the co-op.

A lender also will tell how much interest has been paid during the tax year on a discount loan, one in which the interest was deducted in advance from the amount borrowed. If the amount of interest paid during the year is not stated separately in an installment purchase agreement, the taxpayer may deduct as interest 6 per cent of the average unpaid balance during the year. He may arrive at that average by adding up the monthly unpaid balance amounts and dividing the total by 12.

Because interest payments generally are deductible, a taxpayer should make certain he has not overlooked any, such as those paid on life insurance and credit union loans, or on delinquent Federal taxes.

CHILD-CARE DEDUCTION. Under certain circumstances, a deduction may be taken of expenses for care of a dependent who is physically or mentally incapable of caring for himself or is a child (or stepchild) of the taxpayer and is under age 13. The maximum deduction allowed is $600 a year for one eligible child or dependent, or $900 for two or more. Qualifying expenses include the cost of baby sitters, or boarding or day school or a nursing home. These expenses are deductible if they were paid so that the taxpayer could be gainfully employed. The claimant may be a woman, regardless of her marital status, or a man who is widowed, divorced or legally separated, or whose wife has been institutionalized or incapacitated for at least 90 days. If the taxpayer is a working wife, she must file a joint return with her husband and must reduce her child-care deduction, dollar for dollar, to the extent that the couple's combined adjusted gross income is over $6,000. For example, if their combined income is $6,500, the child-care deduction must be reduced by $500. However, if the husband is incapable of self-support for a period, that limitation would not apply. The income limit also applies to a husband, except for the period his wife is incapacitated or institutionalized.

EDUCATION EXPENSES. In general, education expenses may be deducted, if they were incurred to maintain or improve skills required in the taxpayer's job or business, or to meet an employer's or legal requirements. The Government will not allow deduction of expenses for education undertaken to obtain a new job, to obtain a promotion, to acquire minimum qualifications for a job that is not otherwise available to the taxpayer, or for general educational purposes. There is a broad middle ground. The most recent outstanding case is of the accountant who won a court decision that allowed him to deduct the cost of his training as a lawyer. He convinced the court, as have other taxpayers, that the training helped him improve skills he already had. A person receiving a scholarship, fellowship or veteran's education benefits will find that the value of some of these may not be taxable.

MOVING EXPENSES. An employe may deduct reasonable moving expenses, when transferred to a new "principal place" of employment.

The expenses, including those of regular members of his household, would include the moving of household goods and personal effects and travel expenses, including meals and lodging, from the old to the new home. To qualify, the taxpayer's commuting distance from his former residence to his new place of work must be at least 20 miles farther than was his previous commuting distance. Moving expenses are deductible only if, during the 12-month period immediately after the taxpayer's transfer to the new principal place of work, he was a full-time employe in that general area for at least three-fourths of the time, or 39 weeks. If he was reimbursed for moving expenses, he can deduct the expenses in excess of the reimbursement.

OCCUPATIONAL EXPENSES: An employe may deduct from taxable income certain qualified expenses, such as union or professional association dues, unreimbursed business expenses, the cost of tools, journals and other materials. Uniforms and special clothing, and their upkeep, are deductible expenses only if the taxpayer is required to buy, maintain and wear them as a condition of employment and they cannot be adapted to general wear.

ALIMONY. In general, if a taxpayer itemizes his deductions, alimony is deductible, provided it is taxable to his wife. This would be the case, if the divorce decree or written separation agreement placed the tax impact on the wife. However, to be taxable to the wife and deductible by the husband, the alimony must be in periodic payments. Payments would not be deemed periodic, if the decree or separation agreement called for payment of a principal sum within 10 years. If the husband is in a higher tax bracket than the wife, there is obvious saving in having alimony deductible by him and taxable to her. Some divorced or separated couples work out an arrangement to share this saving. Child-support payments, as such, are not taxable to the wife nor deductible by the husband. However, if the decree combines child support and alimony in one figure, the entire amount may be deductible by the husband and taxable to the wife. Either party can deduct legal fees paid for tax advice in connection with a divorce.

NON-DEDUCTIBLE ITEMS. There are a number of items that many people believe are deductible from their gross incomes, but are not. Some major ones are:

—The cost of travel to and from work.

—Premiums paid for life insurance policies on the taxpayer or his wife. Confusion arises, perhaps, because New York State allows a premium deduction of up to $150 each for the taxpayer and spouse.

—Funeral expenses, the cost of a burial plot and of "perpetual care" of that plot. Confusion here may arise from the fact that such items may be deducted from an estate for estate-tax purposes.

Tax Regulations for Minors: Filing a return, dependency exemptions, minimum-standard deduction, 50 per cent support test, taxable interest, gift taxes

A minor, that is, a person under age 21, according to Federal tax law, must file an income tax return if he earned a gross income of $600 or more. If he is unable to file a return, his parent, guardian or other person legally responsible for his care must file it for him. That person, it is important to note, may be liable for taxes owed by the minor.

As has been noted, there may be two $600 exemptions applicable to a child's life. The child himself is entitled to one, as is any other taxpayer. In addition, if he is under age 19, or if he is older but qualifies as a full-time student getting more than half his support from his parent, the parent also is entitled to a dependency exemption on the child. This is further sweetened by the minimum-standard deduction. A child could earn up to $900 tax-free: his $600 personal exemption and, under the minimum-standard procedure, a $200 base deduction and $100 deduction for his exemption. (The usual "standard" 10 per cent deduction would allow him to reduce his taxable income by only $90.) In addition, a child also could have up to $100 of tax-exempt dividend income. That would put his total possible tax-free income at $1,000.

If that $1,000 is put, say, into a bank account, with no part being used for his support, his father would be entitled to the $600 dependency exemption for him. This would be allowed, if the father provided more than half his support, and if the child were under age 19 and a full-time student. The result: $1,600 of income escapes taxation.

As to the 50 per cent support test, the parent should determine whether he provided more than half the child's support by comparing the amount of support he gave with the entire amount that the child received for support from other sources, including the child's own funds.

Bona fide and reasonable wages (not an allowance) paid by a parent to his child as an employe are deductible by the parent and must be reported as income by the child. The cost of meals and lodging are not deductible. If the child uses the wages to help furnish his own support, the parent's dependency exemption could be endangered, unless he still clearly met the support test.

If the parent names his child as co-owner of a United States savings bond, such as an E bond, the interest would be taxable to the parent, even if the child has the right to redeem the bond and keep the proceeds. But, if the bond is placed in the child's name only, the interest income would be his to report. E bond interest need not be reported until the bond is cashed or mature.

Interest credited on a child's savings account is reported as his income. However, if his parent opens the account in his own name "in trust for" the child, the income is taxable to the parent.

Property transferred to a minor under the Model Gifts of Securities to Minors Act or the Uniform Gifts to Minors Act, or under laws patterned after these acts, constitutes a "completed gift" for Federal gift-tax purposes. Within certain limits, they escape the gift tax (see Chapter 12). The income from transferred property, however, is taxable to the minor, unless it is used to discharge part of the parent's legal obligation to support him. The parent will be charged with taxable income to that extent.

Like any other taxpayer, a minor must have a taxpayer identification number, which must appear on his return. This number, identical to the Social Security number, may be obtained by filing Form SS-5, available at a Social Security or post office, or Form 3227, available from an Internal Revenue Service office. The parent's number must be furnished, if he owns an insurance policy on the child's life, or is co-owner with the child of stock, savings accounts and so on. But the child's number must be provided, if he is listed as sole owner, with the parent perhaps named as custodian.

Tax Regulations for Older Persons: Extra exemptions, retirement-income credit, minimum-standard deduction, sale of a home

Among the benefits available to taxpayers who are 65 or older are extra exemptions for age, exclusion of certain income from taxes, a retirement-income credit and liberalized minimum-standard-deduction rules.

An additional $600 exemption, as has been noted, is allowed the taxpayer or his wife, if either was 65 or older by January 1 of the year following the tax year. Thus, if husband and wife both are 65 or older, they can claim four exemptions totaling $2,400 of tax-free income. The minimum-standard-deduction method allows another $600 of tax-free income—the $200 base deduction and $100 for each of the four exemptions.

Among the nontaxable items are Social Security and Railroad Retirement Act benefits, which generally need not be reported, and certain death benefits from life or accident and health policies. In general, the portion of pension or annuity income that a retired person had financed also usually is tax-free.

The retirement income credit can save a person up to $450 or more in tax, for he can take a credit against his tax of 15 per cent of certain retirement income. To qualify, a person normally must be 65 or older or be retired under a public retirement system, and must have had more than $600 of earned income in each of any 10 years before the tax year.

"Earned income" is compensation received for services performed. "Retirement income" includes taxable pensions and annuities, interest, dividends and rents. For a person under 65, only pensions and annuities received under a public retirement system qualify.

In general, $1,524 is the maximum amount of retirement income eligible for credit computation. However, the maximum is twice that, or $3,048, if both husband and wife qualify, and one and one-half times that, or $2,286, if the wife does not qualify but a joint return is filed.

To compute his credit, a taxpayer would tally his retirement income, staying within his limit, and subtract nontaxable pension payments received during the year. He then would subtract earned income, all but the first $900 if he's under 62 and none if he is over 72.

If between those ages, he would reduce retirement income by half his earnings between $1,200 and $1,700, and by all earnings above that. His retirement-income credit would be 15 per cent of the final remainder.

SALE OF A HOME. The person who is 65 or older also enjoys greater tax advantage than a younger taxpayer when he sells his home. If a person under age 65 sells his home for more than it cost, including the price of improvements, his capital gain would be taxable. He could defer taxation by buying and occupying another home within a year before or after the sale, or within 18 months after the sale if he builds a new home. For him to achieve deferment of the total tax, the price of his new residence must equal or exceed the net selling price of his old residence. The tax actually is deferred, because the tax basis for his new home will be its total cost less the untaxed gain on the sale of the old residence. For example, suppose a person's old home cost him $18,000, including improvements, and he sold it for a net of $25,000. That would give him a capital gain of $7,000. If he then bought another home for $30,000, his capital gain on resale of that second home would be the amount above $23,000 (the $30,000 purchase price, less the $7,000 capital gain on sale of the first home), plus the cost of improvements he may have made. However, if a taxpayer sells his home after he reaches age 65, he may enjoy a once-in-a-lifetime advantage. If he owned and used the home for five of the eight years preceding the sale, he can exclude from income any profit, if the sale price is $20,000 or less. If it is more, the proportion that $20,000 bears to the total selling price is excludable. For example, if the selling price is $30,000, then two-thirds ($20,000 over $30,000) of the profit on the sale is excludable.

The over-65 rule applies if husband and wife own the residence as joint tenants and only one is 65 or older. It also applies if the house, which otherwise qualifies, is destroyed by fire or storm, or is condemned for public use.

If a taxpayer has a loss on the disposition of his residence, no deduction is allowable, unless he had converted his residence into a rental property before its sale. If he had done that, however, any gain would be taxed, since the tax-relief provision applies only to the taxpayer's personal residence.

Late Tax Payments

A person definitely should file his return when it is due, even if he cannot pay all or part of the tax he owes. The Internal Revenue Service will bill him for the amount due, plus interest. If he fails to file on time, he may be subject to civil and even criminal penalties. If, for some other reason, a person cannot file on time, he may request an extension. When he does file, attaching the extension-approval form, he must pay interest on the tax amount due.

12

GENEROSITY CAN PAY OFF

In its purest form, giving can be an art. A person's attainment of that art is apparent in the warmth and thoughtfulness with which he conveys the gift, in his ability to make the receiver feel it can be accepted without a compromise in personal dignity. The artful giver's primary reward is the satisfaction he derives from knowing that he has brought pleasure, comfort and, sometimes, hope to other persons. The beneficiaries may be relatives and friends or, in the case of most charitable giving, strangers.

The gift may take many forms. It may be a gift of service, of time and talent, or it may be one of cash and property. In a sense, the Federal and state governments encourage generosity by providing tax advantages to the generous. As noted in Chapter 11, charitable contributions to qualifying organizations are deductible from taxable income, up to certain limits. Tax concessions also are allowed, as will be noted, for personal gifts of cash and property to friends and relatives. Thus, it becomes apparent that generosity sometimes can pay off in a material as well as a spiritual sense.

Monetary Gifts: Cash, securities, real property, life insurance

Be it a gift-giving holiday or a birthday, money can have its place, and not in a crass sense either. A monetary gift can mark the start of a youngster's college fund or lifetime financial program, or it could give, at least, a feeling of independence to an elderly parent or other dependent relative. The gift may be of cash, perhaps in the form of a "starter" bank account for a child, or it may be of securities, real property or a life insurance policy. The securities or other property may be of the income-producing type, if the recipient's need is for supplemental income, or if the giver's need is for transfer of income for tax purposes.

This brings up the additional benefits that can accrue to the giver of money. Those benefits may be savings in income taxes for himself and his family, or in ultimate estate taxes for his heirs. The saving in estate tax is apparent in the fact that gift giving will transfer assets out of the giver's estate and into the hands of the persons who ultimately would have inherited them when the giver died.

By shifting current income to a relative with no income, or to one in a low tax bracket, the income tax saving could be substantial. Naturally, the higher the giver's tax bracket, the greater the saving. For example, a man in the 50 per cent or better tax bracket might transfer income-producing property or securities to his young son, parent or other dependent relative whose top tax rate might be only 25 per cent or less. But the advantage is not restricted to the greatly affluent. A couple with an income of $15,000 or less and a top tax rate of perhaps 25 per cent might transfer income-producing securities to a dependent whose tax rate would be no more than 14 or 16 per cent.

How may all this be done? Transfer of assets is made somewhat easier by the relatively liberal Federal gift-tax laws. Under the law, a person may in any one year give up to $3,000 each to any other persons tax-free, and has an additional lifetime gift-tax exemption of $30,000. These amounts are doubled for married couples who join in gift giving.

To illustrate, a father can give annual tax-free gifts of up to $3,000 to each of his children for as many years as he chooses. In addition, he can divide among them his extra lifetime exemption of $30,000. These tax-exempt amounts could be doubled—$6,000 a year for each child and an extra $60,000 for all—if the gifts are given in the names of both parents. A married couple may give joint gifts, though only one partner produces the income.

Gifts in excess of those limits would be subject to a gift tax, but it still might be advantageous to transfer certain assets now rather than bequeath them at death. The Federal gift tax rates are 75 per cent of the estate tax rates in the same bracket, but the first taxable gifts would come out of the top brackets of an estate and fall into the lowest brackets for gift-tax purposes.

The transfer is also made easier by certain state laws. For example, laws in all the states make it relatively simple to give securities to a child, provided a custodian is named to act in his behalf. While the gift then irrevocably belongs to the child, the right to manage it remains with the custodian until the child is 21 years old. As long as the donor and the custodian are different persons and the gift is not made in contemplation of death, it will not be included in the donor's estate for estate-tax purposes. However, if the donor dies within three years after giving the gift, it may have to be proved that the gift was not made in contemplation of death.

There was a time when the only practical way securities could be given to a minor was through the creation of a trust, involving drafting of the trust agreement, court costs, periodic accountings and various other details. But this has been simplified by the states' enabling legislation, which was patterned in large part on the Model Custodian Act. That model law was sponsored chiefly by the New York Stock Exchange and the Association of Stock Exchange Firms. The donor may choose to give stocks that are worth considerably more than he paid for them. He thus would avoid paying the capital-gains tax, though it ultimately may be payable by the recipient, perhaps at a lower rate, when he decides to sell.

The person contributing to the support of elderly parents or other dependents may transfer income to them, temporarily, by setting up a short-term reversionary trust. Under such a trust, for example, a dependent parent may receive the income from its underlying securities or other property, paying little or no income tax on it. The son establishing the trust thus would have diverted to his parent income on which he would have had to pay a larger tax. The trust eventually would revert, perhaps at the parent's death, to the son for his own retirement program.

Anyone planning to take advantage of such a plan—or any other gift-giving device, whether it involves a trust, custodial arrangement or outright presentation of property—should first consult with his lawyer, accountant and other appropriate adviser. Aside from being able to evaluate the basic plan, adding their own recommendations, these experts make certain that proper procedures are followed to assure its general and tax legality.

Gifts of securities to children naturally are urged by stockbrokers, who generally note "their potential growth in value" and the inherently "American economic lesson" offered to the child. They and the exchanges publish much pertinent sales and explanatory literature.

Also interested in indoctrinating the young to the products of their business are life insurers, who say that a gift policy has many educational and financial planning advantages, while "starting a child on his own life insurance program and guaranteeing his future insurability." Some of the many juvenile policies being offered are described in Chapter 5.

Money management experts generally suggest that life insurance be considered only as one factor, along with such elements as trusts or gifts of securities, in the planning of a child's financial future. They note, for example, that, while the fixed-dollar guarantee of insurance policies may serve as a hedge against deflation, common stocks could protect against inflation, rising in price with the market and the general economy.

The best thing about monetary gifts is that there is no problem with colors, and little concern with size, unless the recipient is especially humble, or greedy.

Guides to Charitable Giving: Choosing the recipient

The generosity of Americans is evident in the fact that they give more than $7 billion a year to charitable, medical research, educational, religious and other organizations. That these organizations are aware of that generosity is evidenced by their deluge of requests for contributions, particularly during gift-giving holiday seasons. But, before reaching for checkbook or wallet, the benevolent person would be prudent to consider a few factors that could affect his peace of mind and personal finances. His first consideration is the selection of the right organizations for his contributions. This is not as simple as it sounds. Some seemingly respectable charitable or philanthropic groups are outright frauds, while other quite respectable ones spend what may be considered to be too large a part of their receipts on fund-raising and administrative functions.

The donor also should adhere to various tax-reducing guidelines. Doing so may tend to establish the size of his contribution, his method of making it and whether it should be in cash, securities or real or personal property. Consultation with his accountant or other tax specialist would be helpful.

A major guideline in selection of worthwhile recipients of contributions is to determine as closely as possible their purposes and operating costs. A common practice is to return the self-addressed envelope that usually accompanies solicitation literature, asking that the organization furnish its latest financial statement. In this way, the donor has some basis for a judgment as to whether the organization is run in a businesslike manner. The charity also is put on notice that there are those who are interested in how it spends their money. The same request should be made of doubtful organizations, when solicitations are made by telephone or in person. This may be considered embarrassing by some people, especially when the solicitors are neighbors who have been persuaded to become volunteers. Nonetheless, questions should be asked if the prospective donor has doubts.

One veterans' organization that collects huge sums each year spends more than 60 cents of every dollar contributed on "related direct costs and expenses." An overseas orphanage gets only 52 cents of each dollar collected here, and total contributions run to a sizable six figures.

Local Better Business Bureaus are a good source of information on charitable organizations about which a prospective donor may have doubts.

Many donors concentrate their giving on their churches or temples, feeling that such organizations generally keep operating expenses to a minimum.

Making a careful study of charitable organizations before supporting them may seem Scroogelike, but it is the only sensible way of assuring that most of your philanthropic dollars are advancing worthy causes, rather than enriching the commercial "do-gooders" of the giant fund-raising industry.

Charitable Giving Through Life Insurance

There has been a revival in our tax-oriented society of the practice of using life insurance as a vehicle for philanthropic gifts. In the extreme, it can bring to reality the seemingly paradoxical "save-by-giving" concept. In general, sensibly applied programs of philanthropic giving through life insurance can be beneficial to both the donor and the institution receiving the gift.

Essentially, a donor under such a program would name the recipient institution as beneficiary in a new or existing life policy. His designation must be irrevocable, so that he may not name someone else as beneficiary later, after having enjoyed the tax advantage. If the policy is an old one, the donor may claim its value as a deduction on his Federal income tax return. Whether it is old or new, he also may deduct the premium payments.

The tax advantage to the person of low or moderate income is limited. The premium payments would be part of whatever regular charitable contributions he would normally deduct each year; upon his death, there generally is no major estate-tax problem. His prime satisfaction in giving through life insurance is in knowing that his philanthropic goal would be completed whether he lived or died, and that the total gift ultimately would be greater than what he would otherwise have been able to afford.

In an example given in a Young Men's Christian Association pamphlet, a 35-year-old man wishing to give $1,000 to that organization might buy a 20-payment ordinary life policy that "would cost about $690 over the 20 years. This amounts to only $34.50 a year!" On his death, the Y.M.C.A. would get the $1,000.

The greatest tax advantage of charitable giving through life insurance is to high-income or wealthy people, especially in the area of estate taxation. For example, a màn leaving a $1 million estate might save his heirs as much as $70,000 or more in Federal estate taxes by directing some of his charitable giving to the purchase of a $500,000 policy for the benefit of his favorite charity. The premium payments, of course, would be immediately tax deductible.

In buying the policy, he would name the recipient institution irrevocable beneficiary and possibly owner of the policy. However, he would retain what is legally referred to as an "incident of ownership," such as the right to determine the settlement option by which the beneficiary would receive the proceeds. That incident of ownership allows the inclusion of the proceeds of the policy in his total estate, thus increasing it from $1,000,000 to $1,500,000.

In the case of a $1,000,000 estate, the adjusted gross estate, after deduction of perhaps $100,000 in expenses, would be $900,000. The wife would be entitled to half of that, tax-free, as the marital deduction. An additional $60,000 personal deduction for the deceased would leave a taxable balance of $390,000. The Federal estate tax on that amount, not considering any credit for state-tax payments, would be $110,500.

In the case of the $1,500,000 estate, including the $500,000 charitable policy, the adjusted gross estate would be $1,400,000, allowing the same $100,000 in expenses. The wife would be allowed a tax-free half of that, or $700,000. Of the balance, $500,000—the proceeds of the policy—would go, tax-free, to the church, hospital or other institution named, leaving $200,000 from which the deceased's personal deduction of $60,000 is made. The remainder of $140,000 would be the taxable balance on which a Federal estate-tax payment of $32, 700 would be due.

From a charitable institution's viewpoint, the insurance plan could guarantee the completion of a pledge. For example, a 50-year-old man who gives $2,000 a year to an organization could pay for up to $50,000 of straight life insurance with that amount. In direct payments to the institution, it would take him 25 years to give a total of $50,000, and, statistically, he will not live that long. However, while the policy guarantees that the institution will ultimately get the large sum, the question is whether it can survive without the current $2,000-a-year income.

This has been a concern of a number of charitable organizations. As a spokesman for one said, "The only initial gainer is the insurance salesman. We would lose immediate income, which we need, and could only hope that payments on the policies are kept up long enough to give them some cash value that we can use, if necessary, or to collect the benefits when the contributor dies." He and other representatives of charitable organizations agreed that a life insurance program could be only a part of the total fund-raising program. More preferable would be a separate, supplemental plan that would not disturb existing yearly income.

If the insurance program is based on so-called permanent insurance, as most are, there would be two economic advantages available to the beneficiary institution, provided that it also is owner of the policy. Permanent insurance accumulates cash values, which can be borrowed on or used as collateral for other loans. Further, if dividends are paid, the institution can take them as income. In the case of the $50,000 policy taken by the 50-year-old man, the dividends might amount to $200 to $300 in the second year and grow to $600 a year by the 15th year, provided that the dividend scale remains unchanged.

Term insurance, pure death protection that generally does not accumulate cash values, is generally used in only special situations covering a specific span of time. For example, a few persons might take large term policies on their lives to cover a major loan that a church has taken and plans to repay in a given number of years.

The United Lutheran Church Foundation, in its booklet on "Ways of Giving Through Life Insurance" outlines the procedure and gives examples. One of these involves the assignment to the church of benefits on air-travel insurance.

Most, if not all, fund-raising programs based on life insurance are initiated by life insurance agents, who see great sales opportunities in this area. However, the experience of some has been that the dual task of selling life insurance and the charitable institution is a difficult and sometimes impossible one.

Insurance companies supported their salesmen's efforts in the fund-raising field as long ago as 1920, especially in the sale of small policies to new college graduates, who named their alma mater as beneficiary. But the new graduates later discovered that it was not as easy as they had thought it would be to maintain premium payments, and many of them dropped the policies, sometimes bitter at having been persuaded to buy them in the first place. Canceled policies generally mean a loss to the company, because they usually are not profitable until they have been on the books for up to seven years.

The major proponents of charitable giving through life insurance remain the big-volume sellers of insurance. They are happy to sell large policies for this purpose to wealthy individuals, thus performing a valid service. They are even happier to set up life insurance campaigns for charitable organizations.

13

PROTECTING YOUR HEIRS

That title may sound highflying to the average person, but the fact is, his concern with the economic well-being of his family at his death perhaps should be proportionately greater than that of an extremely wealthy person. Why? Because the man of moderate means has little margin for error. If there is a lapse in a wealthy man's planning, causing his heirs to receive as little as half his multimillion-dollar estate, that would be unfortunate, but not tragic. They would have quite enough money to live on. But it would be tragic if the same thing happened to the estate of a man leaving only $50,000 or less, for his family could be left in dire economic distress, particularly if the primary survivors are young children or aged parents unable to support themselves.

Whatever a person's economic status, he would want to feel assured, should he leave minor children, that they would be raised by a guardian of his choice, not leaving that emotionally and economically weighty decision to an impersonal court. The same would apply to the trustee who would manage their finances and to the executor who would administer the entire estate. Further, he may want to protect them from heirs who are financially imprudent, or who are incompetent because of age or disability.

The task is one of estate planning, and the foregoing are among its many objectives. Implicitly, the most basic is the assurance to a person that his wishes will be carried out at his death. Other objectives are the protection of his estate, to the greatest degree possible, from erosive estate taxes, probate costs, legal fees, administrative costs and law suits. The suits may be filed by persons seeking to superimpose their opinions on the wishes of the deceased, or simply to get some of his money. A man's estate, at his death, generally must be processed in his legal jurisdiction's probate court, which sometimes is called the surrogate or chancery court. The probate procedure can be time-consuming, often tying up the estate for two or more years, and it can be costly. It has been charged that, in many areas, court costs and the fees of court-appointed administrators, appraisers, lawyers, guardians and trustees are exorbitant. In addition, probate means publicity, in the form of legal notices and, if the estate is large or interesting enough, news stories.

The proportionately greater cost burden is on the estates of persons who die intestate, that is, without leaving a valid will, for all functions and appointments of functionaries are left to the court, which sets or approves the fees of its appointees. Thus, a properly drawn will, stipulating in detail the deceased person's wishes and naming, as applicable, an executor, guardian, trustee, lawyer and so on, can reduce much of the cost and complication. It also may minimize the risk of disbursal of assets according to the law and the court, rather than the decedent's wishes. However, a will would not eliminate the publicity, nor would it necessarily reduce appreciably the amount of time it takes to probate the will and distribute the assets to beneficiaries. Thus, for as long as two years or more, the widow may be forced to live on a small allowance approved by the court, while her children and other heirs may get nothing. Meanwhile, the money and other assets of the estate would not be invested or used in accordance with the deceased person's instructions, and his family may have to scrape, postpone or go into debt to complete certain plans, such as for a child's college education. Neither would a will avoid all of the costs of probate, which generally are based on the size of the estate. Thus, while a will is essential under all circumstances, as will be discussed later, it would appear sensible to keep as much property as possible out of the basic estate, passing it to heirs in other legal ways that are less cumbersome, costly, time-consuming and public than probate. If proper steps are taken, reduction in the size of the actual estate provides a bonus in that estate taxes may be appreciably reduced or eliminated.

Among the devices that may be used to bypass probate are life insurance, "living" trusts and joint ownership with right of survivorship. The major aspects of these devices will be discussed in this chapter, along with wills. Life insurance was extensively covered in Chapter 5, and another probate-bypass device, gift giving, was discussed in the last chapter.

The Necessity for a Will

"We don't have enough of an estate to worry about, so who needs a will?"

"My wife will get everything anyhow, so why get involved with wills and unnecessary legal fees?"

"I just haven't gotten around to it."

These are some typical comments about one of the most essential documents a family can have. But, more often than not, its value is overlooked by individuals and families, even many of those who are conscientious about other financial planning areas. The result is that, through lack of understanding or, worse yet, procrastination, most people do not have wills. At a man's death, absence of a will could pile additional emotional as well as financial burdens on the shoulders of his already distressed survivors.

A will is a legal document that describes in detail the manner in which a person wants his property distributed after his death. It must comply precisely with state law. While there is no legal requirement that a will be drawn by a lawyer, not using one would be courting trouble. A lawyer routinely follows the mandatory and exacting formalities of the law, with which most laymen are completely unfamiliar. Further, the competent lawyer's experience will yield the most practical, legally valid and economical means of accomplishing a man's objectives. While some people do not have wills simply because they "never have time to get to the lawyer's office," many others do not because they are depressed by discussions centering on death. Relatives and friends, particularly potential heirs, generally would not think of suggesting that a man have a will drawn. ("He'd think we were counting his money and the days until he—God forbid," exclaimed a somewhat emotional wife.)

A will is important because it assures the maker that he, not the state, will decide how his property will be distributed. With proper planning, tax liability and administrative costs could be reduced, and in some instances, eliminated. Further, with properly prepared wills, a person need not leave to the courts the designation of a guardian and a trustee for his minor children, should he and his wife die simultaneously in a common disaster.

In illustration of how the states decide on distribution of the property of a man who dies intestate, let's look at the New York State law. Under that law, as amended March 1, 1964, the following stipulations apply to the estates of those dying intestate:

—If there is one child, the surviving spouse gets $2,000 and shares the balance of the estate with the child. (The court may name a trustee other than the parent for the child's share, and in any case requires that the trustee be bonded. A will could avoid this.)

—If there is more than one child, the surviving spouse gets $2,000 and one-third of the balance, and the children share the rest. (The same trustee arrangement applies.)

—If there are no children, but one or both parents of the dead spouse survive, the surviving spouse gets $25,000 and half the remainder, and the parents get the other half.

—If there are no children or parents, the surviving spouse gets everything, and the deceased's brothers and sisters have no claims.

Under all state laws, a spouse generally cannot be disinherited. In New York, for example, the law gives him or her the right to at least a third of the estate (or half if there is only one child). However, a spouse may be left $2,500 in cash and only the income from a trust fund made up of a third (or half) of the estate.

It is recommended that wills be drawn for the husband and the wife, for several reasons. Whoever dies first, there may be legal questions as to who owned what. If both die in a common disaster, or if the wife dies shortly after her husband and leaves no will, property distribution and care of the children might be at the discretion of the law and the courts. The major personal advantage of a couple's having two wills is that they may name the guardian and trustee who will care for minor children and their property, if both parents die. This usually avoids unnecessary expenses and possible custody battles among relatives, factors that could hurt the children, emotionally and financially.

A properly drafted will often could reduce the cost of administering an estate. The person making a will can name the administrator, or executor, who could be the surviving spouse, another relative, a friend, a lawyer, a bank or a trust company. He may be exempted from bonding and may waive his fee. If no administrator is named, the court will appoint one, who must then be bonded, and who will be paid a fee.

The person administering or managing the estate files the will in probate court. Before distributing the property among heirs he must pay all debts and obligations, and all other claimants and creditors, including those attracted by the legal notices and other publicity who must be heard and dealt with by the probate court.

Life insurance does not take the place of a will. If the policy is made payable to a certain individual or organization, the insured's will can have no effect on that payment. If it is payable to his estate, then disposal of the money may be stipulated in the will.

Once a will is drawn, it should not be forgotten. Circumstances change, and to keep up with them, a will should be reviewed periodically, perhaps every three years, or when a major change takes place. Many revisions can be accomplished by the preparation and attachment to the will of "codicils," or additions, a function that should be left to the lawyer. Among the changes that should prompt review of a will are the birth of a child, change of residence (particularly if it is to another state), sale or disposal of property listed in a will, unavailability of a named executor or of a witness to its signing, acquisition of additional assets or some "windfall" that swells the estate.

Wills should be kept in a safe but accessible place, along with other valuable papers. If a person kept the original copy of his will in his safe-deposit box, there would be delay in getting it, because such boxes generally are sealed on notice of the owner's death.

Supplemental Letter of Last Instruction

It is generally recommended that a person deposit with his executor or lawyer a letter of last instruction that would become effective at his death. While it usually is not legally binding, it can contain a good deal of information that would be useful to a person's survivors. It also could include a person's wishes as to how he would like certain matters outside the province of his will to be handled.

The vital information would include the location of the will and other important documents, such as the person's birth certificate, Social Security card, marriage or divorce certificate, naturalization and citizenship papers and his Armed Forces discharge papers. In addition, he may list, with their locations, his safe-deposit boxes and keys, insurance policies, bank, checking and savings accounts, securities, real and personal property and other assets. He also might leave instructions as to the type, cost and location of his funeral and burial or cremation. He might specify, for example, that, as a veteran, he would prefer burial in a particular national cemetery. Instructions concerning his business also might be included, especially if his will suggests or provides that it be continued. If a person feels it necessary, he also might give his reasons for certain action taken in his will, such as disinheritances. Making this explanation outside the will sometimes is recommended, because it tends to avoid a complicated will that might invite costly and time-consuming litigation.

The Value of Trusts: Revocable and irrevocable living trusts, testamentary trusts

While many people associate trust agreements with the wealthy, these legal tools also can be useful to families of relatively moderate means. Depending on its type and structure, a trust may reduce the income tax liability of the person setting it up, reduce the ultimate tax on his estate, or both. In addition, if properly prepared, it can assure the grantor, that is, the person setting up the trust, that its beneficiaries will be protected from their own imprudence, if necessary.

The complexity of trusts and their tax ramifications makes it wise for a person planning to set one up to consult with experts in whom he has confidence, such as a lawyer, accountant and, if life insurance will be involved, an insurance man. These specialists may add their own recommendations, and will make certain the proper procedures are followed to assure a plan's general and tax legality.

Basically, there are living trusts, created by a declaration or deed of trust, and testamentary trusts, created by will. A living trust, also known as an *inter vivos,* personal or voluntary trust, may take effect immediately. The testamentary trust takes effect at the grantor's, or testator's, death and, generally, cannot be changed thereafter. It is the living trust that will allow property to bypass probate, because it keeps it out of the estate. It affords private and expeditious passage of property to beneficiaries, thus avoiding the expense, delay and publicity of probate. The testamentary trust, being created by will, does not have these advantages, but, nonetheless, may be recommended in special situations in which a living trust would not be possible or practical.

A living trust may be "revocable," giving the grantor the right to change it, or it may be "irrevocable," removing control of the property from the grantor, but giving him and his family certain tax advantages. Income tax advantages that a properly drawn living-trust agreement can provide for a grantor and his family while he is alive are discussed in Chapter 12, which includes commentary on reversionary, or temporary, trusts. The revocable trust may be attractive to the person who cannot decide on final disposition of his property, but, for lack of time or specialized knowledge, prefers to have his property managed by professionals—trustees, be they skilled individuals or a bank or trust company. A major advantage of the revocable trust is that it allows a person to gauge the performance of the trustee. If dissatisfied, he can make a change. If satisfied, he has greater assurance that his wishes will be carried out competently at his death, and thus may decide to make the trust irrevocable.

While the estate tax savings afforded by properly drawn living trusts and certain testamentary trusts generally are most beneficial to persons of affluence, they also can be realized by persons of relatively modest means. For example, the estate of an unmarried or widowed person would not have the advantage of the marital deduction, which could make up to half the estate tax-exempt if passed to a spouse. Thus, aside from certain charitable bequests, everything in an unmarried person's net estate above his $60,000 personal exemption would be subject to estate taxation. Increasing numbers of people are leaving $60,000 and larger estates, because of the broader ownership of homes, life insurance and other assets in this increasingly affluent age.

But there are personal considerations that may transcend the tax and other economic factors. A person may want some control apparatus, such as a trust arrangement, to make certain that his wishes are executed or to protect the interests of his beneficiaries or heirs. They may not be competent to manage funds or other assets, because of extreme youth or old age, or because of other limitations. A qualified trustee could do that for them.

In general, it is advisable to provide for "invasion of trust," thus allowing withdrawal of extra cash for emergencies or special needs.

In capsule, trust provisions applicable to the beneficiary may be as follows:

—Income paid periodically to the trustor himself, or to his wife, child, parent, friend or a charitable or other institution.

—Income to accumulate for a minor until he is a certain age.

—Principal to be paid to a named person when he reaches a certain age (he would be the "remainderman"), income being paid in the meantime to that person or another beneficiary (the "life-tenant"). Sometimes principal is paid to the remainderman at the life-tenant's death.

—The principal is to be paid to the beneficiary upon marriage as a marriage settlement.

Care naturally must be taken in the selection of a trustee. He may be a trustworthy individual who not only is expert in finance, but also has the advantage of personally knowing the family and its needs. To assure perpetuity of trusteeship, a person may choose a trust company or bank. A lawyer could suggest a compromise, in which both may be named, or a corporate trustee could be named to take over when the individual trustee dies. Otherwise the court would name a successor trustee.

Various state laws afford some assurance of safety to all persons involved in a trust. While these may vary from state to state, in general they require that a trustee keep accurate accounts of the assets, which must be segregated; that he comply with the wishes of the grantor in carrying out the terms of the trust; that he not take personal advantage of his position; and that he confine investments to those permitted by law for trusts, if he is responsible for making investment decisions. A trustee's compensation may be agreed upon between him and the grantor, or determined by law or court decision.

Assets transferred to a trust would be subject to the Federal gift tax, above the tax-exempt limits allowed. (See Chapter 12)

Advantages and Pitfalls of Joint Ownership: Joint tenancy, tenancy by the entirety

"Of course we both want to be named as owners," said the young man, as he and his wife were about to take title of their new home.

This is the typical, almost automatic declaration of most couples purchasing real estate or securities, or opening a bank account. But, is it the right answer to the ownership question? Not necessarily. However, any other answer might stir feelings of guilt, or be challenged as evidence of distrust, disloyalty or selfishness. ("Marriage is supposed to be a partnership," she cried.) It also might run counter to the widespread, though often vague, assumption that joint ownership is a good thing. Actually, while joint ownership may be valid under certain circumstances, it more often can generate costly, sometimes distressing problems. These may include loss of control of the property, loss of the right to dispose of it at death, loss of income and an increase in tax liability.

Of the several joint-ownership forms, the most widely used are "joint tenancy" and "tenancy by the entirety." The "entirety" form is limited to husband and wife and, in many states, only to their ownership of real estate. Both forms generally carry the right of survivorship, under which total ownership shifts to the remaining tenant upon death of his co-owner. Because joint ownership is not always advantageous, and because laws vary from state to state, it is wise to consult with a lawyer and perhaps a tax expert before making a decision. Substitute legal devices may be suggested that would more effectively achieve the desired results.

The prime advantage of a joint-ownership form that includes the survivorship right is that property passes to the surviving co-owner directly, and is not part of the deceased joint owner's probate estate, which passes under his will. This can save executor's fees, other administrative costs and time. Further, if properly set up, jointly held property, including bank accounts and securities, can be sold quickly by either co-owner in an emergency. In many states, creditors may not have access to jointly owned property, though the same property may be available to them, if it is individually owned.

To many married couples, jointly held stock provides an appealing tax advantage. There is an exclusion from taxable income of up to $200 in dividends on such stock, compared with a $100 maximum on individually owned stock. Joint ownership of property also permits splitting of income or gains. This would benefit unmarried co-owners or couples who find it more advantageous to file separate Federal and state returns. It also helps couples in states that do not allow joint filing. Income of real estate jointly owned by a couple may be split between husband and wife without gift-tax liability. If the property were owned by one spouse who transferred half the income to the other, the excess over $6,000 a year would be subject to the gift tax.

On the other side of the ledger are the disadvantages of joint ownership, one of which is loss by the individual of control of the property. This poses little difficulty unless the co-owners are in dispute or, in the case of married couples, separated or divorced. Income can be lost by the individual, because joint ownership frequently gives the other co-owner a legal right to his fractional share. This would not appear to be a problem for a married couple.

A person who places property in joint ownership generally gives up his right to dispose of it in his will. Where there are enforceable survivorship rights, the surviving co-owner would receive the property outright. But, where there are not such rights, a co-owner may dispose of only his partial share by will.

Among tax disadvantages are the creation of a possible gift-tax liability on creation of joint ownership, or upon its termination while the co-owners are alive. In both cases, the transfer of property might be viewed as the giving of a gift. This would not apply to a home that is jointly owned by a married couple.

There generally is no particular estate tax advantage to joint ownership, but there could be disadvantages. When a co-owner dies, for example, the total value of jointly owned property is included in his estate for tax purposes, just as if he had owned it alone, unless the surviving co-owner could prove the extent of his contribution. The total value again may be subject to estate taxation when the surviving co-owner dies. Again, the exception would be a married couple's jointly owned home.

As has been noted, professional advisers could suggest procedures that would satisfy property owners' needs while avoiding the possible pitfalls of joint ownership. For example, if the survivorship right is joint ownership's attraction, it might be decided that a revocable trust could better provide that feature. Such a trust would assure that the property would go to the named beneficiary, while avoiding the costs and delay of estate administration and the publicity of will probate. At the same time, it would leave the person setting up the trust in control of the property during his lifetime, and allow him to change the trust arrangement if he so chooses.

Joint ownership's right of survivorship is an attraction to many people, because they believe it precludes the need for a will. Through joint ownership, people can leave property to each other without benefit of a will, but it is not always practical or legally possible for all property to be jointly owned. Co-owners, moreover, might die in a common disaster or in quick succession. There must be a professionally drawn will to fill such gaps. A man could unintentionally disinherit his children or other relatives by depending on joint ownership of property with his wife and not having a will.

Escheat: State seizure of property without an apparent owner

A recent informal survey disclosed that only one person in 25 polled, a lawyer, was aware of escheat: state seizure of property that has no apparent owner. Yet anyone may be subject to its ill effects unless precautions are taken.

Escheat is practiced, to a greater or lesser degree, by all states. The oldest and most common form is government acquisition of the estate of a person who dies intestate. The next most common, and perhaps most familiar, form is escheat of unclaimed bank deposits. Depending on the state, other property may be affected, such as unclaimed stock dividends, securities, insurance proceeds and wages. As an indication of the range of property that might be included, a Pennsylvania state court ruled that telegraphic money orders could be seized, if neither sender nor addressee could be found.

With the exception of the lawyer, initial reaction of those interviewed was indifference. Typically, an advertising executive said: "Escheat? How do you spell it? It doesn't apply to me. I certainly keep track of all I own, and it's absolutely impossible that anything of mine could be declared ownerless and taken by the state." However, that indifference faded, in most cases, during a discussion of several of the situations in which escheat laws would apply.

For example, when Congress passed the law requiring banks and corporations to report every interest or dividend payment of $10 or more, many married people expressed concern that this avenue for discovering taxable income they had not reported would reveal to their families the money they had secretly put aside for special purposes. These investments or bank accounts might be held by husbands or wives building private nest eggs, or mothers saving, as a future surprise, the weekly room-and-board payments made by children just beginning their careers.

Such secret assets could ultimately be taken by the Government, should the owner die. Survivors, unaware of them, would not file claims. Further, if the family relocated, the bank or corporation might not be able to trace them, and the state would get the property after the prescribed waiting period. Personal property of a couple might be disposed of in the same way, if they died in a common disaster, leaving no will or an outdated one that did not list all assets. Here again, the heirs might relocate—or, if women, change their names in marriage—and perhaps never be traced.

Thus, it would be wise to review wills periodically, at least every three years, particularly at "middle age," to take account of changes in financial and family status.

There are many other situations in which property could be exposed to escheat. A gift of a savings account or securities to a grandchild may, with the passing years, fade from memory. A savings account, considered safe, might be left unattended for years, without even one visit to have accumulated interest entered in the passbook or a letter to notify the bank of a change of address. A paid-up insurance policy may be buried in a pile of "valuable" papers and eventually lost, with no claim ever being filed on it.

In New York State, there must be no communication with, or payment to, an owner of a corporate security, bank account or other personal property for 10 years before it can be declared abandoned and escheatable. In general, banks and other holders of the personal property of missing owners are required to reach them by mail at their last-known address, through advertisements and by posting notices. Among such holders may be corporations that have issued stock, or brokerage houses that hold unpaid dividends, securities and other assets in the investors' accounts.

The nonpayment period varies from state to state, and sometimes with the type of property. A holder of a winning pari-mutuel ticket, for example, had better not wait too long before cashing it in, for, in New York State, he has only a year in which to claim his money before the state takes it. State legislatures, it is said, look to escheat laws primarily for revenue. The public value of such laws is that they use ownerless property for the common good, rather than leave it with whoever happens to hold it.

Escheat related under early common law to the passage of real property to the crown upon death of its owner without heirs. In feudal times, escheat occurred when an owner of land died without heirs capable of serving his feudal lord, or when he was convicted of a felony or treason. In the United States, escheat has been steadily broadened to include a wide range of personal property, especially since 1940, the period in which most states enacted escheat legislation. Before that, common law prevailed in all states but Pennsylvania, which has had escheat statutes since 1913.

In a study, "Modern Rationales of Escheat," in the November, 1963, issue of the *University of Pennsylvania Law Review,* David C. Auten noted that the "most significant rationale of modern escheat is that the state's custody protects the owner." This applies to states, such as New York, that take custody of property, rather than confiscate it, and thus allow an owner to reclaim it. It usually is less expensive and difficult to recover property from a government than from a private individual. However, the claimant still must prove his ownership, often by winning a court judgment.

This raises another point that was well made by Mr. Auten. Many states sell escheated property, and pay a recognized owner the sale price, less costs. Thus, in an inflationary period, the owner would be out not only his and the state's expenses, but also the amount the property might have increased in value had it not been sold. Of course, in a period of deflation or market decline, he would be ahead, if the property had been sold at a price above the then current level.

The percentage of refunds is small. In the 1961–62 fiscal year, New York collected $12.65 million and refunded only $574,000.

A further protection to the absent owner is that the state perhaps is a better custodian than an individual, who might become insolvent, negligent or dishonest.

The prime precaution against escheat is a complete and current will. Provided there are no complications, the legal cost of review is nominal, perhaps $10. If there are to be secrets, they must be shared with the lawyer or executor, lest they become eternal secrets. Among other precautions are the registration of bonds and the engagement of a corporate custodian, such as a bank. The prime advantage is that the owner will have constant reminder of his securities, where they are and what he must do to maintain responsible ownership.

Most corporations will register bonds at no charge, and then notify the owner by mail if the bond is called.

It is worth noting, for anyone still doubtful that personal property can go astray, that there are outstanding more than $300 million in Federal Government bonds that no longer draw interest. These securities would have been redeemed long ago, if the owners or their heirs knew they existed.

Estate Taxes

The primary factor that affects the size of the Federal estate tax bill is the size of the net taxable estate, if any, after all allowable deductions and exemptions. The deductions may include funeral expenses, loans, claims, mortgages and estate administration expenses. The exempt property may include bequests to qualified charities and other tax-exempt institutions. A credit is allowed against the estate tax for all or part of the estate tax paid with respect to the transfer of property to the deceased person by or from a person who died within 10 years before or two years after him. The purpose of the provision is to prevent erosion of an estate by the imposition of successive taxes on the same property within a brief period.

However, the major exemptions are the basic $60,000 allowed the deceased and the marital deduction, which, under a properly drawn will, allows a person to leave up to half his adjusted gross estate to his spouse estate tax-free as an outright legacy or in trust. However, the survivor must receive all the trust income at least annually and must have the power to dispose of the property during her lifetime or on death. The adjusted gross estate is the total estate, less allowable expenses and deductions, but including charitable bequests and other exemptions. Thus, if an unmarried or widowed person expects to leave an adjusted gross estate of $60,000 or less, he would have no concern about Federal estate taxes. The estate could be even larger, if he were planning to make charitable bequests. A married person, allowing for the marital deduction in a properly drawn will, could leave an estate tax-exempt adjusted gross estate of up to $120,000.

The Federal estate tax is the prime concern. All states but Nevada impose either an estate or inheritance tax, but the Federal Government allows a sizable credit for those payments. The prime distinction between an estate and an inheritance tax is that the estate tax is levied on all the taxable property of the person who died, while the inheritance tax is levied on the right of the beneficiary to receive a bequest and is based on his share.

After maximum credit for state inheritance or estate taxes, the Federal estate tax on a net estate (with all deductions and exemptions excluded) would be about $110 (2.2 per cent) on $5,000 in assets, $6,600 (13.2 per cent) on $50,000, $19,500 (19.5 per cent) on $100,000, $162,700 (27.1 per cent) on $600,000, and $286,900 (28.7 per cent) on $1 million.

When you get beyond $1 million, they say, you tend to be less concerned about the size of the estate-tax bite. But, as a wealthy acquaintance recently declared: "Wait until YOU get there!"